Stones
ON MY ROAD

Hope is being able to see that there is light despite all of the darkness

Mª Esperanza Pinzón

Praise for Hope Pinzon

This captivating memoir centers around the protagonist and her determination to find happiness, success and peace in her heart. It is a touching tribute to love and commitment to family, as well as commitment to self love, perseverance and achieving one's goals. This inspiring story will leave readers deeply touched and grateful to have followed along as the author told her tale.

~ Ellen Noah

Copyright © 2025 by María Esperanza López Pinzón

All rights reserved.

Published by Red Penguin Books

Bellerose Village, New York

Library of Congress Control Number: 2025901594

ISBN

Digital 978-1-63777-691-9

Print 978-1-63777-692-6 | 978-1-63777-693-3

No part of this book may be reproduced in any form or by any electronic or mechanical means, including information storage and retrieval systems, without written permission from the author, except for the use of brief quotations in a book review.

This book is dedicated to my mother, the most authentic person I have ever known. You touched my heart in so many ways. Even on dark days, you were my hero, my strength, and my inspiration. Your unconditional love and devotion will always be missed.

Nothing will ever be the same without you.

Contents

Chapter 1	1
Chapter 2	7
Chapter 3	15
Chapter 4	23
Chapter 5	37
Chapter 6	48
Chapter 7	60
Chapter 8	66
Chapter 9	72
Chapter 10	75
Chapter 11	80
Chapter 12	91
Chapter 13	97
Chapter 14	104
Chapter 15	109
Chapter 16	116
Chapter 17	122
Chapter 18	129
Chapter 19	136
Chapter 20	144
Chapter 21	150
Chapter 22	157
Chapter 23	160
Chapter 24	167
Chapter 25	174
Chapter 26	182
Chapter 27	188
Chapter 28	195
Chapter 29	200
Chapter 30	205
Chapter 31	208
Chapter 32	214

Chapter 33	221
Chapter 34	227
Chapter 35	232
Chapter 36	240
Chapter 37	245
Chapter 38	252
Chapter 39	260
Chapter 40	270
Epilogue	279
Thank You	281
About the Author	283
Photos	285

Chapter One

It felt like every other day, except the rain and the wind were tapping on my window while I was writing. I realized that nothing matters anymore because time is the most precious thing we have. I have always wondered if my life would have been different if I had not gone through all of these experiences that shaped me into who I am today. Or, is it true that when we are born our path is already written for us? We didn't ask to be born. We didn't know who our siblings would be. But, when I realized that I could choose what I wanted to become, I was driven by the little I had, even though everything looked impossible. When I learned my reality, I found my strength and I was liberated from my suffering. When I understood that my only option was to be strong, I confronted my fears to accomplish my goals.

I close my eyes. I see an image of a beautiful, strong, intelligent woman who was always ready to fight any battle. For this woman in particular, it did not matter how many times she fell. She would get herself back up, time and time again. How could I forget those beautiful blue eyes of hers? They always looked at me in the most loving way. This woman was my mother, born in 1930. Her name was Herminia Del Tránsito Pinzon Rincon.

My mother grew up in Soata Boyaca, Colombia, in the house my grandparents bought in 1940 when they fled persecution and violence.

My Tía Rafaela remembered her grandmother. Calling the land La Esperanza with "the hope" that this would be the last time my family would have to run from their home. The elders had hoped that La Esperanza would be a stable home for their family to grow and for the children to have the ability to live without fear. My grandparents had ten children: Marcos, Isaias, Julio, Miguel, Elisa, Eva, Segunda, Zocorro, Herminia, and Abraham. I remember four of them.

I have to admit that Soata happens to be the most beautiful place, surrounded by many mountains with incredible weather, but with an irrigation system that is far from adequate. Rarely did it rain. The water with which one cooked meals was frequently brought up from the river. It was always essential to boil water as we were afraid of becoming sick, especially when it came to our children. Water was always in short supply.

I have been shaped and strengthened by memories I will never forget. It's like touching an old scar... there is no longer a fresh wound but an old scab lingering on the body and mind. When I revisit these memories, it's as though the wounds are still fresh. They have not healed and turned into scars. There is a saying, "I cannot change my memories but their meaning and the power they have over me."

I remember dogs barking. It was late, and I walked with the other members of the family in the dark. Joaquin, Julio, Sandra, and I were following her. The neighborhood was silent; it seemed as if the whole world was asleep.

Julio was nervous as he asked, "Mom, are you sure we are going the right way?"

She replied without a second thought. "Yes, of course, it is this way. We have luggage, so we must take the long way." Thank God she knew where we were going. If we had taken the usual route, which was shorter, we would have had to carry the white sacks that contained our entire lives up and down through miles of mountains.

"Do they know we're coming?" Joaquin asked.

"Stop it. Both of you." At that moment, it was as if we could all feel her stress orbiting around her being. We continued to walk for an hour, but to us kids, it felt like forever.

"We're here," my mother said with a sigh of relief. "See?" She gestured for us to look up. "That is my brother's house." The house lights appeared out of nowhere, and before I could take in the bright lights I began hugging my favorite tío, Tío Isaias.

"I am so happy to see you!" I spoke into his chest with a smile so big it hurt my face. He lifted me into the air, and his smile was just as big as mine.

"Me, too, sweetie." He slowly walked toward my mother.

"Herminia, I hope you know what you're doing." His eyes filled with concern, but my mother remained silent.

It felt like an eternity before she decided to speak again. "I am sorry to come here like this. It's only for one night, I promise." She paused, "Tomorrow, I will find a place for us."

"Please don't worry." Regretful of his previous tone, Tío Isiais said, "A place, Herminia? Where?" Concern filled his voice as he began suggesting the answer.

My mother answered with worry, "I don't know yet." Her eyes gazed at the ground.

"Okay, Herminia, let me feed you guys." His demeanor was unapologetic. My mom's eyes were forgiving.

My Tía Rafaela was already in the kitchen preparing food for us. Both my tía and tío were always so generous and good to everyone. These two human beings were the most beautiful people I had ever met.

Tía Rafaela called out loud from the kitchen to hurry up.

"Girls, hurry up! Joaquin and Julio already finished everything," Tío laughed.

"Come, Herminia," my tía called. "Have a seat; you look tired."

Her instinct was to nurture those around her. She hovered around my mother and said, "Eat and rest; tomorrow will be another day." She looked at my mother, smiled with her eyes, and said, "You're pregnant?" My mother nodded. "You have to take care of yourself." my tía said.

Tío Isaias and Tía Rafaela were the most loving people. They were nowhere near wealthy but always managed to share whatever they had. They had five children who also shared their generosity. They were an amazing family.

The next morning my cousins welcomed us warmly. We played for hours, climbing on the surrounding trees and collecting oranges, papayas, lemons, and mangos. It felt like paradise. Joaquin and Julio followed the other boys in the family as they went to take care of the animals. My tío had many animals; cows, sheep, goats, pigs, chickens, roosters, birds, dogs, and a horse.

We all returned to the house chasing one another, and at that moment, I thought how much I would have liked to live here with my family. At lunchtime, we all sat at a long wooden table. There were endless amounts of food; rice, beans, potatoes, fried bananas, salad, avocados and chicken. It seemed as if the food would never run out. It was incredible.

Tía Rafaela was a great cook. Everyone but my mother was enjoying their meal. I was lost in my own thoughts. I quickly noticed my mom was not there. I stayed quiet. I had lost my appetite. Tía Rafaela came close to me and asked what was wrong. She noticed I had stopped eating.

"Do you not like the meal?" she asked with much concern.

"Yes, Tía. I love it. I'm just saving the rest for my mother," I said, as innocence took over the sound of my voice. I was about 7 years old, I was very thoughtful and conscious of everything around me. I guess seeing how much we did not have instilled in me the need to give and take care of those around me, especially my mother. She always gave it all to me, and I could not stand the thought of her not having some of the meals we were experiencing together on this day.

"Don't worry, sweetie. There is a lot of food in the kitchen." She hugged me and pointed toward a beautiful figure walking our way. "Look, your mother is coming. Now you can finish your food."

My mother sat next to me, and I instantly felt better. I grabbed a piece of chicken and started eating once again.

"Did you register your kids for school?" Tío Isaias asked before my mother could even start eating.

"No," my mother answered shortly.

"Herminia, they have to go to school," Tío said, frustrated.

"I know, Hermano, but don't you think I need a job first?" she snapped. "As a matter of fact, I found one." My tío looked up from his plate, surprised. "I start on Monday," my mother said proudly.

"Where?" My tío asked, his voice filled with worry.

"Colombiana De Tabaco," she said nonchalantly.

"You are something else. You know this job?...no one can keep up." He paused.

"Why do you think there are always open positions? It's a very hard job."

"Enough," Tía Rafaela said, breaking her silence. "Can we eat in peace? Let her eat first."

My mother took a deep breath, kissed my forehead, and said, "Isn't your tío a pain in the neck?" We all laughed out loud. I will never forget that weekend at my tío's house.

Everyone got along. I loved them so much.

Chapter Two

The year was 1972. We all woke up early. My mother had already left for her "first day of work." My tío began to pack the amount of items that my family and I could make use of. He carefully loaded up blankets, mats, pillows, pots, dishes, hammocks, and as much non-perishable food as they could give us. I observed him with worry. I couldn't understand what was about to happen. He carefully put everything on the horse. And without any explanation in a loud voice, he told my brother, sister, and me to say goodbye to my tia. We followed our tío out, upset to leave. I thought we were going to stay here for some time. I was confused about why we were leaving, and I could not help but wonder what would happen next.

Baffled, I turned to my brother Julio and said, "I thought we were staying here.

Where are we going?" His face seemed to grow with frustration as he stared back at me.

"Stop," he said. "Be quiet. We cannot stay here." He turned away from me and continued to walk forward. I lowered my gaze and looked at my feet, staying focused on moving forward.

I felt bad for the horse and us. The amount of time we spent walking, to a young child, felt like years. When we finally got to where we were going, I could not help but feel disappointed. An abandoned home stared right at me. This place was incredibly different from my tío's house. I felt like I was going to have a heart attack. As soon as I entered the home, I started to cry. My tío began to tell Joaquin and Julio that it was okay and to start cleaning so that when my mother returned home from work, she would be happy with how the place looked. My tío informed the boys that he was going back home to bring more items, and he left soon after. I took the chance and hid. When Julio noticed my absence he started calling for me.

Julio, who usually called me by my nickname, said, "Pancha, where are you?

Pancha, answer me please!" I chose not to respond on purpose, but it did not take long for him to find me. Next to the home, there was a large oven that my grandparents had built to bake bread. I was sitting inside the oven alone when Julio found me.

He said, "If you continue to sit inside the oven, they will cook you in five minutes." I looked up at him, unphased. "I want to be cooked," I said without hesitation.

"Stop whining, and come out. Let me show you. It's pretty here." I rolled my eyes, unamused.

"There is nothing pretty here." I was annoyed with the situation, but at seven years old, I was too young to express my emotions properly. My fears came off as unsettled, and I was in no mood to try to understand the situation.

"Do not be ungrateful. Our mother said we are going to be very happy here." That was the only thing he had to say. To this day, I swear, when he told me our mother approved, I came out without a problem.

He could not stop laughing as I climbed out of the oven. "Look at yourself. Can't you see what you look like?"

After a moment or so, I responded, "Stop laughing at me; I am not in the mood."

"You should clean yourself off before Mom gets home. Please let me help you." At that moment, Julio took my hand and helped me out of the oven.

Julio reminded me to look around. "See, it is not that ugly. We can plant trees, and soon everything will be as green as it is in Tío's house." We looked around for just another moment before he spoke again. "Let's go now. Tío Isaias is back with more stuff." We made our way back to where our tío was.

Before leaving again, our tío said, "You're always welcome to come to my house, but for now, living here is the better option. You guys are closer to school, and your mother is closer to work." As he dropped off the last bit of food and blankets, he began to speak again. "Your mother will be home soon." He left us again in that ugly place. There was a huge living room and one small room. I never understood why the living room was so big and why the only other room was so much smaller. I soon learned that this was previously a school, and the small room I hated the most was once the principal's office.

When my mother returned from work, she told us this would be our new home.

We used to sleep in this small room, piled up against one another so we would not feel as cold at night. I remember feeling safe while lying next to my mother. Anytime I hugged her, I felt protected. Especially when I heard the noise of the rapids. It frightened me that the current got stronger, that it would take us away.

My mother arranged three stones as a fire pit to cook our meals. The stone oven was in the other corner, and it was there where my mother would make bread for us. I also recall the rooster crowing and how it never stopped singing in the morning. That was how I knew it was time for school. My mother would wake up at five o'clock every morning to make fresh bread in the oven. As I got out of bed, I wished my mother would cook the rooster for dinner so I would have more time to sleep. Nonetheless, my mother would start getting us ready for the day. Every morning we ate a little piece of bread with a cup of coffee. Each morning we had to do things quickly so our mother could make it to work on time. We were supposed to leave the house by seven.

Julio and I would go to school together. Joaquin at the age of 14, of his own choice, did not want to go to school. My mother decided that he would care for my younger sister Sandra who was 3, but he was unhappy about being responsible for her. My mother worked in the Colombiana De Tabaco, a factory that processed dry tobacco leaves for export. My mother would stand for ten hours, ensuring all the leaves were perfect, or else the package would need to be redone. I remember her coming home with swollen feet and hands full of calluses. Her nails were chipped, yet her beauty was still untouchable. Her blue eyes, beautiful long reddish hair, and hourglass figure made it difficult for her to hide from any man, and they would constantly harass her because they knew she was alone with her children. Her husband had abandoned her, but she never seemed to care. Her main focus was her children, and she never allowed the constant harassment to affect her parenting. Each night when she came home, she cooked a hot meal for her children.

We ate the same meal every day for what felt like forever. I still remember the taste of pasta soup made with peas, carrots, and potatoes. It always smelled delicious, and we were all very hungry. We would wait anxiously until the soup was ready, and our mother would always wait for us to ask for more. If anything was left, she would finally eat. On many occasions, I saw nothing left for her, but she always had a smile on her face and never complained. Her love for us was unconditional—it is impossible to explain it with words.

My mother would make a cup of coffee and sit on a piece of wood that used to be a grand tree. Anytime she sat on the stump, a cigarette was always between her fingers. Her eyes would gaze at the clouds like she was taking the time to look for and to speak to God. I always waited for this moment, never missing an opportunity to run between her legs because it was only then, when I was next to her, that I felt truly safe and secure. Although when I was with her I felt as if no one would hurt me, at times I could feel her pain in the silence that was never expressed with words. That day I had the courage to ask, "Why are you always sad?"

She replied, "If we have faith, tomorrow will be a better day." She never gave me a direct answer to my question concerning her well-being. I learned through her that no matter how ugly today might be, tomorrow could be better.

I asked my mother if there was anyone in the world who could count all the stars in the sky. She responded, "I don't know, but if you can find three stars that are together, you can ask for three wishes." To this day, whenever I find three stars together, I make three wishes. Although I'm now older and wiser, I still hope they will come true. With time, I eventually came to understand that this was the only way for my mother to keep me quiet long enough for her to enjoy her cigarette. My mother's work was strenuous; those who supervised my mother's work had unrealistic goals for her to achieve each day. My hardworking mother had to put thousands of sheets of tobacco in one bucket and not stop until she completed her long day of work. Her hands would swell due to the result of touching the tobacco leaves all day long. The tobacco leaves heated quickly, and after hours of handling the heat, my mother's hands would no longer appear as delicate but would tell a story of hard work. It was no shock as to why she always looked so tired.

I remember being awakened from my sleep by the sounds of my mother screaming in agony. I knew it was earlier than usual because I did not hear the sound of the annoying rooster pulling me from my sleep. My mother pleaded and cried for help until my brother Joaquin helped her get to the hospital, leaving Julio in charge of taking care of Sandra and me. Two days later our mother came home, along with my new baby brother. Luis was born that November. He was so beautiful. I remember having him in my arms. My sister and I would play with him like a toy. Our mother had to go back to work right away, and we had to go back to school. My brother Joaquin was the one who had to take care of Sandra and the newborn, as well as take on the responsibility of cooking for all of us.

I understand that it was a substantial amount of work for him to handle as a fourteen-year-old boy, and that was the reason why he was always so angry. He took his frustration out by yelling and punishing us constantly. He used to tie Julio to a tree for hours. Sometimes I would be the one to release him, and we would manage to escape by hiding behind our neighbor's house until our mother came back home. My brother Julio and I would go to La Señora Mercedes's house, the highest point on the hill that was behind our house, to sit outside. She used to cook rice with parsley, and Julio and I would immediately indulge in its aroma, captivating our senses. She knew that the two of us would sit there and we had hoped, on so many occasions, that she would invite us in and feed us, but she never did.

When my little brother Luis was two years old, my mother had to bring him to the hospital because he was running a fever. He had been sick for a couple of days at this point, and tears filled my mother's eyes when she left the house. When she returned home, she came by herself. We all could feel that she was very upset, but no one had the guts to ask her what happened. From that day on, nothing was the same.

My mother grabbed her jacket after dinner, and I had a feeling she was going to leave again. I begged her to take me with her, but she did not. Since my mother came home that first night without Luis, this became a daily occurrence. Each night she left after dinner with no explanation.

She returned home two hours later and sat down on the same tree stump that she always did. She indulged in blowing cigarette smoke into the air. The smoke would cover the tears on her face. She couldn't even imagine that I was observing her from a distance, seated at a small window. I would love for her to come inside so I can comfort her. There were so many nights when Joaquin would find me sitting by the window, and he would pull my hair, demanding that I go to bed, but I never could. Each time I would return to the window and think of all the concepts that were too hard for my young mind to understand. What was it that made my mother suffer so much?

Though I felt the need to wait for my mother each night, she would be very upset with me if she caught me waiting up. That is the reason why I never told her the punishments that Joaquin forced me to endure.

Our childhood was not an easy time for anyone in the family. There were moments when life became unbearable. We were frequently hungry, and the fights between Julio and Joaquin became intolerable, especially for my mother. I could never understand why they could not get along. The number of arguments I witnessed where Joaquin would go against my mother made me feel helpless. He resented her for making him take care of her children. He would raise his voice to her, "I am not the father of your fucking children. I do not want to cook anymore. All we eat is shit in this house, soup with noodles again and again. I have to do all the work here, and Julio gets to go to school like a king. I am sick and tired of it all. I swear one day I will burn this place down." After Joaquin finished ranting, he would leave the house for a couple of hours and return even angrier than when he had left.

My mother was as empathetic as ever. Even after he would scream at her with such disrespect, she would still defend him saying, "It is not his fault the way he speaks to me; it's my fault. He has a lot on his plate. We have to forgive him." Tears would pour from her eyes as she would vent her sorrows in response to her son's distress. Julio and I knew it would be only a matter of time before Joaquin would take his frustration out on us when our mother was no longer around. We all understood that Joaquin had many responsibilities, but none of that justified the cruelty of the physical and mental abuse that we received from him more often than not.

Joaquin would often hit us with his belt. I would hide under the bed, and Julio would run to the river to pass the time. If Joaquin ever found Julio, he would tie him to the nearest tree for hours, and if he caught me untying him, I would be hit with the belt. I always prayed for our mother to return home as quickly as possible. I understood how frustrating it was dealing with us, but Joaquin was out of control. My mother knew about his behavior, and shockingly enough, the abuse inflicted on us resulted in my mother asking my father for help.

Chapter Three

Angel Lopez, our father, is from Macarabita Santander. He and my mother had always known each other. They had first met when they were very young, so young you could say they practically grew up together. They separated when my grandparents left that land and moved to Saota, but by destiny, they found themselves together again. My father was always attracted to my mother and did everything in his power to win her over. By the time my father had his chance to be with my mother, she was already a widow with a four-year-old, Edgar Pinzon. My mother had lost her first love to a war between liberals and conservatives. He was killed when my mother was seven months pregnant, which essentially initiated the first of the many losses she would suffer in her life.

Edgar told me the story of his father and our mother some time ago. It did nothing but instill joy in my heart, knowing that my mother had found true love in the earlier years of her life. It saddened me that she had suffered, but knowing she had once been in love let me know she had once been happy. The time of her love was short-lived.

During the 1940s, acts of violence were commonplace, especially between liberals and conservatives. A normal day suddenly turned to horror when she received the news that her husband had been killed. The day that he died, our family knew that there would be no way to know who was responsible for his death. "The only thing known is that her husband was the great love of her life," Edgar recalled.

My heart was warmed knowing that my mother experienced true love, but my stomach ached with the knowledge that my poor brother never had the opportunity to get to know his father.

It became clear that this was the best time for my father to take advantage of my mother's situation. He asked my grandparents' permission to marry my mother, but with the condition that my mother would leave Edgar behind with my grandparents. My grandfather was very happy with the thought of his daughter being married again. He did not want her to be a single mother raising a child on her own. My grandfather did not think anyone would want to marry his daughter, considering she was widowed and with a child, so he accepted the conditions set by my father and approved the marriage. Though my grandfather gave his blessing, my grandmother could not have disagreed more. From the very beginning, my grandmother had ill feelings toward my father and she could not stand the thought of her daughter suffering in her new life. My mother was my grandmother's darling, and she didn't want her to go through any more pain. The loss of my mother's first husband had brought endless agony, but in the hopes of an improved future for her family as well as herself, my mother agreed to get married.

On Sunday, September 14th, 1958, in Bogota, Colombia, the wedding was held that united my mother and father as one, in a true catholic church. The wedding guests consisted of their parents. The newlyweds started their new life but unfortunately suffered financial instability due to my father's lack of economic status, which was overlooked by my grandparents. Their sole motive was to marry my mother off without considering other factors which would affect their daughter.

Soon after, she realized her husband's characteristics were extremely dominant and strong, which were not favored in this relationship. My parents lived in a small room that they rented in the capital of Bogota. A few months passed before the newlyweds learned of my mother's pregnancy. As my mother's belly began to grow, my father's abusive behavior grew progressively worse. Though my father knew about my mother's pregnancy, it did not stop him from abusing her in each and every way. Not only did my mother experience these abuses from my father, but she was also humiliated further when she found out he had a mistress.

With the fear of losing her unborn child, my mother escaped my father's abuse by returning to my grandparents' house. It was then that my mother begged for help. My grandfather was not happy. My grandmother, on the other hand, welcomed my mother with open arms and took care of her until the baby was born. My mother was so happy to be back with her family. She missed her firstborn son Edgar terribly. I believe in my heart that Edgar was the one who gave her the strength to escape.

When he heard that his wife had given birth to their son, my father went looking for my mother and demanded that she return to their home. With no alternative, she had no choice but to return to her abusive husband. In 1959, after baptizing their son who they called Heli Joaquin Lopez Pinzon, my mother was forced to obey her husband's commands. She left with her newborn son while painfully saying goodbye to her firstborn son Edgar and her mother.

My grandmother suffered substantially because of what happened, and my Tío Miguel blamed my mother for all of the pain and suffering my grandmother went through. These circumstances caused a great deal of resentment and hate between my mother and her brother Miguel. Sadly, over time, all of the hatred shared between my mother and Tío Miguel fell to the next generation.

My father promised my mother that things would improve but it was a lie. Soon after, my mother found out she was pregnant again. My mother endured my father's abuse throughout her entire pregnancy; it never stopped. It was almost as if she was living in hell. Each day she would be reminded of the pain she unintentionally caused my grandmother because of him. Due to those circumstances, she remained quiet for a very long time. If she complained, she would lose communication with her parents and contact with Edgar—even if it was only for a few hours. When my mother and father had their second child in 1961, they called him Julio Cesar Lopez Pinzon, and for some reason, he was always my father's favorite. More often than not, I believe that a lot of the reason why Joaquin and Julio fought so much was because of my father's attitude and preference toward Julio.

My mother tried her very hardest to save her marriage, but nothing worked. When my grandfather passed away, the situation grew worse for my mother, and shockingly enough, my mother was pregnant again. Her situation became overwhelming and depressing. Her relatives were no longer supporting her, and she felt lonely and desperate.

If my memory serves me clearly, my mother told me that it was with the help of her older sister that she planned her escape from her husband's abuse.

This time was different from the times before. She no longer lived in fear; she had the willpower to travel far away to another country. My mother's sister lived in Urena, Venezuela, and while pregnant and with two children, she was able to escape to Venezuela. In 1965, without thinking about the consequences that would begin to unravel, my mother accepted her sister's help. She immediately began looking for a job. She found a position as a cook in a restaurant. The situation was not easy, but she was at peace. She was no longer abused or humiliated by my father. My mother and her sister helped one another, and with support from each other, the situation became a little more bearable. While working, she had a high-risk pregnancy. While only seven months pregnant, I was born prematurely in Urena, Venezuela.

Unfortunately, somehow one year later, my father found my mother. In those times, it was against the law to abandon a home. Knowing the law, my father accused my mother of abandoning their home and endangering their children. The court went on to issue a warning to my mother. The court issued her a warning to come back to Colombia or she would be charged with the following: abandonment of the home and endangerment of children. If she did not return, she would lose custody of her children and the court would issue full custody to the father. Failing to respond to this would result in a five-year jail sentence. Once again, my mother was forced to remain in a miserable marriage. When she traveled back to her alienated home, she found out that my grandmother had passed away six months earlier. At this time, there were not many means of communication, and it took a substantial amount of time to receive messages. The only form of communication during those times was through long distance letters with the hope that the message was delivered. This was a very painful time for my mother, as she suddenly realized that the one person who was there for her was gone, leaving her feeling more alone than ever.

As my mother continued to bear my father's existence, she came to realize that she was pregnant again. My sister, Sandra Lopez Pinzon, was born in February of 1968. Fearful of losing her children, my mother resisted all temptation to leave and suffered a life of humiliation, living each day in hopeless misery. After she announced she was pregnant once again, my father abandoned my mother, with four children, as a result of a love that had grown between my father and his mistress. My mother realized after a few months that she could not economically support the family without financial assistance from my father. My mother couldn't even provide enough food to feed her children. With her liberation and no longer suffering from constant spousal abuse, my mother decided it was time for her to return to her hometown of

Saota. This was a very difficult situation, but a weight was lifted off my mother's shoulders.

Returning to her late parents' empty home, my mother knew that she was not going to be respected by the remaining members of the family. Though my mother was well aware of the negativity of the situation, she was hopeful that, due to the prevailing circumstances, the family would have compassion for her and her children. With time, Tío Isaias drastically morphed into a father for me and my siblings. He, his beautiful wife and their kind children, always treated us with love and respect. Tío Isaias's family always shared what they had and always helped us in any way they could; but in contrast, Tío Miguel and his family were cruel to us without any reason to justify their actions.

Eventually, my brother Edgar joined the military, and at this time, Julio and Joaquin were living with my father. My brothers had been behaving so poorly that my mother could no longer control them. The only reasonable solution was for my father to become their primary caregiver. At this time, my father was living with his mistress, but after a few short months, my father could no longer control his sons. He offered my mother some money to take the boys back. It was not much, but it was better than nothing. Almost a year had passed, and still, there was no sign of hope for my brothers to live cohesively. The continuous abuse from my brother Joaquin toward us was horrible. Joaquin put our little sister Sandra and me in a hammock and continuously spun us in circles. It was as if you were wringing a towel. He flipped and twisted us so often that when he stopped, we vomited. My sister and I felt as if we were dying, yet he found enjoyment in doing it. Anything that came to Joaquin's mind would be easily inflicted upon all of us.

Julio always had it much worse than us. Things began to grow uglier than they were before. The situation between my brothers grew to be so vile that Julio asked my mother to let him go to Duitama to work with our cousin, selling shoes in the villages. My mother was terrified to be separated from him again. It took her a very long time to make that decision. We did not want him to leave again, but deep down, our mother knew the fights between my brothers would continue to get worse, and it would be in everyone's best interest if he left to be with our cousin.

My mother finally agreed to let Julio go. She put him on a bus with a small sack filled with necessities such as a toothbrush, a bar of soap, jeans, and a tee shirt. I was so upset that I ran to the river, threw myself in the grass, and started to cry. It hurt me so much that Julio had to go. I felt so alone without him. I was still so young that I thought maybe it was my fault that he had left. The previous week we had gotten into trouble because we were not supposed to hang around my wealthier cousin's home, but we did so anyway behind our mother's back. We used to watch television through the metal bars that crossed the door of my Tío Miguel's house. This tío, in particular, would ignore that we were family and would act as if our pain was insignificant. I guess he forgot we were just children. It was not our fault that we had to grow up without a father. Tío Miguel believed his reasoning for humiliating us in front of our family was justifiable.

I remember this as if it had happened yesterday. Julio and I enjoyed watching a show called *The Lone Ranger*. The show was about a horse who grew to be my hero. I would do anything in my power to be able to watch that program. My brother liked the show, too; he was the one to take me to watch it so I could indulge in what little happiness we had. We were never allowed to go into the house to watch, but all we needed was that small space from the window to enjoy the show. It always amazed me how Scout was able to help so many people. I wanted to be just like him. I wanted to help all that I could. However, on one unsuspecting day, my brother and I noticed that the position of the television had changed. The television screen was no longer in eye view, and we could only see the back of the television set. At that moment, we understood that we could no longer watch the show.

These memories have always stuck with me because without them, I would not have been able to go back to the places where Julio and I would spend time together. Without my brother, there was no point in trying to watch *The Lone Ranger*. I could not understand why Julio had to go, and now I was the only one who had to deal with the person I feared the most, Joaquin.

I also remembered Tío Miguel's restaurant in town. Julio and I, on many occasions, would stand by the gate and smell the aroma of food…until one of our cousins told us to leave, to stop begging. The next day we would return like clockwork and hang around. That was when we realized that he was constantly turning us away. It was unbelievable how much we were being humiliated by our relatives. Maybe we were too young to understand the humiliation that constantly was given to us by our own family. One day when we were hungry, we stood by the restaurant gates until one of the employees told us to leave. We waited to see if our tía would feed us, but her aura told us that, like the others, she was sick of seeing us at the gate. The food that was cooked smelled so delicious to us. I remember our tía used to take a plastic bag and throw away food from the dishes of the tourists who had not finished their meals. Julio and I would run down to the river with that plastic bag, leftovers, and eat every last bit of rice. This became the main reason why my mother asked us to distance ourselves from our family members. It was evident that our family members did not like or respect us. If our mother ever found out, she would have marched herself right back to their restaurant and, without hesitation, burned the place down. Julio and I knew that we had to keep this our secret.

Chapter Four

Whenever I would return home from school I would have to hide under the bed so Joaquin could not find me. Once, my sister was crying and I could do nothing but cover my ears. I was shaking, I wanted to see my sister, but I did not want Joaquin to know I was home. Even though I was young, I knew that Joaquin was only repeating what he had learned from my father. I always tried to do everything to prevent him from being angry with me, but nothing worked. His punishments were constant, and on many occasions, I avoided telling my mother about the abuse because she had enough to deal with, and it was not fair for me to complain to her. Joaquin's anger continued to grow, and his vicious acts against us became more advanced. I recall his short temper. I feared it and would try to steer clear of any confrontation because I knew from previous occasions it would lead to physical altercations. There were so many times that I just wished that I could have grown up faster. I knew I would no longer have to hide or run out of fear.

Being at school was my only source of happiness, I was always the best in class, and it made me very popular. I used to do homework for my classmates, and in return, they would give me food. I liked how I could help my classmates and receive something in return. This was another secret I had to keep from my mother.

My brother Julio had been gone for some time now, and I missed him. Only he and I knew of all of the good and bad that happened to us. He was my best friend; we shared every moment and always counted on one another. A week before he left for Duitama, my mother punished both of us. It was my fault. I found a pencil sharpener at school and brought it home with me that day. I hid it under my pillow because I knew my mother would be angry that she could not afford to buy it for me. My mother only wanted us to have things that she could provide, and if she could not get them, there would be no reason for us to have them. My mother used to sharpen our pencils with the kitchen knife she used to cut our meals with. Every night before we would do our homework, she would whittle our pencils for us. The night that I brought home the sharpener, she noticed that my pencil had the most perfect point on the top of it. My mother could not make any sense of why my pencil looked as if it was just purchased and pre-sharpened from the store, while Julio and Sandra's pencils looked as if they were in desperate need of sharpening.

My mother decided to follow me until she discovered my secret. She was angry when she found out that I had an actual sharpener. She insisted that I had stolen the pencil sharpener, and without any explanation, she started hitting me. My brother Julio tried to defend me. He tried to explain why I had the sharpener, but my mother was set in her belief and started hitting Julio as well. My mother believed that I had stolen the sharpener and was angry that I brought it home without hesitation. The next day my mother accompanied me to school and made me return what I had taken. I was in utter disbelief and embarrassed. I grabbed my mother's hand and begged her not to make me do this. She looked at me with disappointment and said, "Today you took a sharpener; tomorrow, it will be a cow." My heart fell into the center of my stomach when she said, "I do not want a thief in my house." Though I did not believe what I did was stealing, I knew that my mother was right. I shouldn't have taken anything home that wasn't mine. I stood in front of the class and teacher and apologized for what I did. This was truly a traumatizing moment in my life. I would never take anything that doesn't belong to me.

My brother Joaquin's behavior put a lot of stress on my mother. Still, to this day, I am unsure of how my mother was able to deal with the disrespect Joaquin inflicted on the rest of the family. Not only did he stir up problems within our household, but he also caused the neighbors to frequently complain about how he would take his aggression out on their animals as well as their house. The neighbors insisted he was looking for problems. No one liked him; everyone complained about him. There were many occasions when my mother had to travel to the state penitentiary and pay a fine because he was arrested for bad behavior. No matter what, my mother was always there to bail him out.

One day I heard my mother screaming so loud that devastation filled the air. My mother looked worried as a stream of tears spilled from her eyes. Joaquin had not returned home for a full day, including the night. We lived in a small town, so small that everyone knew each other. It was not long before we found out that the military had taken custody of my brother. At this time, according to the law in Colombia, each male citizen who was sixteen years or older had to serve a minimum of two years before having the option of continuing to serve the country. I must confess I was relieved and very happy when they took Joaquin away, but my mother was distraught for the first couple of days. I knew that under the guidance and training of the military, Joaquin would have a chance to grow and become a much better person.

I knew how upset my mother was, so every moment I could try and cheer her up, I would. I used to make her smile by telling her stories I came up with by myself. I thought of myself as a mini-novelist and tried to make her feel like I was reading an actual book.

My mother would rub my head and would always say, "How could this little girl come up with so much?" I knew I was not able to do much, but just seeing a little smile on her face made me feel like I had done it all.

I asked my mother about Julio all the time. I desperately wanted him to come back. My mother would tell me that Julio was fine just where he was, that he was working and studying at night, and I should be happy for him. I was sad that he was not with me, but deep down, I was joyous for him, believing that he was content as well. Julio was very smart. Without a calculator, he was able to do almost any mathematical equation in his head within seconds, It was incredible. He always knew every single answer. Numbers always made sense to him. I wished he would have had the option to go to a university. He would have done so well if he had the opportunity. I used to call him an encyclopedia because he had an answer for everything, and he used to call me a witch because everything I said would happen did happen.

When I felt lonely I would go to a spot near the river. I used to lie down on the grass, imagining my thoughts becoming reality. It was only then that I could just enjoy the solitude of watching the planes flying over me, wishing one of them would land in my town. I would be the first one to get on that plane and go anywhere. I loved watching them pass by.

After hours of pondering my future, I lost all concept of time, and it was getting late. I remember thinking if I did not get home before my mother, she would be very upset again. I remember repeating to myself, "I have to go back home. I will be in so much trouble if my mother is back before me." It was as if I had a sixth sense because once I stepped onto our property, I knew my mother was home. My heart began to beat out of my chest. I did not know whether I should go back to the river or if I should just kill myself. I knew she was going to punish me. There she was, just a few feet in front of me, screaming, "How dare you leave your sister alone?" I started to shiver.

"You think I don't have enough on my plate?" Guilt took over my entire being. I felt horrible. I knew how much my mother needed help, and instead, I decided to think of my future in the grass.

"The only thing I want from you is to help me with your sister. Is that too much to ask?" She knew what she was doing, and she was succeeding. I felt terrible.

"Let me ask you again." I looked down. "Answer me." She raised her voice and grabbed me by my shoulders. She shook them as if that was going to draw an answer out of me, which it did not. I was terrified and at a loss for words. It was then that she started hitting me.

My mother was very hard on me growing up. She used to tell me, "You are the example for your younger siblings." I was very upset. I cried that day, not because my mother hit me but because I disappointed her without being able to help her. I never wanted to disappoint my mother. That day I was just being a child, daydreaming. I never told my mother where I was because I knew she would not understand. I loved lying down on the grass and waiting for that big bird, the plane, to pass over me. It gave me hope that there was a better place for me. I knew I could not tell my mother because if I did, it would spoil what little bit of hope I had left; but in reality, nothing had changed from my earliest memories. We still had no money, and I did not see a future for myself.

We had just finished eating dinner, and I was waiting for her to grab her jacket. In an innocent yet curious voice, I questioned my mother before she left. "Madre, can I go with you?" She stared into my eyes. I was familiar with that look; it sent shivers down my spine. To my surprise, she took my hand without a single word and took me with her.

Before we could leave, we had to take my sister to a neighbor's house because she could not be left alone. I remember walking for a while, unsure of which direction we were traveling. Once we arrived in town, we walked swiftly to the hospital. She was holding my hand very tightly, as if she needed me.

Everyone in the hospital greeted her as if they knew my mother well. One of the nurses said, "Hi, Herminia, how are you?" I could not understand why everyone was chatting as if they were close.

"I've had worse days," she said with a shrug. My mother was not very neighborly, so naturally, she answered dismissively.

I pulled her hands aside to question her once again. "Madre, do you work here?" Sweetness and innocence took over my demeanor.

"Yes, darling, I'm a doctor." I crinkled my nose in response, and confusion took over my face. My mother laughed, and then I laughed because we both knew it was a joke. Just hearing the sound of laughter spill from her lips created an orb of happiness inside of me.

We sat down on a long couch and waited for about twenty minutes. It took everything in me not to talk. I had so many questions, but I knew it would be better for me to stay quiet. A nurse then called my mother and said, "Herminia, only ten minutes, please. He did not have a good night last night." You could tell my mother was upset after speaking with the nurse. I did not understand anything that the adults were talking about, and I was confused as to why my mother pulled my hand and why her hand was freezing. I watched my mother walk over to a small window, look into another room, and cry. She started to pray without moving. It felt as if she was standing there forever. I was so curious as to what she was looking at.

"Can I see?" I asked. She lifted me without speaking and brought my face closer to the window. I could not believe it. There, I saw my little brother. I had forgotten about him for the longest time. At that moment, I knew I would never forget what I had just seen. My baby brother had tubes coming out of every part of his little body. He was connected to a machine. I hugged my mother; I began to cry and asked her to put me down. "Madre, what's wrong with him?"

"Luis is sick." I wanted more details. "When he gets better, we will bring him home with us." She did not give me the explanation I needed. After seeing my brother, we left the hospital. We had to take the same long walk it took for us to get to the hospital.

"How long will Luis be there?" My mother's shoulders slumped before she could speak again.

"Too long, my love." She was so sad. It was almost as if she smelled of depression.

"Why can't I touch him?" I was so young that I did not realize when my mother left after dinner each night, she needed to be alone. Not only was she dealing with issues that were too complex for me to understand, but she also used this time to cope with her struggles. This was not a place for me to be, and I should not have been a part of this. My mother needed time to be an adult, not only a mother, and she needed time to deal with her emotions. My being there did not allow her to have that experience.

"Because he can't move; he has to heal." I continued asking questions because nothing made sense to me. I wanted to know, but I could not understand. "I will explain everything to you, but not today." She broke down in tears as we walked home. I decided then it was time for me to stop asking questions.

After that day, every time she visited my baby brother in the hospital, I made it a point to go with her so she would not be alone. Sometimes we would bring my sister Sandra with us. My mother used to cry a lot when she did not hear good news about Luis's health. I did not want her to go to the hospital by herself because I wanted her to know that she was not alone.

* * *

Sometimes it felt like all parts of my life were at a standstill. The people of this town were comfortable with the little they had. I could not see myself accomplishing anything if I stayed there. But a small voice inside me told me that I should be persistent.

It didn't matter how many Stones on the Road I had to step over. I wouldn't give up. I did not lose hope that one day I could go far, and make a difference. When my mother saw her children grow upset, she would often take us to Tío Isaias and Tía Rafaela's. Being with our cousins made us very happy, Though my tío and tía's home was always a place that cheered us up, my mother always made sure that we did not go very often because it was not fair to them. They were not wealthy people, but they always gave to us, and we always made sure to never abuse their kindness.

* * *

That afternoon we went to the hospital together. My mother received good news. The doctor said that because my brother was developing enough strength, he was going to be disconnected from the machine that was keeping him alive. I took my mother's hand and said, "Madre, you look very happy."

"Yes, my darling. Today is the best day of my life because I will be able to go inside Luis's room." Excitement poured from her. Something I've never seen. "It has been a long three years, and I finally can have him in my arms again." I knew in my heart that this moment was bittersweet for her. It was a happy moment because my mother could finally hold her son, but it was heartbreaking because, for the last three years, she could not be a true parent to him.

"Madre," I began to question, "why was Luis in the hospital for so long?" My mother let out a long breath I had no idea she was holding.

"Remember when he had bronchitis and a very high fever?" I nodded. "He was very sick that night when I took him to the hospital. He had a broken lung, so they had to take him from me." I was ashamed of myself for disregarding him. I knew my mother visited the hospital daily, but there was no link for me to that night, losing my little brother in our home. He did not die, so it was not as if we lost him to death. We lost his spirit, and I unknowingly forgot about him. My mother continued to talk.

"They had to take him from me so he could recover better. The doctor said that I should not have any physical contact with him. It was not smart for the baby to grow attached to anybody, especially me as the mother, because he could not move."

"It would speed up the healing process because his lungs would heal themselves. Your brother could live with one lung. But the other lung should heal naturally. Do you understand darling?" This was a lot of information, and emotionally it was hard for me to understand. How could I forget about my little brother? I asked myself over and over again. I answered her, "It's kind of like when someone breaks their ribs."

"Yes," she said. I asked, "I'm coming with you, right?"

I needed to have the reassurance that she wasn't going to change her mind. After waiting a long time, they led us into my brother's room and lifted him carefully. When they handed Luis to my mother, I stood at the corner of the room. I lost all feeling in my body; I was completely numb. I could not move. My mother was cuddling him, and all I could think was how skinny and vulnerable he was. My mother soaked up the next few minutes as she applied cream to his skin, covered with sores from being in bed for so long. She could hardly speak as a river of tears dripped down onto Luis's body.

As my mother massaged his legs, she questioned the nurse. "Is he going to be able to walk?" The nurse handed my mother a tissue.

"Yes, Herminia, he will learn to walk again." The nurse held my mom ever so tightly, but her body language lacked sympathy.

"You will see, soon nobody will be able to stop him from running." The nurse gave my mother a poke on the shoulder. "With love and patience, your son will walk again." She left the room showing not one bit of emotion.

My mother was so captivated by Luis's presence that she forgot I was in the room too. It reminded me of how I forgot about Luis all of these years.

"What are you doing in that corner?" My mother broke the silence in the room.

"Come close to your brother so you can touch him." Afraid to do so, I walked beside him and kissed his little legs. He was so skinny, with beautiful brown eyes. I smiled and touched his hair, but he did not smile back. I kissed him again as I broke into tears. The nurse came back into the room and said it was time to go. My mother begged,

"Please can I have a little more time?" to which the nurse quickly responded, "No."

"I'm sorry, Herminia, but a representative from the billing department wants to speak with you." My mother ignored the nurse.

"Can I take him home today?" my mother asked.

"I don't know. My superiors can answer your questions." The nurse grew nasty, and I no longer had respect for her. My mother put the little boy down and followed the nurse to the office.

We walked down a very long hallway, my mother squeezing my hand without realizing it. "Madre, you're hurting me," I said.

"I'm sorry, I didn't mean to." I could tell my mother was afraid. As she tightly held my hand, I could practically see the wheels turning in her head as she thought about the various ways she could pay for my brother's treatments over the last three years.

"Are we taking my brother home today?" I asked.

"Of course, we are taking him home," my mother answered. With not a single penny left in her pocket, I was skeptical as to how she planned on making this meeting go smoothly.

"If we take him home, we can teach him how to walk." Without acknowledging my response, she bent down before me and looked straight into my eyes.

"I want you to do me a favor. God always listens to the good children. I want you to pray to God that we can take your brother home." My mother sounded desperate.

"Okay, Madre, I will." I nodded and began to pray.

Upon knocking on the door of the billing office, a woman welcomed us in and asked us to sit down. She offered me a cookie. Unable to eat, knowing that something didn't feel right, I politely thanked her for her kind gesture and held the cookie in my hand. If anyone else would have offered me a cookie on any other day, I would have eaten it, but I just could not at this very moment. I knew this woman's intentions were impure, and her motive was to wrap up this meeting quickly, as we were just another one of her cases. I somehow felt all the emotions that my mother was holding inside of her.

The woman went on to hand my mother a stack of papers. My mother looked at them and started to cry.

"You know that I do not have this kind of money."

"I know, Herminia." She paused. "I understand. That's why I'm here to help you." My mother was scared. "The first thing that I want you to understand is that this is a hospital, not a charity, but we can work this out in many ways."

My mother was like a ticking time bomb right before an explosion.

"You don't have to cry, and please do not pretend that you thought it was possible to come here with the intention of taking your son home today." The woman acted as if my mother was trying to act as a victim. "Without clearing out the bills, you cannot take him home. My suggestion to you right now is to talk to the pink ladies, the nuns who work in the hospital. They help people negotiate their finances." A look of hope appeared in my mother's eyes. The woman continued speaking, "Go to room 3B and ask for Madre Teresa. She will help you. I will see you tomorrow at the same time." Just like that, the conversation was over.

"So this means that I cannot take Luis home today?" my mother asked.

The woman's tone of voice changed. In an unsympathetic manner, she said, "I have had enough, Herminia. We have been nothing but patient with you. You have had over three years to save money. You knew this day would come, so please do me a favor and resolve the financial situation with the hospital." Speechless, my mother's emotions began to shift dramatically toward anger. "I will give you clearance to take your child once the finances are handled. Until then, we have nothing to discuss. Now, if you don't mind, I'm heading to a meeting." She gestured for us to leave her office.

Still holding the cookie, I thought it best to give it back. "Thank you," I said, handing the cookie back. The woman lifted her glasses as she looked at me, confused as to why I would do such a thing. My mother and I then headed to room 3B, where Madre Teresa was.

"Hello, Herminia. I want you to know that I am aware of your situation, and I understand what you are going through. For this reason, we have waited to solve the problem. We know you are a woman of God, and I want you to know that a good future is waiting for your little boy."

My mother listened to Madre Teresa, her words going in one ear and out the other.

My mother knew she was all talk, and there was no sincerity there.

"The problem is we sometimes close our hearts and prohibit God from helping us."

I knew my mother was not listening to anything the nun was saying. "Are you listening to me, Herminia? I feel like you are not present here. We've had this conversation before." Madre Teresa was right. My mother was not present at this moment. She was thinking about her son and the bills. Of course, she was not listening to Madre Teresa.

"Madre Teresa, I want you to understand me as a mother, my situation, my position. I want you to try to understand..."

"Please don't pretend that this is the first time we have spoken about this situation. What I understand is that you have five children waiting for you at home. If you love this little boy the way you say you do, you will do the right thing for him, which is to sign the papers and give him up for adoption." Before that moment, I had never heard the word adoption before. I had no clue what Madre Teresa was talking about. "There is a nice couple who are very well off and are willing to pay for Luis's medical bills and take care of him. This child will most likely be sick for the rest of his life. Don't you think it would be better to go through with the adoption?" She was speaking to my mother as if she lacked basic knowledge and failed to comprehend what was being discussed. "Instead of making a big deal about it, sign the papers, and we can all move forward."

My mother exhaled once again. "Okay. Can you please give me one more week with him? Then I will sign the papers."

If you knew my mother, you knew she had a plan. She wasn't going down until she tried every single option that was physically possible. She went on to act as if she was defeated and had lost all hope, but deep down, I knew she wasn't leaving any of her children behind.

"Sorry, Herminia, but you had three years."

"I came here because I thought you were going to help me."

"I am helping you," Madre Teresa said. "You just don't see it."

"Is there any way I can work in the hospital for free? I will do anything," my mother begged. "I can come at night after I feed the kids. Please help me. I want to keep my baby." You could hear the pain in her voice.

"Herminia," she said condescendingly, "even if you worked here for twenty years, you still would not have enough money to pay this bill. Your son will be in very good hands. Go home and take care of your other children, and when you are ready to sign the papers, come in." She dismissed my mother just as the woman in the billing office did.

My mother stood up and, with all the dignity in the world, said, "Thank you for allowing me to hold my baby today." The level of sarcasm and pride that emanated from my mother was incredible. Even in the worst situations, my mother found a way to exercise her dominance and hold herself to a level deserving of respect.

Chapter Five

On a day like no other, my mother was acting very strangely. It was the week following our meeting at the hospital. The administrator had instructed us not to return unless my mother planned to sign the paperwork, relinquishing her rights as Luis's mother. That weekend my mother was acting weird. She was packing stuff in a bag and I was in disbelief, wondering if we were moving again.

"We have to move fast," she said.

My confusion grew. "Are we running away again?" I asked.

"Stop!" she screamed, "I am sick and tired of you asking me questions." Fear gripped me. "Come here and help me." Her tone was firm. "We have to move fast," my mother repeated. "It is going to get dark. Hold your sister's hand and follow me." I listened and moved as fast as I could, but at the same time, I was crying. My mother acted as if she did not care.

My mother handed Sandra and me a bag before she picked up hers. My bag was on my shoulder. Its weight was pulling me down, but at my age, I knew not to complain. By the time we got to the park near the hospital, it had grown dark and was very cold. My mother left me with Sandra and with the three laundry bags.

My focus was on the church clock. The hour had changed three times since my mother had left us there. "*Where is my mother?*," I thought to myself. Sandra was crying, and I was scared. The lonely look of darkness only fueled my fears, and when Sandra began to cry, I began to overreact internally. I felt helpless and had no idea what I should do.

After three hours passed, we had not moved from the spot where our mother had left us. Suddenly, a man approached us. He was wearing a hat, shawl, and glasses and had a thick mustache that sat above his lip. He began to draw closer.

"Hola," he said.

"Please go away. I don't speak to strangers. My mother is coming back soon." I responded immediately.

"Strangers?" I heard a huge laugh that I recognized. He pulled the mustache off, and there she stood.

"Madre?" I asked. She knelt on her knees right in front of me.

"I'm proud of you. You're such a good girl. Let's go. We have to take the next bus. We are no longer safe here." I could not understand why my mother thought that. I was holding Sandra's hand, when I heard a faint cough. My little brother was underneath my mother's shawl. I could not believe it; that was my brother. We were all finally together again.

"Are we going to pick up Julio now?"

She looked at me with such a sweet look in her eyes, but she was not in the mood for me and all my questions.

"Stop with your questions." Her lips showed a small smile.

After a rather long, dark walk, we finally reached the bus stop. All four of us got on the bus, and I was relieved as soon as we took our seats. I could not help but thank God for finally taking a seat. My sister and I began to play with our little brother, but he still was not smiling.

"Okay, everybody, this is going to be a long ride. Let's try to get some rest." I tried to fall asleep, but I was too excited. Everything I had wanted for the longest time had now become real. I knew we were leaving, but I had no idea where we were going. Though I was unsure of our future, I was in love with the idea of leaving the town that I hated so much. I believed that wherever we were going would be better than where we were. While the road became dark, I was no longer fearful, as my happiness overrode all the darkness that loomed over me and my family.

"Are there any airplanes where we are going now?" I asked my mother.

"Yes, sweetie," my mother answered. I started planning my future again. First, I have to find a job so I can make a lot of money. Then I will buy a house. In that very house, I will have a refrigerator full of food, and everyone will be welcome. I realized it was getting darker as the sun began to set and daylight became night. We had been on the bus for hours, and now we were on another one. I knew then that we were going very far away from home. My mother hugged and kissed everyone. There I sat, hoping that I was not dreaming again. I looked out the open window, enjoying the cold air on my face. My thoughts began to move as fast as the bus. I was looking forward to having a home again. I wanted to go back to school, and I want to go to college. I knew I wanted to be a lawyer. I always thought I was going to be the one to stand up for those who are vulnerable. I wanted to send all the bad people in the world to jail.

When I finally started working, my initial aspiration was to purchase a television with the money I made. I vividly remember the last time I went to Tío Miguel's house. My cousin closed the fence on me and broke my arm. It was so painful. When my mother found out, she went ballistic. My mother told me I was not a good girl. I should have known better than to go near them. It was then that my mother decided to burst into my tío's house and make a scene.

"Come out, you fucking bitch," my mother called out. "Come and hurt me but not my daughter. Next time you touch one of my children, I will kill you with my bare hands." Thank God the gate was closed because if not, I have no doubt that my mother would have done something drastic. My tía screamed from inside her home.

"Herminia, it was an accident." This made my mother more furious.

"An accident!" my mother screamed. "You guys are despicable. You closed the gate on my daughter's arm because she wanted to watch TV, and you say it was an accident? Where is my brother? Oh, I forgot, he's a coward because only a coward would allow something like this to happen in his house." You could hear the hurt in my mother's voice. She was so distracted by the ignorance of her brother's actions that she lost sight of the pain I was in.

"Don't you call my husband a coward, you piece of shit. Whore! You don't belong here. Why don't you leave this town and leave us alone? It's not our fault that your husband doesn't want you anymore." My mother was tremendously upset, but all I could think of was my arm and how much it hurt. I was in so much pain. I was scared that if I told my mother, she would break my other arm as punishment for going near our family's house.

"I feel bad for you. Your tongue is sharp like a weapon." Disgust took over my mother's tone. "Remember, you have children too, and God doesn't like ugly. I will never forget the pain you gave me and my children." She took me by the other hand and took me to the hospital. It was there that we found out my arm was broken, and they had to put it in a cast. I liked that I had a cast. I used to draw planes on it in hopes that one day I would be able to fly on one.

Then it hit me as I came back to reality. My stomach was turning, and I was no longer feeling well.

"Madre?" I called, but it was too late. I threw up all over the seat. I was shaking. The people on the bus were not happy at all. My mother cleaned me up the best that she could.

She said, "Stop looking out the window and close your eyes. We will be there soon."

"Where are we going?" I asked.

"Duitama." I had no idea what she was talking about. All I knew was that I wanted to be anywhere that was not moving.

"Is it pretty there?" I asked curiously.

"Very pretty," she said, as I suddenly began falling asleep.

My mother woke me up when we were getting off the bus. Sandra and I sat on top of the laundry bags. My mother never put down Luis; she held him close to her because she was scared of losing him again. We had just arrived in the city of Duitama, in 1977, and it was very early in the morning. My mother walked to the public phone to make a call. It looked as if she made a couple of calls, but I could barely see her speaking a word. She came back to us with a worried look on her face. My mother instructed us not to move and to stay there. When she came back, she brought us bread and soda. We had not eaten for many hours. The bread smelled like heaven; it was so fresh and comforting.

After we ate, she returned to the phone, and soon after that, she sat directly next to me.My mother was so vulnerable; she hugged me and spoke while crying."I hope you can forgive me for what I am putting you through." My heart ached for her.

"Please, Madre, don't cry. There is nothing you did wrong. You're the best mom in the world." I hugged my mother back tightly. "Who are you calling?" I asked.

"My friend, Lastenia, but she's not answering. I believe it's too early in the morning for her." My mother and I held hands. It was so cold that the only warmth I felt was from her grasping my fingers. I was scared. My mother was extremely nervous as we walked together again to the public phone, hoping we'd have better luck this time. Finally, she got in contact with her. She took a pencil out of her pocket and started writing down an address. After she ended the call, my mother, Sandra, Luis, and I took a lengthy bus ride to get to our final destination.

Upon arrival, we took our items inside a house in the middle of nowhere. The windows and doors had gaping holes, and the flooring throughout was unfinished. It was evidently still under construction. We found a cow living inside the house as if that were normal. My mother led it outside and then started cleaning the house as best as she could.

She fed us again—bread and soda. The night of our arrival brought nothing but misery.

Our incomplete home was drenched in water due to the non-stop rain.

"Madre, how are we going to live here?" I asked.

"We are together, and that is what's important. A lot of people have less than us, so be thankful."

I nodded. I could not understand how anyone could have any less than us. "Help me take the cardboard boxes to cover the windows." We spent the night there.

The next morning my mother's friend Lastenia came and brought us a few things for the home—pots, pans, food, and blankets. She brought the necessities, but it was everything to us because we had nothing. Lastenia was pleasant, but I could not stop staring at her. Her black hair and gray eyes frightened me. After my mother told me that she was a good person, I felt horrible for judging her. Her actions and intentions toward me and my family were generous, and yet I could not get myself to hug her. I was told to stay inside while my mother and Lastenia smoked cigarettes. I knew my mother did not want me to hear their conversation, but of course, I had to be curious and listen.

"I will pay you for us to stay in your house by washing and ironing your clothes," my mother said. Lastenia agreed.

"Okay, I think that's fair. I just want you to know that this arrangement can only be for a short time."

"As soon as I find a job, we will leave. We will not cause any problems, I promise." Desperation fell from my mother's lips. In the moments following my mother's last words, the conversation turned ugly.

"Are you sure that the police are not looking for you?" Lastenia questioned. My mother was chuckling nonchalantly.

My mother yelled, "They probably are...that's why we're here, so they won't find me. I didn't steal anything from anyone. Luis is my son." She paused to take a breath. "I didn't have a choice; they didn't give me a choice. If you're going to judge me, I'll take my kids and leave now. I am not separating from any of them again, no matter what happens."

"Herminia, I am not your enemy, you are going to scare the children. Calm down.

You can stay here, but this is not a good place for your children either," Lastenia said. My mother cried when she shared why she took Luis from the hospital.

"I understand everything you are going through. I'm just worried about you, my friend," said Lastenia. My mother nodded. "Just be careful you're not in the fields where you came from anymore," Lastenia spoke truthfully. "It's not easy to find work around here. For now, I spoke to three of my closest friends. They need help to clean their houses. Go tomorrow. Let them know that I referred you."

"Thank you," my mother said. "We will be okay. Thank you for what you have done for me."

"Who is going to take care of the kids?" Lastenia asked with sensitivity.

"My daughter Esperanza, she is more than 12 years old." She answered normally.

"She is responsible enough to take care of them."

"They're not going to go to school?" Lastenia asked.

My mother's tone changed. "Do you have any other questions for me?" she answered nastily, avoiding Lastenia's previous question.

"This is not the small town that you came from. There are evil people here; please be careful." My mother was breathing heavily. She could not wait for Lastenia to finish speaking. She put her arms out to hug Lastenia to end the conversation, and they kissed each other on the cheek.

"Don't worry. Tomorrow I will be there early to clean your house," my mother said once again, trying to end the conversation.

After Lastenia left, my mother started putting our three bags of laundry away, and for the first time, my mother could cook us a meal and make the place look like a home.

It was nice to know that we had a roof over our heads and a hot meal in our stomachs, even if it was just temporary.

My mother surprised us one day when she walked into our home with Julio. I was so happy when I saw him. We always thought we could have been twins because we always felt so connected. My mother felt at ease to see all her children under one roof. Julio brought us bread, and my mother made him a cup of coffee. My mother began to tell him about the little adventure that she had to go through to bring our little brother Luis home.

"Now we are together again," was all I could think to myself.

"Tío Abraham was asking for you. Is it okay if I tell him where to find you?" Julio asked my mother.

"Yes," she responded cheerfully. "I would love to see him." Tío Abraham and my mother were the youngest of their siblings, hence their very strong bond with one another. They hardly ever fought and always had a loving relationship. Tío Abraham drove a truck to deliver unleaded gasoline to various cities. His trips took him sometimes three or four weeks to return home, but he made it a priority to see my mother. Tío Abraham always brought food and left money for my mother to help with our expenses. We all loved him; he was the best-looking uncle. His physical appearance resembled a model. All the women went crazy when they saw him. No matter how far he was from my mother, he always found his way back to her.

Julio eventually had to go back to work, but he promised us he would visit. My mother hugged me tightly, anticipating my soon-to-be heartbroken feelings due to Julio leaving. My mother still could not find a job, so she continued to work by washing and ironing clothes for wealthy people, and we were surviving from the money she made. I took care of Luis and Sandra, but I always wondered if I would ever get the opportunity to go back to school. I was afraid to ask because I already knew the answer. If I had a chance of ever returning to school, my mother would have told Lastenia, but I now had to take Joaquin's place in caring for my younger siblings.

Each time Julio came to visit, he would complain about the humiliation he had to endure from our relatives and his co-workers. Julio was working for a distant relative who was not sympathetic. My brother was working as best as he could, being so young, but it never seemed to be enough.

"I know it is not easy," my mother said, "but remember you have food and a roof over your head. You should thank God for what you have." Julio agreed with my mother, but I could not have disagreed more. My mother continued, "There will always be someone out there who needs more than you. Have patience; better times will come. If God gives us what we have, then it is all that we need. What will keep us going is working toward what we want. If you are not happy with what you have, you must work for it. Just be strong." She always made sure that we never victimized ourselves. I sat in the corner, listening to my mother's words. All that was running through my mind was, "How could my mother see all good when everything around her was getting harder and harder?"

That week in particular, the rains were so heavy that no place in the house was dry. Because there were no actual windows or doors, everything was soaking wet. The house was falling apart, and the cardboard boxes we once used as protection had disintegrated as the water saturated them. Once again, my mind drifted into thinking how my mother could stay so positive. I remember feeling so hopeless; I just could not understand.

"Really, Madre? Your God gives us what we need?" I spoke sarcastically. I was so frustrated that I was taking my emotions out on my mother.

She approached me, full of determination. "I don't know what you are complaining about, my beautiful girl. You have the nerve to question God." I expected my mother to find something within her line of sight to beat me with. Instead, she spoke calmly, "Very good. You should use that anger you have toward God to make a difference. Maybe do something positive with it." She beat me with her words. "But instead, you complain. Why don't you work on your goals instead, if you have any? Stop complaining about everything because you are the only person that can change anything." My mother's words were remarkable and have always followed me throughout my life. Her words stung, but they affected me in a positive way. As helpful as my mother's words were, I had trouble thinking of goals for myself, because each day we lived through obstacles that grew harder and harder. Every day that passed was more difficult than the one previous; we continued to struggle. How much more positive could I be?

I stayed at home with Sandra and Luis. My little brother was still unable to walk, so Sandra and I would wrap a large rolled-up blanket around his chest so that we could hold him up without actually touching him. He was able to balance himself on his feet while Sandra and I would carry his weight through the blanket. My mother came up with this idea because Luis was too fragile to hold physically. We would stand over him as if we were lifting objects that were too heavy for us, so we needed something to grasp. Slowly but surely, Luis became accustomed to balancing on his feet. One day, while my mother was working, Luis found enough strength in his legs as well as his heart to push through and take steps forward without Sandra and I holding his blanket. We decided that we were going to surprise my mother when she came home, so when she walked through the front of the house we told her to close her eyes and we called Luis to where she was. When she opened her eyes, she grabbed him before he could walk anymore as tears of happiness poured from her eyes.

Chapter Six

My mother had gotten up much earlier than usual to go to Lastenia's house to wash and iron their clothes upon agreement. My mother also cleaned her niece Socorro's house, who lived in Duitama. They gave my mother clothes and shoes that their children had outgrown. My mother was grateful. She came home exhausted, and I did not know how to help her. I used to massage her feet and soak them in water and that would make her feel better. I knew that each day she would wake up at 5:30 a.m. and would have to walk far to the bus. Her ride would then be another hour, and she would have to walk another twenty-five minutes to work. After a long day of work, she would then have to reverse her commute to return home. Her commute home was never easy because she was always exhausted, and some nights she would come home with bags filled with food and used clothing.

In the month of September 1978, we had very heavy rains, and it became impossible to live in our doorless and windowless home. The water had drenched our beds and everything was ruined.

"I think we have to leave this place," I said to my mother.

"I know, sweetie, it is horrible. I am going to see my friend Carmen next week. She is going to help me with a job." I was very happy for my mother, as it had been about a year since she had a stable job. She told me this job would be a good opportunity for her.

My mother gave me hope.

I often knew, intuitively, when something bad was about to happen. I had a gut feeling that made its presence felt. Because of this, my mother once brought me to a priest to have holy water poured onto my head. The priest thought something was wrong with me, but I just saw life through a different lens than everyone else. It feels like a burning sensation under my skin. It starts at the center of my stomach and surfaces like goosebumps on my skin, immediately sending an instant message to my brain that something is going to happen. This happens in my dreams, as well.

My mother constantly asked me if I was still having these dreams. I would tell her no even though I was. I lied to my mother. I knew if I told my mother the truth about the dreams I was having, she would bring me back to church to talk to the priest. The priest would pour holy water on my head and pray over me. I did not want my mother to worry about me. The dreams had become so frequent that I began questioning if something was wrong with me. I would wake up with pains in my body, and the bad feeling would become unbearable.

I even dreamed that a man would come to our home and take me away from my family. On Sundays, I knew we were going to have to go to church. I did not know if there was a way to tell my mother that I did not want to go. My mother loved when I sang, but the priest who played the piano would have me stand next to him. I truly loved to sing, but I hated the way the priest touched me. It was inappropriate. He would rub the back of my upper thighs, my bottom, and my waist. I knew it was wrong, and so did he, but no one else saw. It made me feel very uncomfortable. That is the only reason I never wanted to return to church.

That Sunday, to my surprise, we didn't go to church. My mother was waiting for someone at the door. Suddenly, a man with a wagon and his mule came upon the home (the man from my dreams). Immediately, she began placing all of our belongings in the wagon. My family and I sat on the very top of all of our items and followed our mother's orders. The man began pulling the mule, leaving behind that place where we lived for a year. I no longer wanted to stay on top. I decided to jump off the carriage.

"What are you doing?" my mother questioned me.

"We're hurting the mule," I said, feeling the animal's pain. The owner of the mule laughed cold-heartedly.

"My mule can carry ten times more than that, young lady." The man did not understand my reasoning, but my mother did. She then got off the carriage and walked next to me and the man. It was a long walk, but my mother still looked at me and somehow smiled.

"Are you sure you don't want to go on top of the mule?" My feet were aching, but I was adamant about staying true to myself and my belief in not hurting a living thing. I was very tired, and I knew this animal had to be just as tired, as well. So here I was again, traveling with my family with no knowledge as to where we were headed. Surprisingly, I was happy, mainly because I did not have to go to church, and I could leave that perverted priest behind me. We finally reached our destination an hour later. All I saw was a garage door. My mother opened it after paying our new landlord. This was to be our new home.

My mother was quiet, and I knew this meant she was either worried or angry about something. And for once I knew it was better for me to not ask questions. My family and I unpacked our belongings, which weren't much after the damage from the rain. My mother fed us milk and bread, we prayed, and went to sleep. The next day, my mother got up and went to work, and as usual, I took care of Sandra and Luis. I began to grow frustrated and I felt like there was no way out. I began to empathize with Joaquin because I finally began to understand why he grew to be so angry and resentful towards us. Having to take care of multiple children at a young age forced him, and me, to forget about ourselves and all that we wanted to accomplish in our lives. My mother often made us think about what we wanted to change in our lives. She would tell us to come up with goals, but I asked myself in my circumstance, what can I achieve? I wanted to help but I didn't know how. I would look around this place. It wasn't that bad. At least we had a door and window. I was too young to find a job, but for now, taking care of my siblings is what I have to do. And wait for my mom to come home everyday.

A lady knocked on the door and introduced herself as Martha. She brought us food and explained that she worked at the same place as our mother.

"I am the nanny where your madre works. She told me about the situation you are in, so I talked to my aunt, and she is going to let you stay here for a month. If you need anything, please ask. If I can help you, I will. I like your mother; she is a very good person."

"Thank you," I said before she left.

Whenever we moved from one place to another, my vivid dreams returned. Some were beautiful, while others were horrible. Either way, they all came true. At this time, we still did not have a television, so I listened to music on a little black radio. I was listening to music one day when a common phrase my mother would say began running through my head: "Every individual has a purpose in life." I still questioned my purpose in life. The only thing that came to mind was how I really wanted to go back to school, but I knew that was not possible.

This day, in particular, was one of the worst days. I will never forget. I was so scared because I did not know what was happening to me. In my naive mind, it felt as if I was bleeding all over, and I had to constantly clean myself. I continued to bleed in my underwear, and I got really scared—I thought I was going to die. I decided it would be best if I stayed on the toilet. I thought I would live longer and not bleed to death if I had just stayed as still as possible. When I heard my mother's voice outside the bathroom, I instantly felt so much better.

"Open the door."

I did. I was so happy to see my mother that I began to cry hysterically. My mother came into the bathroom and noticed I was shaking. When she realized what was happening, she was at ease.

"Don't worry; you just got your period." I did not understand. My mother explained to me in a few words what was happening to me. At that moment, I had no idea how getting my period would change my life in such a drastic way. My life became harder than it already was. That day something changed, not only in my body but in my mother's mind as well.

I began to notice that my mother was no longer sweet, and she was extremely hard on me. I never gave my mother any problems; that was more Joaquin and Julio's department. I considered myself a good girl; I always followed orders and did my best. My mother grew to be so strict that depression was all I ever felt. When my mother would leave for work, I would sit outside and cry for hours. I was appalled at my life, and every positive affirmation my mother ever said disgusted me. I was asking my mother's God to let me fall asleep and not let me wake up. I was not looking forward to anything. I think these feelings were partly from my hormones changing, but my mother's actions toward me only made me feel worse.

One morning my mother saw me crying, and when she sat next to me, she spoke words I never expected her to say.

"I know I've been very hard on you lately."

"Did I do something wrong, Madre? I want to know why you are so angry with me."

"You're a woman now, and this is putting you in a very dangerous situation." I grew more and more terrified as the seconds passed. "This means if you go near a man and let him touch you, you will not be able to stop him from having sex with you. If he touches you, he won't stop, and you will get pregnant." Fear rushed through my veins. "Boys your age are going crazy; their hormones have them acting crazy. Boys are animals. You can never trust them, and if you do, you will get hurt." I could not understand why my mother was being so harsh. "If something happens, you will be the responsible one. Take this as a warning." Was my mother trying to protect me from her past? "Be careful. The only thing I can tell you is that any sign you give them, they will take it the wrong way. So my suggestion is to stay away from them."

I was so terrified to get my cycle. Each month I thought any boy or man near me could catch the scent of my blood. I walked past the boys as fast as I could in the street, or anywhere, for that matter. I never wanted to experience a menstrual cycle ever again. I thought after my conversation with my mother that there would be some changes to our relationship. I so hoped that things would return to how they were before my first cycle, but they did not. It was hard for me to understand why sometimes my mother was kind and how other times she was mean. I did everything she asked of me: cooked, cleaned, and took care of the kids, but all too many times, it seemed as if it was not enough.

My nightmares suddenly returned, indicating that something bad was going to happen. I felt it in my soul.

One horrible afternoon, my mother came home, and for the first time, without any reason, she grabbed my hair and pulled it hard. She started to express her frustration about how the house was not clean. It did not make any sense to me; there was nothing wrong with our home. The house was spotless, and everything was in its place. I decided that my best option was to just go along with my mother's anger because I knew she was stressed about something. I just did not know what it was. My mother was trying hard to find us another place to live because her friend was unable to house us any longer. Each time my mother found affordable housing, she was unable to take the offer because of how many children she had. Many landlords did not want tenants who had children. That's why she could never find a home for us. I thought that this was the reason for all of my mother's stress.

Each time we walked outside, my mother held my hand. It made her feel safe. She wanted us to stay together, and I noticed she did not like the children who always played in the street. My mother noticed how the boys stared at me. I knew that this was the reason my mother grew to be so protective after I got my period. My mother was so worried, but the last thing on my mind was boys. I was too busy cooking, cleaning, and babysitting to think of anything else.

On another day, my mother came home in a horrible state. The sound of her voice pierced my ears as she screamed her disappointment with everything in our home.

"Take a plastic bag with a change of clothes and come with me." As soon as those words fell from her lips, I felt like dying. "Do not ask questions." Before I knew it, I no longer had air in my lungs, and I could not breathe. My feet began to move before my mind could catch up, and I found myself hiding under our bed. My mother followed me with a broomstick in her hand. She was poking me, not to hurt me, but rather to get me to come out. After my refusal for about an hour, she collapsed on the floor and began to sob. I could not stand the sight of my mother being in so much pain, so slowly but surely, I inched my way out from under the bed. She opened her legs, and I crawled in between, and the two of us lay together, exhausted.

"You know I tried very hard to find a place for all of us to live, but no one wanted to rent to our family." I understood for once, but I continued to cry. "I would not forgive myself if something happened to you while I was at work. I know you want to go to school, and my niece Socorro promised me she would take care of you and send you to school at night." I was so happy that I could go to school. "All you need to do is help her take care of her house during the day, and you can finally go back to school." I was speechless. "This would only be for a short time. Isn't this what you wanted? To go to school?" It seemed as if my mother was trying to convince me to agree with her decision, but the decision had already been made, and there was no need for this discussion. I still could not speak. I wanted her to stop talking so badly; I just wanted to know where she was sending me. Like ripping off a band-aid, I wanted it to be quick, but I knew it would sting for a while longer.

"As soon as your older brother Edgar returns home from the military, we are going to look for a house, and we will all be together again." I was disappointed, and all I heard was lies. "I promise," she said. I knew at this point nothing was going to change my mother's mind. I took a plastic bag and filled it with a change of clothes and a hairbrush.

"I'm ready to go." Without saying a single word, I walked next to my mother until we arrived at her niece's house." Socorro was kind to us. Everything had happened so quickly, and I knew my mother did not want to prolong the situation any longer. This was so painful for her. We were both suffering, and I knew it was not easy for her to leave me there. My mother kissed my forehead and told me she would come back the following Sunday to visit. Then, just like that, she was gone.

The only thing I wanted to do at that moment was to die. I ran to the window thinking that she would return for me, but that never happened. Socorro's voice pulled me from my thoughts as I longed for my mother to come back. There she was with my plastic bag in her hands, and she asked me to follow her. She pointed out the area where I was going to be staying. Without wasting any time, she began to explain how she wanted things to be done in her house. She gave me a list of jobs that I had to complete daily, and if it was not done I was not going to be allowed to go to school.

"My children get up very early in the morning to go to school. I expect you to prepare breakfast for them." She was very demanding, completely different from the woman who opened the door to my mother and me. "They have to leave the house five minutes before seven because the bus picks them up at seven. After the kids leave, I want you to clean the kitchen right away." Once again, fear took over my demeanor. "You must keep the house in perfect condition. I would not like to hear any complaints from my husband. If you move fast, you can finish everything in time." There I stood in the corner of the little room that was going to become my home for the next two years. I watched this woman pacing back and forth, barking orders.

"My aunt told me you know how to cook, but I will supervise you until you know how we like things to be done. Once you do things as we wish, you may do it alone."

I was confused because, for the longest time, I had grown accustomed to doing things without supervision.

"After lunch, you will clean the kitchen again. On Fridays, you will do the laundry, and on Saturday, you will iron everything you washed on Friday." We did not own an iron back home, so her words seemed foreign to me. "The most important thing is that the uniforms for the kids be ready for Monday." I was afraid to ask what an iron was.

"Okay," I said, "and what time will I go to school?" I asked. She ignored my question and continued to talk.

"I know it sounds like a lot, but it's a piece of cake." I felt so lost. "Don't worry. I will write everything down so you won't have any excuse to forget anything." She ran her fingers through her hair uncaringly.

"Oh, and about school..." My heart began to race, and I was filled with anticipation. "If you do not hurry up and complete all of your tasks on time, I do not think you will be able to go to school." She began to make a mockery of me. "When you get up tomorrow, you must wear this uniform." It was the ugliest thing I had ever seen in my life. It was a navy blue smock and too large for my size. "Your hair must be up because I do not want it to fall in the food; my husband would not like that." I was going to follow every order she gave me. When she finished her speech, she told me that I could go to sleep, and I did just as she ordered.

The room where I stayed was directly next to the laundry room in the back of the house behind the patio. There was a small mattress on the floor, and it seemed as if Socorro was trying to humiliate me. Little did she know, this was no different for me because I used to sleep in the same condition with my family. It did not matter to me where I slept. All I knew was that I just wanted to be with my mother. I threw myself on the cold mattress and cried myself to sleep.

I remember waking up to the sound of someone knocking on my door. It still seemed to be very early because it was still dark outside. For a moment, I thought I was having one of my nightmares, but I was not. It was Socorro making sure that I was awake and ready to work. She went over my list of chores once again, and I tried to follow all of her rules the best that I could. The only thing that kept me going was the thought that if I completed all that she asked of me, I could finally return to school and see my mother again. I would do anything to make that happen.

The school that I was going to go to was very close to Socorro's home. I could see it in the distance when I would bring her children to the bus stop every morning. Each day, I walked the kids to the bus stop. I could not help but wonder what time the classes were starting at my future school. After the first week passed, I waited eagerly to see my mother on Sunday. When my mother did not come to see me as she promised, I was very sad. After three weeks passed, I began to believe that she no longer loved me anymore. I felt abandoned by her, and I tried to accommodate everyone in the house to avoid creating problems. I knew I was too young and I had so much responsibility, but I never complained. The workload was too much for one person. Socorro was so demanding, and each day I think she forgot a little more about how I was a young girl at the age of 13.

I was angry with God and with my mother. I felt abandoned by everyone. My mother did not even let me say goodbye to Sandra or Luis. The day that I left my home to come here, my mother and I were alone. My siblings were nowhere to be found, and I did not get to say goodbye. I had no idea where the rest of my family was, and I felt that the love they once had for me had expired.

Nearly two months had passed and I was cleaning the kitchen when I heard my mother's voice outside the house. She was talking to Socorro and that is when I decided to run to my room and close the door behind me. I stayed in my room until my mother left. I did not want to see her, even though I missed her so much. I just wanted to be alone. When my mother left, I cried for what felt like an eternity. I was so angry that she lied to me. I was upset because she had left me with Socorro. My mother said that if I came here I could go to school. That was a lie. My mother thought because I had food and a roof over my head that I would be fine. She thought this was the best option for me. There would be no men around me so no one could hurt me. Unintentionally, my mother was the one who was hurting me the most.

The next time my mother came, I could not have run into her arms any quicker. I missed her so much that I gave up being bitter. I told my mother that by that time, I was going to school every night from six to ten. My mother was happy for me and would visit every other month on a random Sunday. We would go to the park, play and have ice cream with Sandra and Luis. When the sky grew dark, a strong feeling of pain took over the pit of my stomach because I knew we were going to separate again. From sharing tears with my mother and siblings I had to return to the nightmare I was living each day. My mother always asked if Socorro and her family were treating me well, but I would lie each time. I would answer yes because I knew my mother's current situation. She would not be able to help me with anything, and I did not want to put any more pressure on her, so I suffered in silence for two long years. My mother was worried about me because I had lost a lot of weight and kept asking if I was okay. I explained that the work was hard and balancing school was even more difficult. I told her I was tired but was happy that I could finally go to school.

Chapter Seven

My birthday is November 8th, and just days before my fifteenth birthday, my mother returned from Paz De El Rio. She came to pick me up from Socorro's home and gave me the good news that we were going to live together again in Duitama. It was the best birthday present my mother could have given me. When my mother took me home that Sunday, I was so happy. For a moment I thought I was dreaming. I was so elated that we were finally going to be together again that I forgot to ask my mother why we were returning to Duitama.

While I was living with Socorro as her housekeeper, my mother, Sandra, and Luis were living in Paz Del Rio. My mother's friend, Carmen, had found her a job as a kitchen-aide in a factory. My family lived in a room inside the cafeteria. The only problem was that my mother's boss could not know that she had two small children with her. She was not allowed to have children with her, so Carmen helped hide them. Carmen would also take food from the cafeteria to feed Sandra and Luis. My mother explained to me that everything was going well until Joaquin showed up at her job unexpectedly. She said that she tried explaining the severity of her situation and that he was not allowed there because she would get into trouble and possibly lose her job. My mother was also worried that if Joaquin continued with his inappropriate behavior, her friend Carmen could be in jeopardy of losing her job, as well. Carmen had helped my mother so much, and my mother would not be able to live with herself if something happened to her because of Joaquin. Unfortunately, Joaquin did not listen to my mother's plea and frequently showed up at her job. My mother left for Duitama before Joaquin could find out where she was going. She had enough money saved up to leave.

She had to start all over again. Luckily, our new home was not as bad as some of our past homes. We had a moderately functioning bathroom and a door that locked.

Though Joaquin's behavior caused chaos in our life, I used it to my benefit because I could finally be with my mother again. She was able to find a good job working at a factory where dry grains were packaged in plastic bags. She sat for long hours in front of a hot seal and sealed plastic bags with controlled temperatures. An hour lunch was always given to her, but she never took it because she wanted to finish her workdays as soon as possible. This job also provided her with great health benefits. Luckily, I was also able to find a job selling cleaning products door to door. Finally, my siblings and I were able to go back to school.

After moving back to Duitama, although I slept, I still suffered from treacherous nightmares. About a year later, I awakened from a terrible nightmare, and my mother intuitively knew. She felt my forehead, believing that I had a fever. I could not wait until the sun rose; it had been such a long night. Finally, when we all awake, I knew something very bad was going to happen. I could not explain how I knew this, and to this day, I cannot. I started crying.

"What's wrong?" my mother asked.

"Something bad is going to happen," I said as tears poured from my eyes. She held me tight.

"Stop! Nothing bad is going to happen." She was my strength and the only person I ever needed. Her touch comforted me and always made me feel better. The next day my mother went to work as usual, and I took care of my siblings like any ordinary day. I did not let my siblings play outside because I was afraid something would happen to them. I could not wait for my mother to get home. She left every morning at 7:30 and returned at 5:30.

For dinner, I was expected to cook rice that would go with the eggs my mother would bring home to fry. That night, I had to feed my siblings rice alone because my mother had still not returned home. I went to school, but when I returned home, my mother was still not there. I grew worried but did not have the option to call anyone. We did not have a phone. Without realizing it, I fell asleep after hours of waiting for my mother. I woke up feeling cold air coming from the small window in the garage where we were living. I looked everywhere, hoping that my mother had come home at some point while I was asleep, but she never did.

I sent my little brother and sister to school and went looking for my mother at the factory. When I arrived at my mother's job, I noticed it was not yet open. I had to wait for about half an hour, and as soon as the building opened for the day, I ran straight to the receptionist to see if she had any information about my mother.

Without hesitation, the receptionist informed me that my mother had suffered a stroke the previous day and was transferred to a nearby hospital. I couldn't breathe, and I couldn't even cry. I experienced every emotion, yet I was numb. I felt like I could see the particles in the air. I was dizzy, confused, and unsure of what I was supposed to do. My heart ached, and the only thing I knew was that I needed to see my mother. I already knew where she was, so I knew where to go.

When I arrived at the hospital, I gave the first nurse I saw my mother's full name, and she instructed me to follow her. When I saw my mother, I knew the news was true. Her face was crooked, and she could not speak. My mother was placed in the intensive care unit. My muscles grew stiff, and I felt paralyzed. I was helpless. I couldn't do anything for her. I needed my mother more than ever, and I could not bear to lose her.

Once again, I was upset with God but knew I could not lose faith. My mother always had faith in God, and I knew if she was going to get better, I had to believe as she did. Faith was the only thing I had left. All of a sudden, I could no longer bear the stress of this situation, and I found myself running to the bathroom. I vomited uncontrollably, followed by a tsunami of tears. I had to pull myself together because my siblings needed me more than ever. Now it was up to me to be the caretaker of this family. I guess this was how my mother must have felt when Luis had first gotten sick. My mother's newfound illness had changed my life. I knew that being the oldest, I had to do whatever was needed to make sure my family was okay.

I had to be strong for Sandra and Luis. I cleaned my face with the sleeve of my sweater, got myself up, and made my way out of the bathroom. I glanced at my mother, unconscious, and I left without saying goodbye.

Before going home, I went to my cousin Arcelia's house. Arcelia was the wife of the man my brother Julio was working for. I asked her to please let Julio know that our mother had a stroke and was very ill. With a promise to relay the message, I told her that my mother was recovering in the hospital. Given that Arcelia was family, I was shocked when she did not bother to ask if we needed anything.

That Sunday, I got up very early to get Sandra and Luis ready for church. Our sole intention of going to church was to pray for our mother's health. We needed her to get better. I had never felt so alone before, not even when I was working for Socorro. I was scared and angry; life began to be too much for me. For the first time, I wondered where my older brothers were. They were never there when I needed them. I was the middle child; how could I go through all of this by myself? I needed guidance and support. I was so young, and I had to be the breadwinner for the family. Not only was I angry with the situation, but I was angry with my brothers, as well.

After church, we went to the hospital to see our mother. The doctor who was treating our mother explained to us that our mother was very lucky. He told us that she had bled from her ears and mouth, and because of that, she survived. She bled so much that the blood flow never stopped in her brain, making her chances of surviving the stroke better. The doctor informed us that although she was lucky, her recovery would be very slow. He said she needed to attend physical therapy to make sure she did not relapse. My mother was placed on medication for high blood pressure, which she should have already been taking.

My siblings and I went back home, leaving my mother in the hospital once again. We suffered for three long weeks without her. We needed our mother to return home as soon as possible because the rent was due, and I did not have the money for our housing. Our landlord was aware of the circumstances but was not very understanding. He was very upset over our situation. He kindly asked us to leave, and I did not know what to do.

My siblings and I stayed in our home, but anytime we saw the landlord, we would hide.

He knocked on our door frequently, but we never answered.

I continued to go to the hospital to make sure my mother was getting better. She was making progress every day. My mother began regaining her strength and was able to walk and talk again. I was happy when I saw how well she was doing. My mother would ask if we were okay, and I would always answer yes. I did not want her to worry about anything. I think my little brother gave my mother the most strength. Once she hugged him, she began to improve even more.

Each time we got ready to leave the hospital, my mother made it a point to tell us to never answer the door. She wanted it to seem as if no one was home. I nodded in agreement.

"Don't worry. I will be home soon."

"Okay," I said and smiled as I continued to nod my head.

My nights felt as if they were eternal without my mother. I had horrible nightmares. I heard the sounds of non-existent noises. Anytime I would fall asleep, I would dream that I was running from someone who was trying to catch me. It was evident that my mother's arrival home was much needed.

Chapter Eight

In 1981, the economy in Colombia was frightful. The Guerillas, better known as Terrorists, had become more active. Many people were out of work trying to find jobs that were nonexistent. I remember hearing the screams of victims who were bombed by the Terrorists. It was an intolerable situation for the country as a whole and especially for my family, who were victims of that mess. We did not know what the next day would bring us, and we did not know if we were going to get caught in the middle of crossfires between the Gorillas.

I returned to the hospital a couple of days later after going to church with my siblings, and my mother was up and ready to go home.

"Herminia," the nurse called out. "You have to stay. You cannot go home yet." My mother continued to pack her bags with only one hand because the stroke had taken over the other. "You must stay another week. Doctor's orders."

"I know," she replied, "but what the doctor doesn't know is that my children are home alone. I'm going home now." I was happy to hear that my mother wanted to come home, but I was worried because she did not look healthy. That night we went home, and the three of us slept close to my mother. In the morning, I smelled fresh coffee and knew my mother was already awake. She was massaging her face, trying to get the movement back to what it was before her stroke.

"What are you doing?" I asked.

"I'm getting ready for work. I don't want to lose my job." She opened the door, and it did not take long before she fell. She had only taken a few steps, and there she was, alone and vulnerable. I ran to her and begged her to go back to bed.

"Tomorrow will be a brand new day, and you will see how you feel." I sounded like my mother. The landlord had seen what had happened from the upstairs window and raced down to help me. We brought my mother back inside the house and laid her down on the bed. I was terrified seeing my mother so weak and helpless. The landlord did not waste any time before speaking about what she needed from my mother.

"I am so sorry for what you are going through, but you haven't paid the rent, and my husband is not happy with you being here. I can't keep fighting with him about this. I hope you understand."

"I do," my mother said. "Thank you for everything you've done for my kids. As soon as I get back on my feet, I promise we'll leave."

"I'm sorry that I can't help anymore. My husband is a stubborn man." The woman started to cry. "As soon as he leaves for work, I'll bring some chicken soup for you."

My mother tried to take care of herself over the weekend. She constantly massaged her face, and I helped by wiping the saliva that dripped from the corners of her mouth. I knew she was not going to be able to go to therapy, so instead, she went back to work the following Monday but was sent home because she didn't look well.

Two weeks later we went to church on a Sunday morning. When we came home after the service, all of our stuff was outside. My mother tried to open the door, but the lock had been changed. My siblings and I started to cry. My mother was calm and played it off as if everything would be great.

"What are you crying about? We're going to a new home. This place was too small for us anyway." I shook my head; only my mother could come up with something like that. "Stay with your siblings, and sit on our stuff so no one takes anything," my mother said directly to me.

"Where are you going?" I asked.

"To call my guardian angel." I knew she was going to call the lady with the gray eyes, Lastenia.

I realized that as people passed us, they would just look at us with pity, and no one actually cared. The reality of the situation was that we no longer had a place to live. After many hours of waiting, my mother came back.

"Get ready," she said. "Let's go. We're leaving."

"We're hungry," Sandra complained.

"I will make a meal soon, I promise." My mother had three lollipops to give to each of us, but I did not want mine. I did not want anything. I was upset with how unfair life was. Once again, my mother made arrangements for the poor mule to come to our rescue. Every time I saw the mule, I knew we were going to have to move again. An hour later, we arrived at a large house with a red wooden door. My mother went inside and asked for Mr. Alberto. A nasty man asked how many of us there were.

"Me and three kids," my mother said.

"Okay, I have one large room or a small room. Which one?" he asked.

"The small room is fine." The man handed my mother a key.

"If you follow the rules, you can live here happily. Peaceful people live here. There are five families, and they all get along well. There is one kitchen, one bathroom, and everyone is on a cooking schedule. I will let you know when you can use the kitchen as well as the bathroom." My mother thanked the man. She took the key, opened the door, and we brought all of our stuff inside the room. The room smelled of herbs.

"Tomorrow will be better," my mother assured me. "I promise." I was not sure if she even believed herself.

The hardest part was that we had to urinate on a schedule, so our mother gave us a container to go in so we did not have to hold it in until it was time to use the bathroom. It was almost impossible to live there, and I knew it would just be temporary. I remember one day trying to use the bathroom in peace, and someone wouldn't stop knocking on the door. There was only one bathroom which was insufficient given the number of residents who shared the facility. I could not wait to leave this place.

A couple of months later, my mother returned with the mule. I knew it was time to move again. Sure enough, she told us to pack all of our items, and we set out for our new home. It was a small house that looked as if no one had lived there for a very long time.

My mother's friend had helped her find this place. This house, in particular, still brings back horrible memories. The stench of mildew was unbearable. My mother tried to mask the odor by boiling water with cinnamon in it, but it didn't do much.

Still recovering from her stroke, my mother frequently tried doing her own physical therapy by massaging her arm with a glass bottle. She worked hard to get the movement back in her left arm so that she could return to work full-time. Unfortunately, her coworker informed her that because of my mother's current circumstances, she had been let go.

My brother Julio returned to live with us as he could no longer work with our cousin. He eventually found a job working in a bakery, but we spent many days hungry. I remember one day, Julio and I opened our window because we smelled food. We were curious to know what our neighbor was cooking, so Julio used a wooden chair as a ladder. He decided to reach his arm through the window and stick his hand in the pot. What he failed to realize, however, was that the stove was very hot. Suddenly, I heard him scream. Julio had suffered a second-degree burn on his hand. To alleviate the pain, my mother put cold water on the burn.

We all cried, especially my mother. She felt responsible for what had happened. My mother had found a job washing and ironing clothing and was even cleaning houses, but still, somehow, it was not enough. To make matters worse, my brother Joaquin had returned home to live with us again. He had gotten a job in a factory as a security guard, but our lives became a nightmare. It was impossible for Joaquin and Julio to live under the same roof. As soon as they were back together, they started fighting. Unfortunately, Joaquin had not changed at all while in the military. He was more arrogant than ever and continued to hurt us, especially Julio. Due to Joaquin's behavior, it did not take long before Julio packed his things and disappeared from our lives for a long time.

My mother was very sad when Julio left. She tried to talk to Joaquin, but nothing made him come to his senses. His cruelty had increased, and we could no longer stand his abuse. My mother asked her brother Abraham to help us move again so that we could be far away from Joaquin. Tío Abraham found us a room, and he moved us there. We had to share a kitchen and bathroom with four other tenants, which was similar to the situation we had in Mr. Alberto's house. Although this was very difficult, it was much better than living in a house where Joaquin and Julio fought all the time. Each time they did, it was clear how much my mother was suffering. My mother could not control the situation between the boys; she was helpless. So it did not matter where we were now living because this was better than before. We had all suffered in one way or another because of Joaquin's poor behavior. I told my mother that we could no longer run from home to home. I was also not willing to run from Joaquin anymore.

"When is he going to stop?" I asked. My mother started to cry.

"Madre, I promise I will find a job as soon as I can, and I will buy you a house so you will never have to work again." My mother put her arms around me and held me tight.

Chapter Nine

Six months later, we received news from my older brother Edgar. My mother was so happy, she acted as if she won the lottery. My brother would return from the military to live with us. In his letter, he asked us to look for a home to rent. Immediately, we looked for a place. With luck we found a home, it was up on a hill, so naturally, we had to walk a little farther than usual, but it could not be more perfect for us.

My mother and Edgar would communicate through letters. She would always read to us out loud. It was her dream for all of us to live together, and finally, that day came. He surprised us all when he arrived at the house, and we were finally reunited. Edgar had married a very nice woman and she was pregnant. My mother looked happy for him but was very surprised to know that she would be a grandma for the first time.

My brother's wife was very friendly. She was very respectful to us, especially when it came to my mother. They had a very special relationship, so much so that every time my mother was hospitalized for her high blood pressure, my mother would ask to see her.

When Julio found out about Edgar's return he wanted to live with us. Julio started working as a waiter in a restaurant, and I was still going to night school and selling cleaning products door to door in the morning. Everything in our lives returned to normal; we seemed to be a perfect family. I have to admit that was the best time for all of us. We have great memories. We were also looking forward to the birth of Edgar's firstborn. I was excited to meet my nephew. Unfortunately, the baby was born two months earlier than expected and was very sick. He needed intensive care, but his mother was exceptional; she took care of him morning and night. His birth brought so much joy.

We all spoiled him, especially my mother.

That morning we were all at home, and suddenly my mother called out, "Someone is knocking on the door!" I was the one who opened it and was paralyzed with fear when I saw who was standing there. It was my brother Joaquin! No one seemed pleased that he had returned except for my mother, who ran into his arms and gave him a welcoming hug. She was so happy and cooked a special dinner for him. A couple of days later he found a job. Joaquin was always lucky with finding employment. Unfortunately, since his return home, living together was not the same. My mother was always in the middle trying to stop the fights so that we would get along. Nothing could have been worse than when we got the news that my older brother Edgar had gotten a better job opportunity with a transfer to the capital city of Bogota, and he took it right away.

How could I forget that afternoon? My brother and his family were leaving. My mother's sad face was hard to explain. My mother cried and cried that night. She finally admitted to herself that if Joaquin had not returned home, Edgar would not have gone to the capital. I was so angry. I asked my mother, "Why don't you ask Joaquin to leave the house?"

"Take a look at my hands," my mother said as I was drying her tears. "Do you see how my fingers are all different?" I nodded. "This is the way I see all my children. It does not matter how different one is from the other. I need them, and I will love them no matter what. One day you will be a mother, and you will understand me." I sat offering my mother support, not saying a word, just being there with her.

I woke up early that morning. I was ready for anything. Not only was I angry but I wanted a change in my life. I felt paralyzed. It was time to do something for myself. I was in need of finding a real job. I went out daily to supermarkets, restaurants and cafeterias. No one would hire me because I was a minor. I was not going to stop until I found a job.

Chapter Ten

One day I saw a poster that said, "Person With Experience In Glass Installation." It sounded good, so I went inside and asked about the job. The owner of the shop raised his eyebrow and started laughing.

"What is so funny?" I asked seriously.

"I'm looking for a boy, not a girl," he scoffed. "Go home and find something to do in the kitchen or help your mother with washing clothes."

"I have older brothers," I replied. "Please tell me what they have to do, and I'll bring them tomorrow."

"Well," he said, "your brother would have to go to a house where there is broken glass and offer our services to the owners. If they are interested, he would have to get the phone number of the person and bring the information back here. I will do the rest."

"That is very easy," I said.

"Yes, you're right. It is very easy," the man responded.

"Okay, thank you," I said as I made my way out of the shop. "I will see you tomorrow. *The job is mine*, I thought. I returned home and made a plan.

I was going to start my job without yet being hired. I knew I was going to make it work no matter what. My family needed the money for next month's rent, and I did not want to move again. My brother Edgar was now gone, and I had to help my mother more than ever. I practiced speaking to homeowners for the rest of that day.

"Good afternoon. Are you the owner of this home? My name is Esperanza, and my father and I started a small glass company. We are new to the market and would like to give ourselves the opportunity for the community to get to know us better. I see that your window is broken. If you would like, I can take down the measurements of your glass, and my father can call you a little later to tell you the price for the repair. We would do the installation for free."

In the beginning, it was hard, but I was not going to give up so easily. My plan was working, and I was very happy. Many people allowed me to take measurements of their broken glass, and many even offered me a soda. This was great. It looked as if I could sell anything. I was fascinated with all the work I was doing and was very excited about it. One night, I realized it had gotten very late, and I had to get home. My mother was very upset with me and asked where I had been. I did not want to lie, so I remained silent. My mother knew I had not gone to school. She was very angry with me.

"Why are you doing this to me?" my mother asked the following day. I started to cry. "Tell me where you have been all this time." I did not answer. "Please answer me," she begged. "Please don't tell me you are still hanging out with that Olga girl. She is not a good influence. She's a flirt. I see her in the park talking to men all the time."

I needed to break my silence. "Please, Madre, don't say that about her. She is my good friend, and she is very nice to me. You've always said we can't judge people, and now you're doing it." I paused. "I'm very sorry I was so late yesterday. Do you want to know where I was? Okay, I was looking for a real job, and I'm not going back to school." I took off before my mother could speak another word to me.

I continued with my new project, and I went to face my potential new boss. There he was, doing nothing but sitting in the same chair I left him in before.

"Buenos días, Señor." I said.

The man raised his head from his desk. "Oh, it's you again," he said smugly. "You have nothing better to do? Get out of here," he said rudely.

"I'm sorry to bother you again. I'll go, but before I do, I would like to offer a proposal." My eyes were filled with power and confidence. "In my hands, on this very paper, I have twenty-five potential clients that could benefit both of us. Would you be interested?"

He looked at me and smiled. "Let me see what you have there," he said.

"I don't think so," I said. "I'm sorry, but that was not the answer I was looking for. I want to know how much you are going to pay me if I keep bringing you potential clients?"

"How can we work this out?" he replied. He said sarcastically, "Would you like to be my partner?"

"Yes!" I said. The man laughed and ignored me. He lowered his head and continued to read his paper.

"Okay, look," I said, finally breaking the silence, "If you are not interested in my offer, I have no problem finding another glass shop." He did not speak or move. "Thank you," I said and started to leave.

The man finally got up from his chair and called after me. "Hold on," he said. "How many did you say you have?"

"Twenty-five," I answered, "and I will bring even more every week."

"If this is not true and you made me waste my time, you will be in a lot of trouble, young lady," he said sternly. "Where is your mother?"

"Do you want the clients or not?" I asked.

"Yes, but I do not want problems with your parents."

"You won't have any, I promise."

He read the list of the clients I had prepared for him. "I can give you three percent after the glass is installed."

"You have to be kidding me. Ten percent." I said.

"This is my store, and I make the rules. Five percent, or you can get out of here."

"Okay, but after the first month, if I prove to you that I can do better than this, you have to up the commission." He shook his head but said yes anyway. I had no other choice but to believe his words. At that time, taking someone's word meant everything. It could have more value than any document and was the start of any negotiation.

From that day on, I worked for that grumpy man who turned out to be a wonderful person. We worked hard, and I was pleased because I was helping my mother with the house expenses. I also continued going to school at night again, and I worked for him for some time. Joaquin was giving my mother a hard time with his continuous fights and delinquent behavior. We all knew he would never change. The only difference was that no one was willing to take his crap anymore. My family and I would fight back if we had to. It did not make much difference, but it felt good to let him know we were no longer afraid of him.

Every Saturday afternoon, my family and I went to the marketplace to buy the food we needed for the week. My mother always bought an extra pound of wheat flour, and I always argued with her because she always acted as if she didn't hear me. What I really wanted was to buy one can of sardines, but each time she would take the sardines out of the cart and put more wheat flour in. It really bothered me. I loved rice with sardines, but I had no idea what she was going to do with the extra pound of wheat flour.

The next morning I woke up earlier than usual and found her at the door of our house with a pot of hot soup, giving food to the poor. She was giving to the old people who slept in the street, and I remember getting very upset. I told my mother that we did not have enough for ourselves, so how dare she give our food to others? I will never forget the lesson that I learned that day. My mother told me to serve each one of them so I could feel the pleasure of giving what we had.

"When you give something to others, you must share what you have, not what you have left. Remember that, my beautiful girl. Your good actions and generosity will always be rewarded. Giving without asking for anything in return will bring the best to your life." She taught me such a beautiful life lesson that day. Since that day, I noticed that there is more pleasure in giving than receiving.

Chapter Eleven

My mother always believed in me, and she always had trust in me. I remember one day when I was about seven years old, my mother was preparing breakfast for everyone, and I began to question her, as usual.

"Why are there only two eggs if there are five of us?"

"Simply because my eggs are magic." I looked at her, confused. "Let me show you: two eggs and a little water and flour." She smiled. "But don't say anything to your brothers. It's our secret." I nodded. Over time, I realized that the real reason we did not have five eggs was that she was economically unable to purchase more than we had. I always heard my mother thank God for each day she was able to get through. She was an extraordinary woman who never complained about how hard her life was. My mother suffered many illnesses in silence to ensure her children's survival, knowing that if she gave up her high blood pressure medication, it could lead to death.

I knew I needed to earn more money somehow, and the glass business was beginning to slow down. It was time to start looking for a new job. My friend Olga told me that the fabric store was hiring. I applied for the job, and two days later, I was hired.

During the week, I worked full-time selling fabric for uniforms to the catholic school and earning both a salary and commission. On the weekends, I continued working at the glass shop to make extra money. To this day, it amazes me how I was able to manage a full plate and still go to school at night. Through experience, I learned quickly, and in no time, I began cutting fabric. All my bosses were satisfied with my performance. I was happy doing the work until I started having problems with the store manager, who began groping and touching me from behind with the impression that no one was looking.

This man always managed to ruin my day, and I wanted to hit him. Everything in my life seemed to be going so well, but this situation was very unsettling. As the sexual harassment became more frequent, it became unbearable, and I decided to notify the store owner. No one ever took any action against him after I reported his inappropriate behavior because he was the owner's brother. This man continued with this sexual harassment until one day when I finally reached my breaking point. I kicked him in his testicles as hard as I could and ran out without looking back. I sought comfort in my friend Olga. I told her everything and she always listened, reassuring me that everything would be alright.

I went home, laid on my bed, and thought about what I could do. I knew I could not go back to work, and helping my mother would become a hurdle once again. When my mother arrived home, she was shocked to see that I was there.

"Why are you at home so early?" she asked.

"I lost my job, but I promise I will find something better." I paused and took a second to think.

"Please don't worry. When something bad happens, it's because something good is going to come from it." My mother's words comforted me. I closed my eyes, pretending to be asleep. I was so upset I did not want to speak to anyone. The disgusting man caused me to lose my job, and at that moment, all I could think about was that if I were a man, this would never have happened. I wanted to get physical, I wanted to hurt him the way he hurt me. If I had his power, I would not have abused it. Anger festered inside of me, but I knew I needed to let it go. I did not want my mother to start asking me questions or to begin worrying about me. To make myself more relaxed, I decided it would be best to listen to the radio to put my mind at rest. A commercial filled my body with excitement. It sounded very interesting, and I needed my mother to listen to it with me so I knew this was not a dream.

"Dreams come true... Come to us, and we will teach you how." The words transported me to another universe. I listened to the commercial four times before I could write down the address in full. I thought my ears were betraying me because it seemed too good to be true. I could not believe what I was hearing. At that moment, I knew I had the answer to all of my problems. My mother looked at me as if I had gone mad. If I saw myself the way she did, I probably would have agreed.

I got up early the next morning to make sure I would arrive on time at the dreammaking place. My mother let me try on some of her dresses, but nothing she had seemed to fit well. I decided on a pair of pants that I usually wear with my favorite shirt.

Upon arrival, the hours of operation on the door indicated the store's business hours were nine to five. I was early and decided to pass the time by sitting on the sidewalk of a beautiful building. I had time to kill, so I had to keep myself occupied somehow. Though I was thinking non-stop, time did not pass as fast as I would have liked it to. I was not going to leave this building today without a job. At around 8:20, a car finally pulled into the driveway. A man stepped out and opened the trunk, which was filled with boxes. I ran to the man and asked if he needed help, but he kindly declined. Minutes later, the gentleman realized he did need help after all. One of the boxes opened, and a surplus of books fell out. I explained I had arrived here early for an interview that was scheduled for 9:00, and I had the time to help him.

"That's great; early interviews are always better." He smiled and accepted my help. The gentleman and I brought all of the boxes to the elevator, and we went up to the third floor. He thanked me when we got to his office, and he took money from his wallet. He handed it over to me, but I refused.

"Good luck with your interview," he said.

"Thank you," I said. I took the elevator down to the main floor and asked the doorman for the office I was looking for. The man looked confused.

"How did you get into the building if we are not open yet?" I explained I was helping a kind man who works on the third floor with his boxes, and the doorman laughed. I was puzzled because I did not think offering my help to someone was funny.

"What is so funny?" I asked, annoyed.

"The office you're looking for is on the third floor." I grew slightly embarrassed for getting annoyed so quickly. "Where did you say you were helping the man with the boxes?"

I felt stupid, not because of what the man was saying, but because I had to go back to the office I had just left. I returned to the third floor and did not think twice before knocking on his door.

"Did you forget something?" the man asked as he opened the door.

I blushed and said, "The doorman informed me that this is the office where my interview will be held." The man looked puzzled. "Can you tell me who is going to interview me?" I asked.

"I do not remember scheduling an interview for today. I think you might be mistaken."

"Is your office the only office with an ad on the radio?" I asked.

"Yes," he said.

"So I am in the right place," I said with a smile on my face. The man smiled back.

"Please come in," he said. "Take a seat, listen... sit and listen. I'm looking for a professional with experience, an educator... How old are you, sweetheart?" "Eighteen." I lied.

"Do you have any identification?" he asked.

"No, but I can bring it to you tomorrow."

"You came to an interview without identification?" he asked in disbelief.

"I'm sorry, señor, but I am interested in working with you and your company," I said, almost begging.

"I understand." The man took a moment to think. "I'm sorry, but I don't think you are qualified for the position."

My stomach dropped. "Señor, please," I begged. "I really need this job. I can clean, make coffee, whatever you want. Please give me the chance. I will make you proud." "What's your name?" he asked.

"Esperanza, and yours?" I tried to keep the conversation flowing.

"Jorge Gomez."

I shook his hand. "It's a pleasure meeting you," I said calmly and professionally.

He smiled. "Have you ever worked before?"

"Of course I have. I have lots of experience." I felt my chances were growing. "I promise I will not disappoint you."

He smiled again and said, "If you bring me identification tomorrow, you can work in the office." My heart began to explode with happiness. "You will prepare the coffee, pick up the mail, and clean. I nodded. "Nine to two. Does that work for you?"

"Yes," I said. "Is it alright if I make you a cup of coffee in gratitude? I'd like to start now if that is okay with you. You don't have to pay me for today. I know you need a hand," I said, gesturing at all of the boxes we brought up earlier.

He smiled once again and agreed. "Bring your ID tomorrow."

I nodded. "Look behind the door, and you will find a uniform." I did as I was instructed. "Help me with these folders." I was ready to jump right in. A new opportunity presented itself, and I knew I was going to do well.

Señor Gomez asked me to put a folder in front of each chair in the conference room. He encouraged me to rush because he was expecting a group of educators shortly.

"Please make the office sparkle." I looked up at the clock that was on the wall, and it was already 9:20. I was impressed that within twenty minutes, I was able to get myself a job and begin working.

"Not bad," I whispered to myself. I was proud of my achievement. As the moments began to pass, I could not help but think about what I was going to do about bringing my ID tomorrow. Considering I was still a minor, I did not know what would happen. I told myself to not think about it for the remainder of the day. Instead, I focused on cleaning everything meticulously so at the end of the day, Señor Gomez would be satisfied with my work.

A few minutes later, the secretary arrived, along with two other gentlemen. I offered the three of them coffee without asking questions.

"Who are you?" The woman asked.

"I am Señor Gomez's assistant." I responded as the woman laughed.

"I thought I was Señor Gomez's assistant." My eyes widened. "My name is Gloria." She held her hand out to shake mine, "I'll take that cup of coffee." Gloria walked into Mr. Gomez's office. Within no time, I started to overhear her conversation with the boss as she said, "Ready to start the interviews?" "Are they all here?" Mr. Gomez asked.

"They are all in the meeting room," Gloria responded.

"How many people are missing?" Mr. Gomez asked with a concerned look on his face.

"Six," Gloria said with fear in her voice.

"Alright, hopefully, we finish the interviews today so we can start training on Monday." Mr. Gomez desperately wanted to do so, but with the missing individuals, it was evident that he was not sure if it would be possible.

I did not understand what was happening. On a positive note, I was sure the position in the company was mine, and no one could take that from me. Interviews were happening all day. Men came in suits and ties, and the women dressed in skirts and high heels. At that moment, I thought I could never wear high heels. I now understood why I did not qualify for the educator position. Mr. Gomez was right. The day went by fast, and around 3:00, my superiors sent me to pick up a pizza. When I returned to the office, Mr. Gomez and Gloria were sitting at a table. They kindly invited me to join them to eat. I was embarrassed because I had never had pizza before. When I tasted the symphony of flavors, I was in heaven. I wanted to devour it all, but I knew it was inappropriate. I felt guilty at the moment given that my brothers and sister had never had pizza either.

I listened to the conversation that Mr. Gomez and Gloria were having. Mr. Gomez was dissatisfied with the candidates he had interviewed. Gloria suggested holding another round of interviews the following day, to which Mr. Gomez agreed. The office was usually closed on weekends. This extra day was the only hope they had to target qualified applicants for a position within the company.

After finishing his lunch, Mr. Gomez left the office. Gloria asked me to take out the garbage, and once I did so, I was allowed to go home. It was important for me to come back early the following morning so that I could be of assistance for the second round of interviews. I was pleased to be called in because this meant my superiors were satisfied with my work ethic. Before leaving, I asked Gloria what I should do with the remaining slices. Her direct response was to dispose of them. I was in disbelief when she told me to throw out the food as if she had no clue what it was like to face starvation. The box contained nine untouched slices.

"Can I take the pizza home with me?" I asked without knowing where I found the courage to ask.

"Whatever you want to do is okay with me," she said nonchalantly.

"Thank you." With a big smile on my face, I took the pizza box home with me on the bus. Everyone on the bus was uncomfortable, but it did not phase me. I was excited to get home and share this new food with my brothers and sister. I could not believe I was working in a professional building and eating pizza for lunch. I felt satisfied and significant knowing I was able to share that experience with the rest of my family.

As soon as I got home, my mother began asking me a thousand questions. "Where did you get that pizza? How did you get the money to buy it? Please tell me the truth," she begged. I always told my mother the truth, but somehow she doubted me. The last thing I wanted to do was to give her more stress. She was always worried about me, especially when I started a new endeavor. I will never forget the smiles on my younger siblings' faces when I brought home the pizza for the first time. My mother ate that night as well. It was just amazing. When my mother was in a better mood, I told her about my new job. We sat and laughed together. I loved seeing her happy. She was beautiful, especially when she was happy.

The next day I arrived at work on time, and the day went as planned. We closed at noon, and Mr. Gomez was happy with the work accomplished. He had found all thirty people he was looking for, and the training would begin on Monday. Mr. Gomez was so busy he forgot to ask me for my ID—I was elated. I went to work in the glass store for the rest of the weekend. On Monday, I returned to my new job happily, but I was curious to know how much money I would be paid. I was worried because I needed the money for rent, but I decided it was best not to ask because I didn't have an ID. I was appreciative that I was still able to work at the glass shop on the weekends, but it was not enough to cover all the expenses.

The following Monday, I went to work early to make sure everything was in order. I noticed there was a lot of tension in the office. Mr. Gomez asked me for a cup of coffee, but he already had one in his hand. With a smile, he handed me two boxes of pencils and asked me to sharpen them. I was so happy to be part of a team, even if I was not completely qualified.

For three consecutive weeks, meetings were held to provide sufficient information regarding customer service in sales. Mr. Gomez gave so much information that was expected to be memorized by the end of the three weeks. I admit it was a lot of information to learn and memorize, and everyone looked overwhelmed. I continued to do my job the best that I could, bringing water or coffee any time anyone asked for it and distributing pencils and papers. It was an easy job for me. Mr. Gomez spoke highly about his company and persuaded his staff to also speak in such a manner. Afterwards, he would ask the group to open their folders which were always placed directly in front of them, with all of the information they would need.

To begin each day, Mr. Gomez would start with an inspirational speech. Anytime I heard the word knowledge, I remembered why I had gone to ask for a position at this company. It was important for me to do my job, but I aspired to learn more than just my job.

I did not think anyone would notice, so I used it to my advantage to learn the course with the staff members who were training. Every single word that was spoken was important to me.

Mr. Gomez discussed the contents of each single paper in the folders. At that moment, I knew that whatever was in the folders was valuable, and somehow, I needed to get my hands on them. This week, in particular, Mr. Gomez opened the box and took out a leather briefcase.

"Your future is in front of you," Mr. Gomez said with a powerful pause. "Today, you all have a folder in front of you; tomorrow, it could be a briefcase. How many of you would like to own one?" He stood in front of the room with a commanding demeanor, hoping to encourage the staff members to make their dreams and aspirations a reality.

"The folder contains five posters that, when unfolded, will become a large informational illustration for all of you to learn. Through our customer service, we will sell encyclopedias. The first poster features *biology*, the second is for *math*, the third for *history*, the fourth for *languages*, and the fifth and most important presents *The First of Knowledge*. *The First of Knowledge* is the foundation for all education and is what we will use for the rest of our lives. This fifth book will be given for free after the initial purchase of any other encyclopedia. This last encyclopedia is my favorite because it contains a little knowledge of each subject. It is highly recommended and only for children at the elementary level.

I was fascinated every time that Mr. Gomez spoke. Every time he opened a box, there were endless supplies of books. The smell of the books inspired me to want to read.

I never had so many resources in front of me except for the town library.

On one occasion, a trainee asked Mr. Gomez if he could borrow a book. He answered, "No, it's not possible." But if he desired he could stay in the office and would be able to read any of the books. No books should leave the office. After finishing the daily meetings, everyone would leave with their folders, and I had to put everything back in place. I used to touch each book as if it were gold. I wanted to read them all, but I knew there would never be enough time. I had an idea, to borrow a book without anyone finding out. I put the book under my blouse without anyone seeing me take it. I read as much as I could at night and tried to absorb as much information as possible. The next day, I would put the book back. I took a chance each time I borrowed a book, not knowing if I would get caught. I could be fired if my superiors knew what I was doing.

My desire to read the books was stronger than getting caught.

I wanted to have one of those folders, but it was impossible. They were all accounted for. The objective of Mr Gomez was to educate them so they would be prepared. The goal was to create an interest in purchasing an encyclopedia for their home.

Every time Mr. Gomez finished his training, he would repeat, "Remember everything you have learned. Go home and practice in front of the mirror. This will help with your self-confidence. I have faith in all of you; I am sure you will all be successful in this company. Remember, the owner of the company will come next week, so it is imperative to study the brochures so each family can understand the benefits of having an encyclopedia for their children at home." I looked around the office when I realized that the group was cut in half. It was apparent some had not returned. Mr. Gomez ended by saying have a great weekend.

Chapter Twelve

That afternoon I was summoned into Mr. Gomez's office. I was so terrified, thinking that he had finally found out about the books that I was taking without permission when, in reality, he began complimenting me on my work ethic and telling me I was doing a great job, which made me proud. My hands were sweating, and I realized I was nervous from the guilt of hiding what I was doing behind Mr. Gomez's back.

"Tomorrow, the big boss is coming in, so please make sure that everything is in order." I nodded. "And one more thing, why haven't you brought your ID in yet?" My secretary has to pay your salary.

"Excuse me. Tomorrow I will bring it," and I scurried out of his office. I began to worry that my job was on the line. I would muster up some sort of identification. I was thinking all day I must get a fake identification or I would be in trouble. I loved working for this company. Reading their books inspired me. I was eager to educate myself. Sometimes I would lose track of time and end up being late for school. Finishing high school was very important to me.

That night when I got home, I sat with my brother Luis and pretended that he was going to be one of my future clients. I gave him the speech that I had practiced alone many times before. I realized I had all the knowledge to answer any questions that came my way, just like in Mr. Gomez' class.

My mother inquired, "Isn't your job to clean the office? I hope you're not getting into trouble! Are you selling books now?" she asked.

"No, Madre. I work in education." I continued to practice with my brother and the more I practiced, the more enthusiastic I got. It was then that I began to understand that life was not always fair. I wanted to be part of something that I wasn't qualified for. I was not going to spend a minute complaining about it.

I was ready to fight for what I wanted, even if there were stones in the road. I wanted to keep going.

That Sunday, we went to church as usual. It was important for my mother to thank God for all we had and to ask for protection. Sunday mass was a priority for everyone in my family. My mother was a practicing Catholic, and her faith was never questioned . The only thing I wanted that weekend was for it to pass by quickly. My subconscious told me that something good and positive was going to occur in my life. It was hard to explain, but at that moment, I knew something was going to happen.

When I returned to work that morning, Mr. Gomez asked me to please make sure everything was in order because he wanted to impress his boss.

"The owner of the company will be here soon. I hope everyone is well-prepared for any question he may ask." Mr. Gomez chanted to the room filled with educators. They broke off into small groups pretending that they were families with children waiting for an educator to present to them. I understood perfectly that their task consisted of selling a product. I knew that in order to sell, they needed to have extensive knowledge of the product they were selling because, without it, the consumer would not feel confident in the product. For some reason, I felt and understood the stress the educators must have experienced at that moment, which made me nervous as well.

*　*　*

Every time I brought books home my mom would look at me confused. She asked, "Why do you have those expensive books with you? Don't get into trouble!" She was right, but I didn't have an option, even if my mom's look was valid.

"He's here! He's here!" Gloria said. A short man with a spectacular smile and a huge beard entered the office. He asked for a cup of coffee, and I got it right away.

"Welcome, Mr. Perez," Mr. Gomez said firmly.

"I hear you have an incredible group here," Mr. Perez said as the two men started walking toward the office. The gentlemen conversed for some time while Gloria was going crazy in the conference room with everyone waiting for them to start. Even if I wanted to forget that day, I could not because it was one of the best days of my life. Given that everyone in the office was extremely nervous, the need for coffee had doubled from the usual orders for the educators. My boss came to the meeting room and introduced Mr. Perez as the owner of WJMY. Dressed in a perfectly fitted suit and holding a very nice portfolio in his hand, he began his speech.

"I am very happy to welcome you all, and I want to thank you for choosing to be a part of my company. I am very excited to open our doors and expand our marketing in the city of Duitama. Parents will be thrilled with the idea of being able to supply their children with an education from their very own homes. Doing homework will become so much easier for everyone involved." He paused and glanced at all the faces in the room.

"All of you are very lucky. Mr. Gomez is one of the best educators in our company. Each of you will be very successful. I would love to come back next year and hopefully have all of you participate in the International Book Gallery that will be presented in Bogota, the capital. Here you have extraordinary material in your hands, and it is your job to create the awareness of how beneficial this is. I am looking forward to signing a lot of commission checks for all of you. My company is generous." He smiled and added, "Also, bonuses will be given." I was unsure what everyone else in the group thought about Mr. Perez's speech, but I thought it was empowering. I wanted to have all the benefits the company provided to its employees; it was just amazing.

Everyone in the room had their folders with them except me. I was frustrated, but I did not have a choice. I had to remain quiet, which was hard to do.... Mr. Perez wanted to know each and everyone's name, and after a few minutes of silence, Mr. Perez asked who was going to give the first presentation today. The room grew silent.

"What Mr. Perez is trying to ask is which one of you would like to introduce what we have because he needs a good encyclopedia for his home." Mr. Gomez jumped in, trying to save himself as well as everyone in the group, but everyone sat in their seats as though they were paralyzed. They were not moving or speaking. I felt terrible for Mr. Gomez. It was then that the students in the class all began turning their heads, looking to see who would be the first to present. The silence was awkward and painful, and I suddenly realized that this was my opportunity to show that I was capable of more. I put the coffee on the table, cleaned my hands, and spoke with my trembling voice.

"I am Esperanza, and I have worked for this company for a while and would love to pitch my product to you." Everyone laughed because they thought I was joking, but Mr. Perez looked me dead in the eyes.

"I do not have much time, but I have a moment to spare," Mr. Perez said as he went on to improvise with me during my presentation. It boosted my confidence to continue. "Mr. Perez, I want to share with you the importance of keeping your children home after school." I shook his hand and asked if I was able to have a seat with him. "How many children do you have at home?" "Three," he said, and I nodded.

"If you would allow me to have a few minutes of your time, I will tell you and your family the benefits of having the right material to help your children when they are occupied with homework." Without looking directly into my boss's eyes, I continued. Mr. Gomez would have never approved of what I was doing. I opened the displays on the table and talked about each encyclopedia without stopping. I presented and answered every question he had.

"Is this expensive?" Mr. Perez asked.

"My company offers payment in installments; this way, it's financially easier on the customer." Without thinking twice, I asked Mr. Perez my final question. "How would you like to pay? Installments or cash?"

"In cash," Mr. Perez said. He then got up and applauded me on my presentation, which led to everyone else in the room following along. "You are going to get very far, young lady." I smiled, proud of my achievement. At this time, everyone was more relaxed, and they continued with the presentations for the rest of the day. I continued to serve coffee, but I noticed by the look on my boss's face that he was unhappy with my actions. I was called to his office shortly after everyone left.

"We no longer need your services. Gloria will notify you when your check is available for pick up." I went home and was very quiet, which was abnormal for me. My mother knew something was wrong, and I went on to tell her every detail without holding back.

"You are the best saleswoman in the world, and if I had money, I would buy all the books from you." My mother always knew how to uplift me with her words of wisdom and kindness in times when I felt like a failure. At that moment, we laughed together as she hugged me tight, but still, the pain of knowing that I had lost my job didn't stop growing.

"I lost my job, Madre."

"But I did not lose my daughter." She was suggesting there was little reason to be upset.

"Madre, I learned a lot when I was there." She nodded proudly.

"When you learn, you never lose; you always win."

"You're right, Madre. I feel better now." I smiled, finally feeling some peace.

Chapter Thirteen

The next day I woke up and made my way to the nearest payphone to give Gloria a call. She informed me that my check was ready to be picked up. I went to the office as quickly as I could.

"Mr. Gomez is waiting for you in his office," Gloria said as soon as I arrived. Upon entering Mr. Gomez's office, I was shocked to see Mr. Perez. I was under the impression that Mr. Perez had returned to the capital. An uneasy feeling took over my being, and a million things ran through my mind.

"How did you know so much about the company if you have not taken the course?"

I was stunned by Mr. Perez's question. Every nerve in my body began to shake, and it felt as if I was speaking a foreign language. As calmly as I could I explained that I would listen to Mr. Gomez's lectures as I served the educators, and admitted to taking books home at night and returning them the next day. My mother raised me to be honest, so I told him the whole truth and begged for forgiveness for my inappropriate actions.

Mr. Gomez spoke sharply. "I asked her for any form of identification, but she never brought it. I believed in her. I did not imagine she would have been a problem for us."

At that very moment, I understood that Mr. Gomez was in trouble for my actions. Mr. Gomez was always very good to me, generous and kind, and I betrayed him. Tears began to well up in my eyes, and before I could stop them, they began to cascade down my cheeks.

"I have never stolen anything from here, I swear. I just took the books to practice at home in front of a mirror, just like Mr. Gomez taught the educators to do." I took a moment to catch my breath. "I read every line but returned each book to its place. I swear!" I took a deep breath and began to pull myself together. "Mr. Gomez gave me this job, and I abused his trust. For this, I am so sorry. I hope you can accept my apology." My heart ached. I wanted to better myself by gaining all of the knowledge that Mr. Gomez dispensed, but I did not consider the repercussions.

"How could you not see so much talent?" Mr. Perez asked Mr. Gomez.

"I did, but she is very young. Your apology is accepted. You did not do anything wrong." I did not believe him. If I did not do anything wrong, he would not have fired me.

"You have great potential, but correct me if I am wrong. Aren't you fifteen years old?" Mr. Perez asked.

I shook my head. "No, I'm sixteen years old."

Both men smiled. Mr. Perez asked, "We would like to speak with your mother."

I nodded in agreement. "I will bring her tomorrow." I paused, telling myself to bite my lip, but I did not. "Do I still have my job?" I asked innocently.

"We will talk tomorrow."

Worried, I was left to question my future in this company, given that I loved it with a passion. Though the day was not over, I felt like I had been up for days. Every single emotion I experienced was weakening my strength. I then focused on my love for airplanes, as they always had a way of de-stressing me. On days when I was overwhelmed, I would go to the airport and listen to arriving and departing flights. I did not know when, but I knew that one day I would be on one of those planes bound for bigger and better things. That night when I got back home, my mother was sitting in her chair waiting for me. She was worried because I was late. My mother cared for me so much that it nearly broke my heart to know that I was the cause of her stress.

I then went on to tell her about my day. I was hesitant at first, but I was eager, given the circumstances. I told her that my superiors requested her presence. "They want to talk to you."

"What?" she said.

"Didn't they fire you?"

My mother didn't look enthused by the news. Intuitively, she felt nothing good would come out of this. She got up from her seat and said nothing. But she didn't say she wasn't going either.

The next day, my mother was preparing herself to get ready to leave with me. We traveled to the office to have a meeting with my bosses. The two gentlemen spoke to my mother first. Then she asked me if I understood what was going on.

I nodded yes and suggested my idea of what they had said to her.

"I'm a minor, and they want you to sign a paper, right? Is that the truth?" I asked. My mother took my arm and pulled me away so we could speak in private.

"Hija, no, it's not as simple as it sounds. Do you understand what you would be doing here? You are going to be selling books. Who in this city is going to buy a book?" She paused. She looked into my eyes. "Nobody! Why do you always worry me?

You're not going to be paid a salary. Everything is based on commission and if you sell a book. What they are saying is that the checks given would be under my name because you are a minor. You know what I think? You're crazy?" she said. "I'm not going to sign the papers."

"I think you should go back to the fabric store. It was going so well for you. I don't know why you left."

Little did my mother know that she opened a wound I had hidden from her, believing I could heal on my own.

"Madre, I will never go back to that place." Frustration took over. "I don't understand why you think it is so bad to sell these books. Everything is possible if I just try. If not, I will never know the outcome. You said that you would support me in everything." I began to beg. "Don't be scared, Madre. I have a good feeling about this."

Her expression grew soft, and she looked as if she was giving in. "Please, Madre." She raised her hand, gesturing for me to be quiet.

"Enough! I don't want to hear anymore. Go, that man wants to talk to you."

I went into Mr. Gomez's office, and he explained to me how they would keep my position within the company. I smiled and asked when I would start.

"I don't want this to go poorly for you. Your mother explained your needs to me. If you would like, we can try this out. If it does not work for you, just let me know, and I will give you back your old job." I nodded.

"One more thing, the way you carry yourself and your appearance will not benefit you in this business. My humble suggestion would be to cut your hair and dress a little better. That will definitely help."

I was not offended because I saw how the female educators dressed, and I did not look the same.

From a young age, I had never taken anything personally. As a child, I frequently looked different from the children around me because I did not have as much, but it never affected me because I was okay with what I had. Mr. Gomez's constructive criticism came from a place of goodness, and I knew he was just looking out for my best interest and potential as the businesswoman I was destined to become.

"Of course," I said. "No problem. Thank you so much for the opportunity." I left the office practically floating on air. I got my chance.

I did not have any new clothes, but I knew I needed to get them quickly, not to mention high heels. I had never worn high heels before in my life. I went to my cousin Blanca's house. She was always very special to me. I told her what happened, and she kindly gave me three dresses and a pair of shoes. I had to have the shoemaker repair the heels before I could wear them. The dresses were too big for me, but my mother adjusted them to my thin frame.

The next day I was ready to start my new adventure. I felt invincible. I was going to be the best saleswoman that month. I would win the briefcase in no time. I started going door-to-door in my neighborhood, but within no time, I realized that these people weren't my target customers. All the families in my neighborhood were living below the poverty line and did not have the means to make unnecessary purchases. They were just trying to make ends meet. My next destination brought me no luck either, and within three long weeks, I had not sold one single book.

Given that I was now working on a commission-based salary, I would get home later than usual. I was trying my very hardest to visit as many clients as possible. My mother was not happy, and I tried to explain to her how difficult it was. She pretended to understand, but I knew she was worried about the situation. I was working long hours and wasn't making any money. These times were very difficult for me. I was so depressed that I asked my mother to cut my hair. She did not like that idea and denied my request, so I took matters into my own hands and cut my hair in front of her. When I looked in the mirror, I started to cry. I looked horrible. I felt the odds were against me. My mother hugged me and tried to undo the disaster I had done to myself. We both knew that my frustration was because I did not have any sales. My hair was now short, and it made me look older than my actual age. I just had to get used to my new "look." It was just a matter of time. But this was not an excuse to not continue working. I would walk for endless hours. My shoes would give me blisters.

My mother would have a bucket of salt water to soak my feet waiting for me when I arrived home. It always felt so good and helped with the inflammation. My mother knew I was not going to give up so easily, so she tried to help me to the best of her ability.

When I looked in the mirror I missed my long hair, but I pretended that I was happy with my new look. My boss liked my appearance, and everyone in the office complimented me. I always looked pale so I put on lipstick and applied a bit of blush on my cheeks.

Unfortunately, the whole group was going through the same, regarding sales. The people loved the presentation but the excuse was always the same: *We can't purchase it at the moment.*

Mr. Gomez had an idea that we all meet in the park and break into pairs. That way we can figure out what the roadblocks were. We would meet up again at the park, talk about our experiences, and learn from one another. We knew every single line because of how repetitive the process was. My partner was very nervous. She always wanted me to approach potential clients first in exchange for doing the rest of the work, but somehow I always ended up doing everything.

Each morning, we were greeted with a motivational speech from Mr. Gomez before we went out to sell the product. This would give us a better understanding of the process. But the thing that worried me the most was it was almost the end of the month and I didn't know how to help my Madre with the expenses at home. I always left with the same attitude. "Today I will get my first sale." There were instances when people would open the door and not allow us to speak. On other occasions, they would not open the door at all. I knew it would not be easy, but I had no idea it was going to be this difficult.

I had put all my time and effort into this project and was *not* losing hope.

Chapter Fourteen

Sunday morning, my mother asked me if something was wrong, yet I think she already knew the answer.

"I'm sorry, Madre, but I can't go to church today."

"Are you sure you are feeling okay?"

"Madre, I'm fine; I promise. I will be home later." I took the bus and got off at the first stop. I went with the intention that if I did not manage to sell any books today, I would go look for another job. When the bus came to a stop, I hopped off and walked toward a beautiful home. An old man sat in front of the house reading a book. It was hard to tell what he was reading from a distance, but the book had caught his attention. He was so focused that my presence, standing two feet in front of him, didn't seem to phase him.

"Seems like an incredible book you're reading," I said.

"It is," he said without looking up. "It's a classic." His eyes moved across the page, never losing his concentration.

Trying to figure out how I could catch this man's attention, I realized that my only hope was based on his interest in books. I knew he would be interested in my product. Although I felt as though I was bothering him, I had to make a sale. I owed it to not only myself and what I learned, but also to my mother, given that she had done so much for us.

"I don't want to bother you, but I think I have something that will benefit you and your family."

He lifted his head gently. His face was sweet, and the wrinkles on his face brought to mind an old blanket. He looked like a safe place, and for some reason, I trusted him.

"You work for W.M. Jackson?" he asked. I nodded. He noticed my logo on my folder. "Please come in," he said as he got up from his chair. In any other situation, I would never have agreed to go into someone's home, especially someone I did not know. However, something told me I could trust him, so I did what he asked. I followed him into his grand home, and the first thing that caught my attention was a shiny brown piano.

His living room was the size of my entire house. "Please, sit." I did as I was told once again. "How long have you worked for the company?"

Without thinking, I blurted out a response. "Three years, sir," I said, with all the confidence I could find in me.

"And how old are you?"

I felt like a deer caught in the headlights. "I don't think that matters, sir. If you don't mind, let me start explaining our product to you."

He agreed with a smile on his face. "Of course, I would love to hear what you have to offer." He sat down and placed his book on the table. He gave me his full attention, making me even more nervous. Throughout the training, the instructors advised us to only speak about one specific encyclopedia at a time, depending on the client's needs. The initial question I should have asked was what kind of books he owned. Instead, I began my presentation by talking about every book I learned about through my training.

The man, whose name I still did not know, listened to me speak for over an hour without any interruption. He was my angel.

"What do you think?" I was hoping he had something to say so I could finally shut up. He smiled again.

"Great," he said. "I finally have a chance to speak." I wanted to die. My face grew red, and at that moment, I knew I was not going to make the sale.

"I think you talk too much, like a wet parrot."

I knew that parrots in their ordinary state mimic humans with no problem, but when they're wet, they make sounds at their highest volume.

"You don't ask questions, and you don't tell the truth." My heart sank into my stomach.

"Now you are going to listen to me, young lady."

The man pulled out a piece of paper and a pencil and wrote something down. On it was the word opportunity. After a moment, he explained, "Opportunity. Do you know what that word means?" Before I could answer, he began to speak again. "Sometimes, you are given a chance to do something you wouldn't normally have the power to do, but it's all up to you to take that leap of faith. Most of the time, you only have one shot." He paused; my heart sank.

"Many years ago, I used to be a salesman like you. That was how I made my living. Back in the day, the only way to achieve your goal was to be persistent." He paused and then said, "My darling, the first thing you need to do is create a connection between you and your client. Don't go into your sales pitch right away. First, you must establish some type of camaraderie. You want to appeal to your client like they are a friend." I nodded. "The most important thing is to listen; the less you talk, the better. It is very important to understand your client's needs so you know exactly what to offer them, and they don't feel you are wasting their time."

He asked me to stand up. The man pointed to his library, which was in the adjacent room. I was so nervous that I didn't even take a moment to appreciate the room.

"I want you to look around my library, and if you are selling something I don't already have, I will buy it." I was finally presented with an opportunity to make my first sale, but I was so consumed with the thought of making the sale that I did not even consider what this man might need. I walked around the library, speechless. The room was covered in books.

As I walked around the room, I was impressed with how immaculate and organized it was. All I could think about was how I could lure this man into purchasing a book when it was evident that his house consisted of a bookstore. It was then that I reached the corner of the room and found a framed photograph. I immediately picked up.

"Is the baby in the photo your son?" I asked.

"No, it's my grandson... he's seven years old."

I was thrilled. "Does he like to read?" I smiled, knowing at this moment I was going to make a sale.

"He loves to read." The man seemed amused.

Without hesitation, I said, "I have something for him. It's called *The First Knowledge* and consists of four books." I was thrilled because I knew he did not have these in his library. "This book will teach any child, in the simplest way, how to do their homework without getting frustrated. This is a great present for your grandson, don't you think?" I asked excitedly, awaiting his response.

He laughed hysterically. "Great! You learn fast." I smiled and nodded. I knew he was a man of his word. "May I have two of those encyclopedias? I have two grandkids." He wrote a check to the company, and just like that, I made my first sale.

I said, "I'm sorry. I lied to you. I have only worked for this company for less than a month. This is my first sale."

He laughed and said, "You learned quickly. I have a feeling you are going to get pretty far in life."

My nerves were still out of control, but I was happy that I completed my goal of making a sale.

He said, "I have a gift for you."

I crinkled my eyebrows, shocked at the thought of what more this man could give me.

"I'm going to give you ten referrals." I was speechless.

These referrals would provide me with more confidence and make it less necessary to go door to door. I would be able to prepare in advance, which would enhance my sales abilities.

"I want you to remember that these ten people are ten new opportunities. Only you can decide what to do with each of these new clients." I took the referrals and smiled.

"Good luck to you, my darling."

Little did I know this was only the beginning.

Chapter Fifteen

I have been told, "The first sale is always the hardest. Once the initial sale is complete, it's just the beginning of one's sales experience for bigger and better." I learned how to schedule appointments and work with referrals. Life became so much easier when families were referring me to others because of the great reputation and name I had created for myself in the industry. Any time I mentioned to a client the person who referred them, I could almost guarantee to make the sale. It was like magic. At times, I thought I was dreaming. I couldn't believe this was happening to me. After about six months, I had made some money and was so happy. I wanted to buy my mother something—anything she wanted.

"This is the last time you will ever have to give up buying your medicine in order to purchase food. I want to make sure you are able to take your medicine every day." This was the first thing I told my mother when I was able to save some money. That day, we went into a store and bought a new stove. The stove was green and red. My mother was so happy. We also bought a television so my mother could watch her novelas. After splurging on those luxury items, I made my way to the supermarket with the rest of my money to buy everything else she needed. I wanted to reassure my mother that if she ever needed anything, all she had to do was ask. I made it my mission always to have food on the table for my family.

My life changed for the better that day. I met the mystery man who loved to read, I ended up holding the "best saleswoman" title with the company for eight consecutive months, and everyone in the company was pleased with my work.

One day after pushing myself to do the absolute best when it came to selling the encyclopedias, my boss called me into his office and told me that national management wanted me to partake in the international book fair. To do this, I would have to pretend to be someone else because of my age. In the year 1982 the book fair was going to take place in the capital, Bogota, where my older brother, Edgar, lived. I told my boss that I would have to speak to my mother first and to make sure that I could stay with my brother before giving him a definite answer. I started to feel intimidated because I had only ever lived in my small city, and to go to the capital on my own was overwhelming. Traveling to Bogota would be a challenge for me, and the last thing I wanted to do was worry my mother.

That day I went home and explained my boss's proposal to my mother. She was anything but thrilled. She said, "A rose petal does not move without God's permission." I stayed quiet, but I knew what she meant. "Ask Edgar if you can stay with him." The only way she would let me go was if things fell into place easily. She knew that if this were the right thing for me to do, God would let it happen. I did not tell her I had already thought of asking to stay with my brother—I did not want her to think I was going behind her back. Soon after speaking with my mother, I called Edgar, and he picked up instantly. As I explained the situation, I felt my intestines grow tight. He seemed happy for me, but he wanted to speak to my mother before any decision was made.

That weekend, my brother came home from Bogota to talk to my mother. He promised her that he would take care of me and not to worry as I would only be staying for two weeks. Edgar thought this was a great opportunity for me. He knew it would be my one chance to network and meet different professionals in various fields.

In July 1982, I arrived in the capital, Bogota. The weather was cold, I felt it all over my body. While I waited for my brother Edgar to pick me up at the bus station, I realized the city was huge; nothing compared to where I came from. I realized I was very young when I first left the capital. When my brother finally arrived I asked him, "Do you like living in the capital?" To my surprise, he answered abruptly.

"No! Not at all!" I was shocked.

"I would much rather go back Soata, but I can't." I knew he was here because of work, but at the same time, it made me happy to know he missed our town. The city looks overwhelming. You are very intelligent, you will adapt quickly. said my brother.

"But don't you worry, your brother Julio and I are here to help you." We will all figure it all out. I was reassured by his plan.

The city streets were so confusing. They mimicked each other. My brother lived in the southern region of Bogota while the book fair was being held in the north. The distance between the two terrified me and all I could think about was my commute and how I would get there on time.

When we finally got to my brother's apartment, I saw his wife and my nephew, Edwin, for the first time in a year. I was so happy to see them. Edwin was so cute and had grown up so much. We sat down to have a nice dinner that they had prepared for me.

Julio said, "Okay, Esperanza, listen carefully. You will go from the south to the north, and this is how you are going to do it. It's a piece of cake, so don't worry about it." I didn't think it was going to be easy and began to panic.

"It's one bus with only two stops," Julio said as I grew anxious.

It was then that Edgar said, "Julio is going to take you tomorrow to show you the ropes. However, you're on your own after that, so you better pay good attention." I nodded, expressionless.

"You mustn't talk to anyone... this is the capital, and it is very different from Duitama."

I just listened to my brother's helpful advice. After some more conversation, my brothers told me that it is common for thieves to stake out victims on buses. These thieves were fast and efficient. They would cut open a victim's bag using a blade and steal whatever fell out. By the time the person realizes their bag is empty, it's too late. I was terrified. I lived in such a friendly neighborhood that I felt like I was now in another country.

With fear festering in my mind, I could barely sleep that night. I woke up before the sun, and as soon I was ready, I told Julio it was time for us to head out. My brother and I left around half past seven as I did not want to be late. I was anxious, and my brother became frustrated with me. I kept asking him every five minutes, "Are we there yet?"

We reached our destination ten minutes before nine o'clock. "Happy now?" my brother commented sarcastically. "Wow, this is a really nice place." He looked around, astonished at the building. I introduced myself to the receptionist. We took a seat and waited for Mr. Perez. As soon as he arrived, I introduced him to my brother Julio. He said hello and left shortly after. Mr. Perez directed me to where I needed to go for the fair. I was excited to make my first sale in Bogota. I didn't have time to think about how I would get home that evening. The only thing I desired that day was to make a lot of sales.

Speaking to people has never been a problem for me. As I got more comfortable making sales, my confidence grew, and it became easier to make connections with these clients at the fair. On this day in particular, I made so many sales and gained many referrals. I even had the opportunity to meet professionals from other companies. Everyone was so friendly. Throughout the day, I noticed one man staring at me constantly. It was clearly evident that he was watching me. With every move I made, I could tell his eyes were on me. It was unsettling, and I began to feel uncomfortable knowing I was being watched.

On the final day of the fair, the man who had been staring at me for the past couple of days approached me. He handed me his business card and said, "If you ever get tired of selling books, I would love to have you work for me."

I was embarrassed. In my mind, I believed this man was looking at me in a weird way when in reality, he had been admiring my work ethic. I took the card, thanked him, and shook his hand. Placing the card in my pocket, I did not think much of it.

I worked very hard at the book fair, and we surpassed the number of books we initially intended to sell. My boss was so happy that he suggested I stay longer in the capital. My boss believed I would have a better future in the company if I continued to work out of Bogota. When I received my paycheck, I nearly had a heart attack. I had never made that much money before. I promised my mother that I would return home, so I knew there was nothing left for me in Bogota. I did not want to break my promise to her.

When the fair ended, I thanked Edgar for letting me stay with him and his family and let Julio know I was leaving. Julio once again took me to the bus stop, and I began to make my way home. When I was on the bus, I could not help but miss my mother. My stomach growled just thinking of the food she made. My mother was the best cook that I had ever known. When I finally arrived home, my mother was ecstatic to see me. She acted as if I had been gone for years. My siblings were excited to see me and because I brought them many presents. We all went to sleep that night, and when morning came, life was back to normal...or at least that's what I assumed.

When I woke up, my mind was running a mile a minute. I could not get Mr. Perez's words out of my mind. I took all the referrals out of my pocket and could not help but ask myself how I could pass up all of these opportunities. Just knowing months ago, I was given ten referrals from a kind old man and a big lesson. Thanks to him and his small kindness I had tasted success. I couldn't help but ponder how much I was actually willing to give up. If I wanted to move forward, I would have to move to Bogota. I didn't think this would go over well with my mother. In reality, for the very first time she lived a very peaceful life and it wouldn't be fair to destabilize her.

That month the sales in the company went down drastically. Everyone in the company was struggling. Anytime anyone would enter the office, each salesperson began complaining about how they could not meet sales expectations. It was a bit worrisome. All I could think about was the words that Mr. Perez had said, that I would accomplish a lot more in the capital.

My mind was telling me to move, but my heart did not know how to tell my mother. After battling with myself for what felt like forever, I finally had the courage to speak to my mother. We had a conversation about how moving to the capital would help me grow into a bigger and better position within the company. My mother listened to me. After I finished explaining myself, my mother grabbed her bag and went out. She did not say a word.

At the end of the day my mother and I reunited to have dinner. You could cut the tension with a knife. She finally broke the silence between us. "Is this what you really want?" my mother asked with concern in her voice. She knew me so well she knew from the bottom of her heart that nothing was going to change my mind. It took everything in me to talk to my mother. I explained how I wanted to grow my position in the company and how the process would be easier and much faster if I were to live in the capital. She did not have much to say that night, but the next morning, she continued the conversation.

"If this is what you want…it's fine, we'll go." I could not believe my mother was not only going to let me do this, but she agreed to move with me, as well.

Chapter Sixteen

In the year 1983, my brother, Edgar, helped us find a place to live. We rented the space from a very nice couple. We organized our things exactly like my mother wanted.

She left the place sparkling as if you were to have tea with the queen.

I told my mother I wanted to graduate from high school. Having a HS Diploma was very important to me. My mother loved the idea. I signed up for night school right away. All of us had trouble adjusting at first. It was not easy getting used to the capital, especially for me.

I had trouble with directions. I kept saying to myself in due time I will get it. Soon everything will be back to normal. My younger sister Sandra, expressed that she wanted to work. I thought it seemed ok to do it. My only condition was that she continue to go to school. She started working in a bakery.

On the other hand, my little brother Luis was the polar opposite of Sandra and me. He did not like school at all. I would scold him when he would not attend his classes. Anytime I would lecture him, he would give me hugs and kisses to deflect. I could never stay angry at him for a long time. Every day was the same struggle.

My mother would try to wake Luis up, but he would refuse to go to school. The only thing that made him happy was finding things around the house to assemble and disassemble. The only stress of my mother was to educate Sandra and Luis. My sister Sandra had a high temper. And the stress with Luis was to attend school. My brother Julio was a great help to me. He taught me how to find an address in such a big city. On occasion, he would accompany me when I had late appointments. We would ride the bus together. When I got to my destination, he would wait outside until I finished with my presentation. Afterwards, we returned home together. He wanted to make sure I was safe. That year was hard but I was very successful. I took advantage of every referral I got at the fair. I was doing pretty well. Somehow, I always managed to find new clients to call.

I remember that night I came home to an unusual situation. I could hear Sandra's screams. Through her tears, she explained that the bakery owner had closed the business without giving their employees any notice, and she had lost her job. I tried to calm her down because I knew she would eventually find another one. Her classmate, Rosa, offered to help her find a job in a restaurant. In the meantime, I tried to cheer her up and show her that there was a silver lining to every situation. Sure enough, one week later, my sister was working at a restaurant as a cashier. Unfortunately, we did not know that this job would change her life forever.

Moises, the owner of the restaurant, was also renting out an apartment in his multifamily house. My sister knew we were looking for another place to live, given that we finally had the money to rent a bigger apartment. When she heard the apartment was for rent she came home excitedly to inform my mother and me about the situation. It could not have been more perfect. That same day we met Mr Moises for the first time. He was very friendly with us. He offered his help in everything. He didn't even ask for a referral or the deposit that was required. He also offered to help with the move. My mother was very grateful for what he did. Everything was going so well.

Who would ever imagine that a fifty-year-old man would be interested in a very young girl? It did not take long for my mother to realize his true intentions. Distraught, she confronted him immediately. He denied all the accusations my mother made. He said his intentions were pure and that he just wanted to help my family, but my mother knew better. She did not believe a word he said. After the uncomfortable conversation, she sat down to talk to us. I know you don't have a father to watch over you. But there are sick and twisted men in this world. And they use this benefit to love and convince girls like you to make you think you need them. Immediately Sandra answered nastily, "Mother, I can't believe these accusations. If you are talking about my boss, I would like to remind you that I am his employee and we live in his house."

"Well just to inform you, young lady, this will not be a problem because as of tomorrow not only are you quitting but we are moving immediately."

My sister Sandra stormed out of the room leaving just my mother and me. After a short silence, I asked my mother, "Can you explain what's happening?" She started crying.

"I can't believe you don't see it! He began showering Sandra with gifts. He drives her in his car. That man does not have good intentions with your sister. Tomorrow we need to find a place to move."

From that moment on, my sister and my mother had a tense relationship which became hurtful and more tense as time passed by. I spoke with Sandra personally but she insisted everything was a lie. By the following week, my mother had already found us a new place. She communicated to us that we were leaving. But Sandra refused to move.

My mother wanted to teach Sandra a lesson, so we moved without her.

Before Luis and I left, I tried to convince Sandra to move with us. I stressed how she was a minor, but she did not care to listen to anyone. Her mind was made up. My mother believed that Sandra was ruining her life, and she wanted no part of it. We left without my sister. My mother was convinced that if Moises was smart he would bring her home to avoid any legal trouble.

Sandra was strong-willed, and I knew she could defend herself, or at least I hoped so. My mother was very anxious about leaving her. Just as my mother suspected, Sandra was furious and did not want to go but agreed after Moises explained the legal trouble he could be in because she was a minor. She asked him to drop her off at Edgar's house because she refused to go with my mom. Sandra's move was contingent upon her and Moises's commitment to never to stop working together and continue seeing each other secretly.

Although this situation made my mother suffer immensely, she found some peace knowing that Sandra was with my brother. Sandra, however, did not want to listen to anyone other than Moises. She disregarded the appeals of her own flesh and blood for a man more than double her age. Just as any mother would, my mother wanted to shield her children from anything negative in the world. My sister still did not understand that what she was doing was wrong. Sandra thought, despite her age, that she had the right to decide who she could be with.

Sandra continued to live with Edgar while still seeing Moises in secret. Edgar was aware of the situation prior to Sandra moving in, though when he dropped her off, Moises declared that he no longer wanted anything to do with her—an obvious lie. Sandra, on the other hand, had plans of her own. She was no longer just "friends" with Moises; she was dating him right under Edgar's nose. I think, deep down, Sandra knew that sooner or later, she would get caught. Eventually, Edgar found out what Sandra was doing and immediately spoke with my mother. Sandra was blatantly disobeying my brother, and he no longer wanted to take responsibility for her. He was so frustrated and felt so disrespected that he packed up Sandra's things and dropped her off where my mother, younger brother, and I were staying.

It was no secret that my family had struggles. My mother was a hardworking woman who overcame many obstacles. She faced abuse, poverty, illness, hunger, and the last thing she needed was to deal with a defiant child. Nobody wanted the additional drama. It was not an easy situation for anyone, especially for my mother. I felt very bad for her. She suffered in silence, watching her daughter waste her life away on a man with whom she should not associate.

After Edgar dropped off Sandra, she and my mother had a long conversation, and Sandra promised never to see Moises again. Unfortunately, she did not uphold her word.

My mother blamed herself for Sandra's behavior because we had essentially grown up with no father. She believed that Sandra was seeking attention from Moises to fill the father-figure role in her life. After my mother countlessly begged Sandra for weeks, she felt there was nothing else for her to do but to punish her. My mother was exhausted from punishing Sandra so often.

One morning, I woke up to find my mother hysterically crying. I then discovered that Sandra had run away from home because she knew her behavior was making my mother suffer. Sandra thought the best way to save my mother from pain and strife was to leave the house. She believed that if my mother no longer saw her, she would no longer suffer. The only thing I knew was that Sandra had not come home the night before, and we had no idea where she was. It did not take us long to find out that she was renting a room from someone in the neighborhood while continuing to work at the restaurant. My mother tried to get her to come home, but Sandra said that if my mother really loved her, she would no longer interfere with her life.

"Please, Madre, do not call the police. No one is forcing me to do anything I don't want to do. I love this man and I am not leaving him."

That night my mother came home and cried until sunrise. Since then, my mother has chosen to no longer interfere. No matter what, my mother still loved Sandra and would set food aside for her every day and dropped it off where she lived.

Chapter Seventeen

My mother's health was slowly deteriorating. After her stroke a couple of years earlier, she was no longer the same. I became focused on making my mother's life as peaceful as possible. I tried to help her avoid stress at all costs, but it was difficult for my mother because she was a worrier. No matter how old her children were, she was still concerned about their well-being. At this point, I did not want my mother to work anymore. I was making enough to support both her and Luis.

I wanted to give my mother a bit of happiness. Her grandchildren, Edwin and Edgar, managed to bring so much joy to my mother's life, as they were the fruit of her womb. She was partial, however, to Edwin, Edgar's eldest son. Although I did not like that my mother had favorites, her happiness was all I wanted, regardless of the cost. I knew she delighted in her grandchildren.

Luis wanted to work and make money; he believed school was not for everyone, especially him. It was hard for me to punish Luis because we had all spoiled him. Luis got away with everything; all he would have to do was look at us with his one-of-a-kind smile, and that was it. Luis knew he could manipulate my mother, but at the same time knew that would not work with me. I walked into the kitchen and asked my mother where he was. I wanted to strangle him.

"Where do you think he is?" I looked up. "In the backyard, covered in dirt." I made my way to the backyard and kneeled next to him.

"Give me a reason for this behavior," I snapped. "Make sure it's a good one." I was so angry; all I wanted to do was pull his hair. Deep in my heart, I just wanted to understand him better and see why he hated school so much. He remained quiet.

"Do you know what I have given up for our family all these years?" I asked as tears started to stream down my face. I was so overwhelmed. I had bottled these feelings up for so long that they just came pouring out of me.

Luis turned toward me, hugged me, and said, "You are the best sister in the world. You have done so much for our family." He paused. "All I want to do is help, but please, please," he begged, "do not make me go back to school. I don't want to. I want to be a mechanic. I want to fix cars."

"Really," I scoffed. "So mechanics don't go to school? How do you think you're going to learn to become a mechanic if you don't go to school?" He remained silent. "If this is really what you want, I will support you, but you have to go back to school." Luis trusted, admired, and obeyed me and my wishes. I wanted to believe that Luis was going to do the right thing so I could do the right thing by him.

My mother had dinner ready for us by the time we walked inside. As usual, we washed up, had dinner, then went to sleep. I told my mother not to worry about anything. I promised her I would wake up early and make sure that Luis went to school. That night, I woke up in the middle of the night to get a glass of water and noticed the light was on in the kitchen. Luis was on the ground putting a car together. I bought Luis a little car a week before, and he took it apart. I was so disappointed because I had just spent money on a gift for him, and he took apart the pieces and tossed them in a plastic bag. Before I knew it, he had put the car back together like nothing had happened. I took a seat next to him and gave him a hug and a kiss.

I asked him, "What are you doing?"

He looked up at me. "I don't want to lie to you. Please don't send me to school."

I shook my head in disbelief. "Do you want to make an ass out of yourself?" I asked unapologetically.

"No!" Luis cried. "I just want to be a mechanic." He kept repeating that he wanted to be a mechanic but did not want to put in the work required to get there. I decided to make us a cup of coffee so we could talk things over. Just as I brought the mug to my mouth, I noticed the hairs above Luis' upper lip. He had grown a mustache. I could not believe how much he had grown up over the last couple of months. I was so busy working that I had not realized he was not a little boy anymore. Time had passed so quickly—it had been just over two years since we had been living in the capital.

"Look at me. I worked and attended night school at the same time, and I did it," I said. "All you have to do is go to school. You don't have to worry about anything." I was so frustrated trying to convince Luis that going to school was the right decision. I began to sound like a broken record. No matter what I did, he did not want to hear it. I needed help. I could not let him stay home and waste his beautiful mind.

After I tried convincing Luis through various talks, I reached out to my brother Edgar and asked for his help. I wanted to know Edgar's thoughts on Luis not wanting to go to school and see if he could help in any way. Edgar was adamant that he knew how to persuade Luis to go to school.

"Don't worry..." Edgar began, "I will be around this weekend, and I'll handle it." As always, Edgar assumed the role of a father figure and did all that he could to protect us as well as push us to do better. Even though Edgar was now a father to his own children, he still made sure to keep an eye on us. He was always willing to listen to all of our problems and offer advice.

As promised, Edgar came by that weekend and sat down with my mother and me to have a long conversation about Luis. After a while, the three of us concluded that Luis would go and work with Edgar for six months. My mother cried at the thought of not being able to see Luis every day, but she knew it was the best decision for him. Edgar had to ask his boss if it was okay to have Luis work as an apprentice, and once he got the approval, Luis would be on his way. Edgar promised my mother that he would make Luis's life so miserable that he would dream of going back to school.

Luis would come to visit us every other weekend for the six months that he was working with Edgar. No matter how difficult Edgar made his life, Luis was not changing his mind. He could not wait to get a real job, considering he was learning so much working with Edgar every day.

Even though I had not stopped working, sales had gone down. I was always the first to arrive at work and would use the phone to book appointments to follow up with referrals. The economy was not strong, and no one was buying books at this point. This situation always worries me. I couldn't let my guard down. I had responsibilities at home.

After a long day at work, I went home a bit earlier and decided to clean my room. I found a business card that someone had given me at the International Book Fair. The card read National Manager: Piso Limpio, Francisco Gonzales. I figured I had nothing to lose, so I tried to book an appointment with him. I made several phone calls to the company, but I did not have any luck. I would leave messages, but no one would return my calls.

I did not understand why no one had contacted me back, so one day, I took the bus to where the business card said they were located and found myself in their lobby. I walked toward the reception desk and introduced myself. My name is Esperanza.

"May I speak with Mr. Francisco?" I asked.

"You need an appointment to meet with him," the woman behind the desk said with a cold exterior.

"What makes you think I don't have an appointment with him already?"

"I'm sorry, ma'am, but I do not see your name in my book. Are you sure it's for today?"

"I did not say it was for today. Mr. Francisco gave me his card two years ago, and I decided to come today." The receptionist looked at me in a weird way. "All I am asking you is if you could please give him this card and see if he is willing to meet with me." The card was not in good condition. It was bent and dirty. All I knew was that it was authentic, considering his signature was on the back of it. "Please let him know that I am the saleswoman he met at the International Book Fair two years ago." She looked at me like I had three heads.

"Could you please sit and wait?"

"Yes. Thank you." An hour later, I went back to her again. She looked unamused.

"It's you. Again."

Now I was angry. "I am not going anywhere without speaking to Mr. Francisco." It took everything in me to stay composed. The woman then got up and went into the office, and returned with Mr. Francisco. I had no idea what she had said to him behind those walls. When he saw me, he could not believe I was at his office. A smile came to his face.

"What took you so long?"

I smiled and stood up. He put his hand on my shoulder and guided me toward his office. "Come in," he said as I followed him. "I have so many new products. How did you know? As a matter of fact, I was just thinking of you. You would be perfect to spearhead this new promotion." At that moment, I felt a little intimidated. He was already hiring me without asking me any questions. He kept talking, like a wet parrot and all I could do was keep quiet and listen to whatever he had to say. Mr. Francisco grabbed the mop that was on the top of his desk and asked if I knew what it was.

"Yes, a mop," I said, thinking that question was too easy.

"No, it is not. It looks like a mop, but it is much, much more. It is everything that a housewife needs to clean the home easily." I was dumbfounded but admired his enthusiasm and passion as he explained his new product. After he finished his presentation I asked.

"Does your company only sell mops?" He affirmed proudly of course.

Am I really going to leave my company to sell mops? I thought? Absolutely not. Who in their right mind was going to buy a mop willingly? Although I could not wait to get out of there, I said, "Let's talk about money. How much would I make selling these mops?"

"You will make a minimum salary, as well as a ten percent commission per sale."

I had never received a salary before. The current company I worked for was solely commission-based, which made it more difficult when sales would go down. I was speechless; I thought that was incredible. I couldn't believe that I would no longer have to worry about making enough each month to cover my expenses.

"I have to think about it." I did not want him to call my bluff. "Let me give it some thought. I will get back to you over the weekend."

He nodded. "Please do not take too long, I need people now, and this is a great opportunity for you." As soon as I left, I could not help but think about how I was going to carry the weight of two jobs. I decided that the best thing to do was to speak with my current boss. My mother always said to be honest and not burn any bridges, as you never know. WMJackson had taught me everything I knew about sales, work, and life, and at that moment, I knew exactly what I had to do. I was so grateful to them for giving me a chance. I did not want to feel guilty about anything because if I did, I would not be able to move on. I was surrounded by great people, and I was going to miss them all. But I should think about myself.

The following day, I made an appointment with my boss and told him what I was planning to do. It was difficult to leave this part of my life, but my boss was happy for me and knew this was the best opportunity for me at this point. He also mentioned that if I wanted to, I would always have the option of selling books on my own time. He gave me a big hug and wished me the best.

Chapter Eighteen

In the year 1984, a new chapter in my life started. I signed a contract for one year with Pizo Limpo. After a two-week training period, I was assigned an official location. My life solely revolved around mops. My job was to sell the products, and that is exactly what I did. I was selling more than what was expected of me. People were fascinated with this mop; it was designed for the average housewife. The positive features of the mop were that it could be cleaned in a washing machine, was reusable, and had a head that would twist on and off.

Just like in my other sales positions, I was given a script to memorize and was expected to succeed. My initial plan was to work Monday through Friday with Pizo Limpio company and sell books on the weekends, but I was doing so well at this new company that my boss asked if I could work on the weekends, as well. Although I still wanted to stay loyal to Mr. Gomez, I knew that leaving the book company was the best decision.

When I received my first check, I was astounded at the amount of money I made selling mops. I even had enough to put a down payment on a fridge. My mother was happy when I gave her the surprise. I wanted to work harder and buy her more things. I dreamed of buying her a reclining chair. I realized it was two hard years. I worked seven days a week. But it was worth it because I saw great results.

In the meantime, Sandra was still living alone and would occasionally come to visit our mother. We knew she was still romantically involved with her boss. Every time Sandra stopped by she looked sad. My mother and I knew something was wrong. But Sandra never complained. I worried about her but she was of age now. I only reminded her that I loved her and she could always count on me.

After working with Edgar for six months, Luis had to return home and go back to school. My mother and I had no problem with Luis coming home, but we wanted him to go to school. Each day I would come home exhausted and have to deal with the same problems. Each day Luis would disappear and return in the afternoon like nothing happened. It made me upset to find out that he was disobeying my mother.

"Help me understand why you are blatantly disobeying. How does a child not want to go to school," I asked Luis as all the frustration boiled in me.

"I'm not a child; I'm already a young man. You know people. You have the connections. Why can't you just help me find a job? I guess you forgot how old you were when you started working." He had a point. My head had been hurting from the long day I had. I told Luis I would try to find him a job. But I could not promise anything.

The next day I met Edgar at his house and asked for his help. He had a friend who worked at an auto body shop called Soto Brakes, so Edgar called him. He explained the situation and what we were going through. The owner was really nice. He promised me not to worry and that within no time, Luis would be back in school. Washing screws and being full of oil and dirt was not enjoyable. With these conditions Luis started to work there.

Luis woke up bright and early so he wouldn't be late to work. To everyone's surprise, this became constant. On occasion I would ask him how the job was going, and he would respond that it was going great.

"Soon I am going to learn how to repair cars."

I noticed his hands were dry and cut up from the gasoline he was using, so I tried putting cream on them to make him feel better.

"This is what you want your hands to look like instead of going to school?" I asked.

"Yes, this is what a real mechanic's hands look like." His answer somewhat took me aback, but it solidified that this was his truth. This was what he wanted to do.

* * *

Each Monday, every salesperson was expected to report to the main office of the company. This was when we would get our weekly assignment and find out if there were any location changes. I heard my co-workers talking about a grand opening for a new supermarket. My boss had the flier on top of his desk, and I picked it up.

He said, "We're invited to that grand opening."

I turned around, and my boss was looking right at me.

"We?" I asked, shocked he was talking to me in front of all of my coworkers.

"Yes, you are coming with me because every single person coming to this grand opening will be leaving with a mop, right?"

"Yes, sir," I said and nodded with reassurance.

"We will be given a booth, and you will be working with two other ladies from our company. You will be in charge and handle the microphone, and the other two will handle the product and the sales." I was scared because I had never spoken in front of so many people before, but I was always up for a new challenge. The grand opening was only three days away, leaving barely any amount of preparation time to figure out what I wanted to say. I was working every day of the week with no time for myself. With that being said, I thought the best way to prepare was to wing it on the spot and use honesty to steer customers to the product. I decided I would just give a testimonial on how I viewed the product, and hope for the best. Sure enough, my tactic worked. Our sales and customer interaction were incredible. As the grand opening was coming to an end, a man from the side began applauding us on our outstanding work. He was in complete shock as all he could say was, "Wow!" It was then that he began approaching the table.

"Let me introduce myself, young lady."

The man seemed to be forty-five to fifty years old and was elegant. When he spoke, it was always in a sophisticated manner. Just through his speaking, one could tell he was educated and knew what he was saying.

"My name is Leonel Ortiz, I am the President of Industrials La Coruna. Have you ever heard of the company?"

Mr. Ortiz's company was known for exporting and importing elite food products. This company was well recognized within wealthy communities because of the renowned caviar and delicacies they sold.

"Yes, sir. I do know of the company. But it does not interest me because you sell products that, unfortunately, I could never afford." He looked at me and smiled.

"I appreciate your honesty. You're not only a good saleswoman, but you're funny, as well. I don't think all my products are as expensive as you think. With your permission, I would like to give you some samples."

I was very excited. "For free?"

He nodded. "Yeah, for free," he said nonchalantly.

Throughout our interaction, he would pause to shake other people's hands. It was evident that he was a well-respected businessman who knew everyone in the industry. I walked with him to the parking lot and took the samples that he gave to me. I shook his hand as he gave me his business card. He told me he was interested in working with me and asked me to give him a call when I was ready to interview. It was then that he drove away, and my two co-workers ran toward me.

"Oh, my god, what was he saying to you?" one girl asked.

"You know he is frequently known for being a womanizer. It's rare for him to be seen with the same woman twice," the other interjected.

I said, "So what? What does this have to do with me? He just gave me some samples. Would you like some?" I shared the samples he had given me: prunes, grapes, cherries, and a bottle of olives. I was excited to bring this food home to my family and share it with them. To my surprise, none of us enjoyed the food he gave me. Although it might have been expensive, it was nowhere as good in comparison to rice and beans with a fried egg on top. We all laughed.

The following day I went back to my usual location, and to my surprise, Mr. Ortiz came to my booth around noon.

"So, what did you think?" he asked.

I did not know what to say. "About what? Your product?" I said as I looked into his eyes.

"No, the interview."

I was confused a bit why he would come to find me when he had already given me his business card. I was not interested in working for him because I was content and pleased with my job.

Mr. Ortiz said, "I strongly believe you would do very well at my company."

To which I responded, "To be honest with you, I am really happy at this company, but thank you for the offer."

I continued with my demonstration of the product and didn't pay attention to him.

"I believe you will do very well in my company. Please think about it. If you change your mind, the offer is still on the table."

Since that day, every time he would supervise his employees in the Supermarket that I was working at, he would find a way to strike up casual conversation and ask how I was doing. He was always respectful and never made me feel uncomfortable. It seemed as though he was really interested in my work ethic. I could not help but wonder why people were always approaching me when I was succeeding. My current boss had approached me at the book fair when I was doing extremely well selling the encyclopedias, and now the same thing was happening again. I did not want to make the wrong decision and leave my current place of work, but Mr. Ortiz kept insisting I had nothing to lose by going on an interview.

After that day's work, all I wanted to do was go home and talk to my mother. This woman always had an answer for everything. After dinner, my mother could tell something was wrong with me. She came behind me, and I felt her soft hand touching my hair. She kissed my head, and I felt her love and that gave me peace.

"What's wrong?" my mother asked.

I grabbed her hand and kissed her. "Nothing, don't worry." She remained quiet.

"I got another job offer."

"God heard my prayers."

I crinkle my nose in confusion. "What?"

"You work too much, sweetie. You don't even have a day off for yourself. You don't sleep enough." She paused. "I know we have expenses, and you take care of all of us, but maybe you should check out this new job. Maybe you'll have a day off." I knew my mother would have the answer. The next day, I called Mr. Ortiz and scheduled an interview. The interview was scheduled for Monday at 5:00 p.m. That weekend was the worst weekend for me. I was reluctant about the decision I was making. I felt stuck and had a feeling that this may be the highest position I could receive, but I believed in opportunities. If I were meant to keep growing as a professional, I would take every chance I was given. Sales were never a problem for me. I was more concerned about the kind of product and economy that I was going to sell. Mr. Ortiz's products were expensive and only catered to a select clientele.

In the mid 1980s Colombia was the world's second-largest coffee producer, but international coffee prices fell. Colombia's rise in petroleum earnings compensated for the loss, but this was not enough. The middle class was heavily affected. The economy was terrible, and everyone was afraid that their job was in jeopardy. I didn't know if it was the right moment to switch jobs. If the economy crashed more than it already had, who would have money to spare?

Chapter Nineteen

Monday rolled around much quicker than I anticipated. I was extremely nervous and did not know what to expect. When the receptionist hung up the phone, she gave me her full attention.

"Can I help you?" she asked.

"I have an interview with Mr. Ortiz," I said calmly.

"No problem. He is busy at the moment but will be with you shortly."

I was the only one in the waiting area, and the woman decided to strike up a conversation. "Have you known Mr. Ortiz for a long time?"

I gave her an ambiguous nod. "I often see him at the supermarket where I work. He approached me and said that his company had a better opportunity for me, but if I am being honest, I am a little nervous to transition over."

She nodded. "My name is Selena. It's a pleasure to meet you. This company indeed offers great opportunities, but to be honest with you, you have to be careful of Mr. Ortiz." It was nice of her to warn me, but I did not care. "Mr. Ortiz definitely has a thing for beautiful women. You know he's divorced?"

I couldn't care less who Mr. Ortiz was attracted to. My sole priority was work and being able to provide for my family.

Minutes later after our conversation Selena asked me to follow her. I knew it was time for my interview. I stood up as the receptionist pointed in the direction of Mr. Ortiz's office. It was nicely decorated with elegance and class. He matched well with the theme of the office, dressed in a gray suit with a red tie. He was perfectly well groomed.

He stood up and smiled and stuck his hand out.

"Welcome. Please have a seat. I am so happy that you are here. Very rarely am I wrong, and I know this is the right place for you. You are going to do great things here." His words excited me. I kept waiting for him to say something that would turn me off, but as time passed, Mr. Ortiz sold me on this position. He made me an offer that was hard to refuse. I would earn twice as much, be given additional medical benefits, and be granted a commission for every sale I made. Before finishing the interview, he said, "If you enjoy sales, this is the right place for you. All employees are treated equally and given opportunities to grow, but it's up to you to decide if you are willing to take this chance. You will be working with elite products. All beginnings are difficult." He paused. "What do you think will hinder you from challenging yourself?"

"Fear," I answered automatically and without hesitation. "The hardest thing to overcome in life is fear because when a door closes, you are afraid to knock again.

Fortunately, my life has taught me that I have to knock more than once." I took a moment to pause. "If you can overcome those obstacles, nothing can stop you." Mr. Ortiz looked at me with a fire in his eyes.

"This is the attitude I want to see in you, not just today, but always." Mr. Ortiz was a sales expert. I admired him from the moment I met him. I knew I would learn so much from him. For once in my life, I did not have to knock on a door for an opportunity. This time the opportunity was knocking at my door, and I would be foolish not to open up.

Although fear was trying to hold me back, I dared myself to take the opportunity.

After the interview, I was impressed with his proposal. He offered me benefits: life and medical insurance and room for growth within the company. As soon as I finished the interview, I went and looked up the word elitist in my dictionary. Mr. Ortiz mentioned the word so many times throughout our conversation that I wanted to make sure I had a full understanding of what he meant. The term elitist is defined as exclusive.

Exclusive? I knew I could not sell one bottle of olives in my neighborhood. A bottle of olives, a box of cherries, and a container of prunes from this company were the equivalent of buying two pounds of rice, two pounds of potato, and a bottle of oil.

Before I went home that night doubting this new position. I called my friend Olga and asked if she was able to meet with me so I could get some of this stress off of my chest. We met for coffee, and she let me vent as much as I needed. I knew leaving was the best decision for me. Throughout the years, I had to make big decisions in my life that ultimately affected not only myself but my family and my future. It was time to move on.

I had been selling mops for the last two years, so I should take the risk.

I gave my current boss two weeks notice and felt in my heart that this was the right decision for me. My boss was not happy with my decision. Firmly but coldly, he shook my hand and wished me well. He also said I would be welcome to return if I changed my mind. I felt an impending sense of guilt. The next two weeks went by so fast. I finished my work with honor and trained the person that would replace me. I did not want to burn this bridge.

In the year 1985 , the first week at my new job was nothing like I expected. On my first day, I thought Mr. Ortiz would give me a sales assignment like my previous job, but I was wrong. Instead, he sent me to the factory, where his products were packaged and shipped out. The goal was for me to learn about each product from start to finish. Mr. Ortiz wanted me to taste, smell, feel, and memorize each product I was going to sell. Through his eyes I understood the vision of the company. His reasoning for sending me for a two week training made complete sense.

The following week, I was assigned to a new supermarket. My job was to supervise the product that was already on the shelves. I was in charge of keeping the products clean, organized, and facing forward. Keeping the products aesthetically pleasing was everything to this company. Appearance was what would grab the attention of customers.

This company understood sales as a science and not just a mechanism for profit.

I stood next to the products all day. People would approach me and ask questions about the products, and I would answer them perfectly. Every night I would go home and study the products to make sure that I knew what I was talking about. Over the weekends, I would set up samples for shoppers, and of course, they would have questions. A week later, I knew these products inside out. Work became a piece of cake. I loved talking to people, sales came easy, and the time passed quickly.

Before I knew it, I had already been working for the company for six months. I went to Mr. Ortiz's office and was handed my bonus. My eyes nearly fell out of my head when I saw how much money I made. Not only was I handed a bonus by Mr. Ortiz, but he also promoted me to a supervisory position. My task now consisted of going to multiple supermarkets to make sure that all sales associates were doing their job. I was now managing 12 supermarkets, and Mr. Ortiz expected that under my supervision, sales would double in revenue.

On many occasions Mr. Ortiz would personally supervise me. He wanted to make sure I was doing my job correctly. I remember on many occasions he would ask if we could have lunch. Remembering Selena's advice, I politely declined. I was at the peak of my career. Mr Ortiz did not exaggerate about the opportunities that were being given in the company. I was going to take full advantage.

Whether his intentions were good or bad towards me, I did not have time to entertain that. I was so focused on work and that was it.

Time flew by quickly. Sales in each supermarket went up just as Mr. Ortiz projected. I was called into his office once again, where a travel position opened. I recalled in the interview he asked if I had a problem traveling or relocating. I said I had no problem. He then said to speak with Selena. She will be in charge of all the details; flight, hotel and itinerary.

While Mr Ortiz spoke, I tried to contain my emotions. I could not believe that one of my dreams was finally coming true. I would fly on the same plane that, as a child, I watched take off from the river.

When I went home and told my mother of this new opportunity, she could not believe it. She was so proud of me. My heart was warm, and I was proud of who I had become. All the sacrifice was worth it. I could see a clear future. Now I knew nothing was going to get in the way of me reaching my goals. I counted the days until my flight. My mother helped me pack my luggage. I was very anxious that morning. I got her blessing, and headed to the airport. Mr. Ortiz was waiting for me. We entered the airport together. I could not feel my legs. I was hoping he could not tell how nervous I was. Not only was this the first time I had stepped into an airport but it was my first time flying on an airplane. I had to keep my composure over everything, when I finally sat in my seat.

My head was spinning. My mind had many questions. What would happen if the plane crashed? I would never see my mother again. Suddenly, Mr. Ortiz extended his hand to shake mine, and I instantly noticed that my hand felt like the inside of an ice box.

"Are you nervous?" he asked.

"No." I shook my head, lying straight through my teeth.

"Good. Get used to it." My heart stopped. "This time we will fly together. Next time , you'll be doing this alone. After a while this will be repetitive," he said.

Nearly all the air in my lungs escaped every time I stepped on a plane. We flew to many cities; Medellín, Barranquilla, Montería, Pasto, Boyacá, Sin Lejo, Pereira, and Cartagena. He introduced me to the manager of every supermarket we visited as a new supervisor in the company. Mr Ortiz was always greeted like royalty. He was well respected. You could tell that everyone appreciated him.

Not only did this job allow me to travel, but it educated me on everything there was to know about my country. I had never left my city alone before this. Mr. Ortiz and I traveled together for six weeks to all locations. Medellin was one of my favorite places to go to. Medellin happened to be one of my favorite spots to visit. I highly recommend the *ajiaco, arepa,* and *bandeja paisa. Ajiaco* is a soup, and *arepas* is a dough that is split down the middle and filled with anything you can imagine. The *bandeja paisa* was a big rice dish consisting of meat, beans, and fried egg. It was delicious. Seafood, commonly referred to as *mariscos,* is an accumulation of abundant Caribbean shellfish. This is commonly recognized as the most flavorful dish around.

I carried a bottle of water with me everywhere I traveled because only bottled water was safe for consumption. Mr. Ortiz ordered wine every night at dinner. I, on the other hand, had never had an alcoholic beverage and had no intention of doing so. This was one of the most incredible experiences I had ever had. I knew I would remember this for the rest of my life.

My life changed a lot after that trip. I was flying, visiting new cities, and following up with clients. I was even opening new accounts. I enjoyed this opportunity because I was constantly meeting new people, but I was away from home most of the time. My mother was not happy about that. Every time I spoke to her, I tried to explain how fortunate we were. There was no better feeling than doing what you love. I did not feel like I was working. A year later, I was awarded "Best Seller of the Year."

The capital city had grown to become a very dangerous place to live. The streets were no longer safe. My mother told me that while I was away, two men raped a young woman on the bus. It happened at 9:00 a.m. in front of everyone. These two men then took this woman off the bus and threw her into a car. No one did anything to help her.

My mother was so worried about me because I was always traveling alone. I promised my mother that I would be careful, but I was not going to stop living my life because something bad happened to someone else.

Every time I had to take a plane, I had to assure my mother that I was going to be safe. She would look me in the eyes and beg me to come home safely. Although I could not control much of that situation, I always reassured her that I would.

Once, I even brought her a newspaper and read her an article.

"Colombia has railroads and highways with important inland waterways. The airplane is particularly important in maintaining communication with other countries. Colombia has one of the best flight transportation records in the world; there is only one called Avianca. Avianca was established in 1919. Over 5.5 million people use the airline annually without accidents being reported."

I took a breath, "So what makes you think it will happen now? Madre, relax. I'll be fine."

After I finished my speech, she looked at me unapologetically.

"Sweetie, if that plane is meant to fall down, it will... no matter what." Every time that I returned home, she was so happy. I always tried to spend a lot of time with my mother before leaving for my next trip. My mother's favorite pastime was attending church on Sundays, so I made it a point to always try going with her. I loved to take my mother to breakfast after church.

My worries never subsided as the company's expectations of me were so high. My family completely depended on me. I was going to ensure that we would never go through any pain like we had in the past. We were not going to go hungry, and we would always have a place to live. I was sure of it, I would do everything in my power to do so.

Chapter Twenty

Every day was a challenge considering the economy was doing so poorly. The government increased the cost of living in all aspects, including food and housing. If you could think of it, the government put a price on it. It was up to me to support my family, and I had to do everything to ensure I did not get fired. Every time I returned home from one of my business trips, I felt a sense of pride. My mother was always waiting for me by the front door with a big smile and was very happy when I returned home safely. Upon my arrival at the office, I was awarded for being one of the top sellers for the quarter. I could not complain about anything, knowing how bad the economy was.

By this time, Luis had been working at the auto body shop. He would come home so happy each day, hug me, and kiss my mother. I waited every day for him to come home frustrated and tired, claiming that he hated his job, but it never happened. After several months, I decided to go to the shop and speak to Luis's boss. I wanted to remind him that Luis was supposed to hate his job, not love it. According to Mr. Soto, he told me that my brother had a real talent and was doing perfectly fine there. I was very angry with Mr. Soto. He apologized to me but had little explanation as to why he could not encourage Luis to go back to school. Customers were asking for my brother by name to fix their cars. Luis was passionate about the work, and everyone wanted him to do the service they needed.

Before I knew it, Luis had been working for a long time. Mechanics from all over the place would call Luis for help. He was able to help other mechanics by phone. All they would have to do was give him the make and model of the car, and Luis was able to tell them what needed to be done. I was fascinated with how well-equipped he was. I was so proud of Luis; I promised him that after I bought our mother a house, I would buy him an auto body shop so he could have his own business. Luis gave me a big hug.

"Gracias, Hermana, I will make you proud."

Luis liked to dress well, and he especially loved sneakers. Since he was making some money, he would purchase them and pay in installments. People would come to the shop selling sneakers, and he would buy them. He always liked to dress sharp. That night, Sandra came over and gave Luis a funny look.

"Where the heck are your shoes?" she asked.

"Please do not tell me you did it again?" my mother begged Luis. Sandra and I looked at her in confusion.

"If Luis sees someone without shoes, he gives them the ones from his own feet no matter how expensive they were." Sandra and I looked at him like he was crazy.

"Oh my god, what is wrong with you? You pay for those in installments! You probably have not even paid them off yet," Sandra exclaimed.

Anytime we said anything to Luis, he would just laugh at us. He never complained and never stressed. After Luis got home from work, he would take a shower, eat whatever my mom had made, and then go to the park to play soccer. He loved soccer and girls... who were always following him around. My mother and Luis had a special bond. She was never able to go to sleep until Luis returned home. She always waited up for him no matter how late he would stay out. I frequently had to reprimand Luis for coming home so late. I wanted my mother to be able to sleep and relax. My brother respected and frequently listened to me but would inevitably do it again.

Everyone who knew Luis loved him. He was like a little bird, not attached to anything. He liked to be free, afraid someone was going to take away his wings. On many occasions, I tried to ask Luis why he wanted to move through life so quickly, and he would tell me there might not be a tomorrow.

At this time, our weekends were very enjoyable. My older brothers would try to see my mother, and my sister would sometimes stop by. My mother always hoped that when Sandra would come to visit, she would decide to stay with us for good. Joaquin finally came to see us after meeting the love of his life, his wife. My mother seemed to be very content. Everyone had settled down comfortably, and she was so happy to be a part of her grandchildren's lives.

After my siblings left, she would have tears in her eyes. I asked why she cried, and she told me it was because she knew all her children struggled. At that moment, I wished my siblings would not tell my mother what they were going through. They would come home and stress my mother out, which was unfair to her. It was not like she could do anything to help them. All it did was make her feel guilty. My mother wanted to help them financially, but she was not able to do so. She was so concerned with their finances that she even asked if I could support them in some way, but my mother was my main focus. I had many responsibilities other than to support my adult siblings.

Everyone was healthy in my household, and my mother was finally doing okay. She continued to worry about my brothers, however, which is why I promised her that if I continued to progress and do well financially, I would help them all. My mother believed me because I always kept my promises to her.

One morning when I got to the office, I found it curious to see a little boy sitting in the waiting area. I smiled at him and he smiled back. When I got closer to Selena's desk she whispered it's Mr. Ortiz's son. From what the receptionist told me I knew he was separated from his wife and lived with his son in an apartment close to where Mr. Ortiz's mother used to live. From what I heard, she had passed away not long before I started working for the company. Mr. Ortiz and his mother had been very close, and after she passed away, he supposedly did not take it well. I never asked questions or thought it okay to get involved. I respected his privacy and believed that everyone had a past. I went directly to my office to prepare for my next flight. Before the day ended he passed my office and introduced me to his son. It was a pleasure meeting him. There was something special about this boy. His eyes looked a little sad, but he was so sweet.

There was a lot of excitement in the office because the company was throwing an end-of-year party, the first one of these events I would attend. . There would be raffles, extra bonuses, and a catered dinner with music. This party was only a week away. Selena asked me if I had something to wear. I didn't even think of that, and it was a great idea to go shopping. I remember that day my mother looked at me so proudly when she saw me in my new dress. My mother complimented me on how beautiful I looked. I thought she was exaggerating. When I got to the party music was playing, and everyone danced salsa, merengue, and cumbia. We all had a great time. Mr. Ortiz took the microphone, and the first name he announced was mine. I won one of the raffles and received a bonus for being the best employee of the year. Many of my coworkers received many prizes. It was a great celebration.

A little while later, I was sitting at my table, and Mr. Ortiz asked me if I wanted to dance. Although I was a little nervous, I accepted. Before that night, I didn't know he was such a good dancer, and I never danced so much in my life. Realizing it was getting late, I grabbed my bag and made my way to the door. I needed to catch the bus. When I neared the exit, I heard a voice.

"Why are you leaving so early?" Mr. Ortiz said.

Suddenly, fear began growing in my stomach. "It's getting late and I have to get home."

I walked quickly and he stood in front of me and said, "If you'll let me, I can take you home."

I looked at him, my eyes widening. "No, thank you. I can take the bus." I said.

"Goodnight, Mr. Ortiz."

I left and waited for my bus. Thirty minutes had passed, and I was still waiting.

Mr. Ortiz drove by slowly and opened the window to his car.

"I don't think that bus is coming. Let me take you home, please." Mr. Ortiz said. He was right.

I accepted, but I told him, "Please leave me a block away from my house. If my mother sees me in your car I will be in trouble."

He found my request a bit odd. He found it strange and I could tell by his smirk. The only thing I was interested in was getting home and not having any problems with my mother.

"Whatever you desire, young lady," he answered sarcastically. He opened the door like a true gentleman and I got out of the car.

Mr. Ortiz followed my rules and dropped me a block away as I requested.

After I got out of the car, he said, "I will pick you up tomorrow morning at the same place. We can go to work together."

I did not answer him and could not wait to get home. I knew my mother would still be up when I got home and she would have a million questions about the party. The last thing I wanted to do was answer questions, at least not tonight. I ran into my room and smelled my hands. His cologne was all over them. It was so crazy. I ran into the bathroom and washed my hands until his scent was gone. Only to imagine that Mr. Ortiz was trying to go out with me freaked me out. He did not take women seriously, and I was not going to make a fool out of myself.

The next day I took the bus to work, as usual. When I arrived at the office, I found a box of chocolates on my desk. I acted like I didn't notice. Mr. Ortiz called me into his office.

He said, "I was waiting for you this morning like we agreed. Everything okay?"

"I am perfectly fine. I took the opportunity to clear some things. Listen, Mr. Ortiz, I am not looking for someone to give me a ride to work or to leave a box of chocolates on my desk. As a matter of fact, you can take them back." I took a minute to think. "You have it all wrong. I am here at this company because I love my job. So I would appreciate it if things could stay professional between us." It grew quiet. Mr. Ortiz looked at me like I was crazy.

"I understand," he said. "I did not leave those chocolates on your desk. Have a nice day." He lifted his arm, suggesting I leave his office. It was evident that Mr. Ortiz did not like how I spoke to him.

Chapter Twenty-One

Soon after that awkward moment in his office our relationship changed. Nothing was the same between us. We ignored each other at all times. When he needed to talk to me it was in a professional way and very cold. The truth is, I felt ignored completely. This situation bothered me, yet this is what I asked for. Therefore, there was no reason this should bother me.

Not only was I stressed about my work relationship with Mr. Ortiz, but I was worried about my mother finding out. I was scared that her curiosity would begin to grow as she questioned what was wrong with me. In reality, nothing was going on. My mother had been down this road with Sandra, and I did not want to put her through the same situation again.

Mr. Ortiz could have easily been my father, His oldest daughter was my age. An impending sense of doom took over my being. I did not want to be home, so I spent my time at the park to avoid my mother. I felt like a fool. I thought of everything Sandra went through. Once again, I thought, *I am no different than my sister.* I was in my late teens at the time; it did not make the situation any better. I decided to avoid Mr. Ortiz as much as possible, but I did not succeed for very long.

Without notice, and after having been ignored for months, Mr. Ortiz approached me and asked if I wanted to have dinner with him and his son. My answer flew out of my mouth faster than my mind was working. The three of us went to a very nice restaurant, and the night went by quickly. From the moment I met Orlando, he captured my heart.

There was just something in his eyes that reminded me of myself at that age.

Orlando and I became inseparable. Unknowingly, he brought his father and me much closer to one another. We continued to see each other more frequently behind my mother's back, something I wasn't proud of. The only condition I asked for was that he had to bring his child every time we went out. He introduced me to his younger sister, who was about to start working for the company. We were the same age so we got along well and had a great friendship. She invited me one day to her summer home. I asked my mother for permission. We went with some of her friends to the home. We were so excited to vacation. One of the girls from the summer home, to my surprise, told me she was Mr Ortiz's girlfriend. I was not surprised by what I heard. I knew about his reputation with women. There was no reason for me to be upset with Mr. Ortiz. I was mad at myself for being part of this game. Even though there was nothing between us, it was clear to me he was trying to court me.

The following Monday, I returned to work. All I could think about was turning in my resignation letter. I did not want anything to do with him. At that moment, that's all I desired. I knew I had a lot to lose. I worked hard to get a position at this job. It was all my fault that this was happening to me. Now I had to make a drastic decision, even though I would have to start from the beginning. I tried to relax a bit. I tried to think of another plan which wasn't quitting. I had a thought, so I went into Mr. Ortiz's office as if nothing had happened. With pride I asked him if he could transfer me to another city.

"Why?" he asked, confused.

"Mr. Ortiz, every day the city is getting dangerous. I would like a town more peaceful for my mother."

"So you're trying to run away from me?" he asked. "I don't know what's going through your head, but what I do know is that you are very important to me. I think I am falling in love with you," he said without a thought.

Instantly, anger took over. I thought of his audacity to tell me he was falling in love with me. I could not believe him. It was all lies. Was this one of his tricks? Was this just a game he grew comfortable playing?

"Are you serious? How can you speak about loving me when you have a girlfriend?" I demanded.

"Do you have proof of that? People can say many things, but you have no proof." I could not believe the words coming from this man's mouth.

"Yes, I do. This past weekend, I met someone who introduced herself as your girlfriend. What more proof do you need?" The words shot from my mouth as ammunition would fire from a machine gun. I was no longer willing to play his game.

"Girlfriend?" he asked, confused, "I don't have a girlfriend."

"I've had enough," I said firmly and walked out of his office. I went back to work as normal. I started to send my resumes to finally get out of this. I should have done this a long time ago.

A week later, I found out that Mr. Ortiz traveled to the city with another trainee. Every single day of the three weeks he was gone, Mr. Ortiz sent something to my house; flowers, chocolates and letters. Upon his return, Mr. Ortiz showed up at my front door with a bouquet of flowers. He requested to meet my mother. He wanted to ask for her permission to date me. At this time, asking for a parent's approval was customary to establish respect and rapport with the family. Asking for my mother's approval was nice, but it was unnecessary unless he asked for mine first.

I wanted to hide the situation from my mother as much as possible, but she let Mr. Ortiz in and invited him to have a seat in the living room. He professed his love for me and asked my mother's permission to court me. To my surprise, my mother handled the situation shockingly well.

"I think you're making a big mistake here. Do you realize she's very young...and you're a grown man?" My mother spoke unapologetically. "She could be your daughter."

"With all the respect you deserve I could be her father but am not." My mother looked at me in a very sad way.

"At the end of the day, it's not my decision. Isn't that true, Espernza?" she said.

Her eyes were disappointed, and I knew she could tell I had feelings for him. As much as I tried to deny it, they were there. I stayed silent, and my mother grew frustrated. She no longer wanted to speak with him.

"You can finish having this conversation with my eldest son, Edgar. He's like her father."

"I have no problem waiting for him. When is a good time for me to talk with him?" I was impressed.

"I don't know. He lives far away from the city."

My mother was rubbing her hands over and over again as though she had just put lotion on. She was strong-willed yet always managed to keep herself cool, but I could tell this made her uneasy.

"Señora Herminia I would like to do this correctly. Tomorrow is Saturday, so why don't we all take a trip, and you can introduce Edgar to me? This is very important to me, and I want to do it right."

He had an answer for everything. He spoke so calmly and had everything in control.

"Is this what you want?" my mother asked, and all I could do was nod my head. I was so embarrassed.

"Señor Ortiz, we will be ready for you tomorrow," my mother said. As soon as he took off, my mother made her displeasure apparent. She cried and looked at me with disappointment. She asked what she did wrong and why I was doing the same thing as Sandra.

"Are you in love? Answer me!"

I did not have an answer. I did everything in my power to stay away from him. I asked God to help me.

We both went to sleep that night and prayed to God that Mr. Ortiz would not show up the next day. I wanted to leave this all behind me. All this brought stress to my mother. How was I supposed to know what love felt like?

The next morning Mr. Ortiz was at my door bright and early. Before I knew it, three hours had passed, and we were sitting with my brother. Edgar was waiting for us in his home with a cup of coffee. After he and Mr. Ortiz spoke for a bit, my brother approached me and said, "I am no one to tell you what to do. You are of age, What is happening is just a formal thing. I want you to understand that marriage is not a joke and this gentleman wants to marry you. Is this what you really want? I just want to wish you the best, because you deserve it. Personally, I worry about the age difference."

Our return home was much better. There was no more tension. My mother felt relieved after talking to my brother.

After that trip he never left my side.

Six months later, he asked me to be his wife. The night he proposed, he dedicated a song to me, "Alma Corazon y Vida," and asked if I would marry him. The words expressed a soul to know you, a heart to love you, and all my life to live with you always.

When I shared the news with my mother, she told me, "Sweetie, you don't have to get married. You have a whole life ahead of you, He can be your father." She then added with sadness, "I know this is all my fault because you didn't have a father figure by your side." I didn't say a word.

We started preparing for the wedding but soon found out that we could not get married in Colombia because divorce was not legal at that time. The only thing legal at that time was the separation of bodies and property. We had to go to another country that would be willing to marry us under those conditions. Venezuela was the closest country to us. We started all the paperwork. As soon as we had the appointment with the judge we flew together to Urena, Venezuela. In 1987, that same day we arrived, after we checked into the hotel, we spoke to the judge for the final details. We thought that was the best thing to do, knowing that the ceremony was planned for the next day. When we arrived at the office we got some disturbing news. The secretary informed us that the judge's mother had just passed away, and that our wedding was being canceled. We were surprised with the news.

We explained that we had a long flight and we do not live in this country. The secretary felt bad and said please wait out here. After a while she said the judge will be leaving the office in one hour.

"Can you get married right now?"

Leonel answered, "Yes."

The secretary explained that we needed two witnesses. "We do not know anyone," he said. Our witness was going to be someone that lives in the city, but they are not with us at the moment. We went outside the courthouse and asked the man who was selling lotto tickets to be our witness, and he agreed. The woman who cleaned the courthouse willingly volunteered herself. Less than 15 minutes later we were in front of the judge.

Ten minutes after that we were husband and wife.

As soon as we got to the hotel, I couldn't hold it in anymore. I started to cry, I was so disappointed everything we planned didn't follow through. My beautiful dress was hanging up in the hotel. Leonel was very happy. He insisted we were married and we didn't have to make another trip. Leonel tried to make me feel better with his words. "Tomorrow we will go into the city so you can put on your dress and we can take pictures and enjoy one another on what was supposed to be the happiest day of our lives."

The next morning, his sister called and said that Orlando was running a fever. We were supposed to be in Venezuela for ten days enjoying our honeymoon, but we decided to cut our trip short and travel home right away. He was very worried and so was I and we rushed home.

Chapter Twenty-Two

When I finally met the rest of my husband's family and friends, everyone had the same reaction as soon as they saw me. I was too young for him.

I was also scared and confused. As Leonel and I were making our way home that afternoon, he could tell I was overwhelmed.

"I am bothered by all the comments everyone makes."

He pulled over, stopped the car, and looked into my eyes with frankness.

"I didn't think you worried about what people thought of us. Everything in life has a price. I cannot guarantee happiness to anyone. I don't know how long this will last. The only thing I ask is for honesty and respect. Under one condition, promise me that the day you don't want to be in this relationship, I will be the first one to know. It doesn't matter if our love lasts one month, one year, or one day."

This conversation made us feel better. I was willing to start a family with him under one condition; my mother was always going to be a priority in my life. Under no circumstances was I going to compromise on providing for her. Leonel smiled at me with his kind, caring eyes and reassured me, "I will not stop you from taking care of her."

Soon after, we bought an apartment. This was not just a place to live but somewhere for Orlando to feel safe. The three of us needed each other mutually. I started my life with a man that brought me peace and security. A huge responsibility was waiting for me. Orlando needed us more than ever. Living together was never a problem. I felt like I was taking care of my younger brother Luis. My only concern was that he followed the house rules. Truth was I was too young and I didn't want to confuse him. I wanted us to be friends but there were rules to follow. The day we moved in, I wanted to speak with him to let him know.

"Orlando, I want to be in your life, but only if you want me to be."

These words were hard to speak, but I knew what it was like to be raised by a single parent and did not want to interrupt the dynamics Orlando had already grown accustomed to.

I said, "I want you to feel comfortable with me." I paused before continuing, "I won't pretend to be your mother. I can be whatever makes you comfortable...a friend...a sister, a cousin...I just never want you to see me as your enemy because we have to live together. Do you understand?" He nodded his head. It was easier said than done.

Orlando's mother lacked a presence in his life, which was difficult for him to grasp during those very important years of his childhood. He was angry, and his feelings were valid.

Children need consistency surrounded by a positive home environment in order to thrive in school, as well as other areas of their life. Divorce tends to be traumatic for children, and Orlando was no different. School was his second home. Because of being in this situation, he was acting out in school and seemed to be having a difficult time adjusting. I had faith that, eventually, things would work themselves out. I was never a quitter growing up, and I certainly was not going to quit making this one of the most important relationships in my life. I was committed to making a positive change in Orlando's life. I wanted him to see me as a beacon of light instead of darkness.

The first thing I needed to do was establish trust. Some days my husband would come home and see me very upset because Orlando was not behaving. After many months of Leonel coming home to see me frustrated and tired, he finally snapped. Leonel told Orlando that he was going to live with his Tía. Instantly, my mind drifted back to the moment when my mother left me at my cousin's house. I felt terrible then—vulnerable and abandoned. I could not let Leonel do the same thing to Orlando that my mother did to me. Even though the circumstances were different, I could not have this beautiful boy grow to resent his father. I wanted Orlando to trust me, and this was not the way to do it. I begged Leonel to let Orlando stay and promised myself that I would never put Leonel in a position to choose between me and his son again. Even though I did not expect to have so much say in this family, it was in my hands to keep this family together. I had to learn as I went and adjust to all of the obstacles thrown my way.

After that terrible day when Orlando was nearly sent away, Leonel became very happy with the new dynamics of our household. Orlando and I got along beautifully, and the more time we spent together the stronger our bond became.

Chapter Twenty-Three

Our apartment was centrally located in Colombia's capital, Bogota, commonly referred to as the business city. The people in this city dress to impress. It has become so common that it is now standard. Not only are the people well put together, but they also are extremely talented and educated. Everything in Bogota is based on perception; if you looked and dressed better, you would be treated better. Even though Bogota was considered a big city, it was pretty small, and it was common to run into people you knew on the streets. On many occasions, Leonel's associates would come into town, and we would have them over for dinner. I went from being a girl who was just an employee to Mr. Ortiz's wife. I had to behave like a first-class lady when, in fact, I was still a teenager.

During the months from March through November, Leonel and I were extremely busy. Our careers made us both incredibly successful. I was humble, especially given where I came from, and always reminded myself how my family still needed me. Bogota was a beautiful city. It was just like springtime in New York City, except it lasted all year long. The temperature was always a pleasant sixty-five degrees at its warmest and a chilly fifty-five degrees at its coldest. All the memories I recall from living in Bogota were positive.

Upon the Spanish colony's takeover in the 1500s, Colombia was given its name after Christopher Columbus. By the end of the 18th Century, Bogota served as the capital of the region that included Venezuela, Ecuador, and Panama. The country had been free from Spanish rule since 1819. After that, the country was dominated by wealthy drug traffickers who organized cartels and globally produced the largest amount of cocaine. Like many other Latin American countries, Colombia maintained the tradition of a civilian government. This meant that Colombia allowed free elections. Nonetheless, Colombia's history was marred by violence such as The War of a Thousand Days (18991902), when a total of 600,000 civilians were killed.

Colombia has many mineral and energy resources but suffers from high unemployment. It is the world's second-largest exporter of cut flowers and coffee. It produces first-grade stones and emeralds that are among the most perfect in the world.

Futboll is Colombia's main sport; commonly, families gather to watch the games together as a pastime. No matter how difficult life got, there were always moments to appreciate and a silver lining to hold onto.

Leonel and I talked about buying a house in the near future. My mother needed me more than ever. I wanted my mother to live with us.

At the time, my mother lived in a neighborhood not too far from us. I tried to see her at least once a day, either before or after work. As always, my mother's health was my main concern, and I had to ensure that she had her medicine and whatever else she needed. It was also important for me to check in on Luis. He was growing up so fast, working and making money, not to mention all of the girls that were always hanging around. Although my mother lived with Luis, she still longed for Sandra to come back home. Living with Luis was not the same as when Sandra and I were home with her. I wasn't comfortable with my mother living alone, and deep in my heart, I wished Sandra would just go home.

One day I stopped by my mother's house, and she noticed I was not looking like myself. I was pale, exhausted, and had dark rings under my eyes. She asked me what was wrong, and I responded that I thought I had a stomach virus. I was nauseous, and every smell bothered me. My mother looked at me with her big beautiful eyes and said, "Mija, you're pregnant." I thought my mother was insane. Leonel and I had agreed that I should go back to school before having a baby. We already had Orlando to care of. For the time being, another child was not in our plans. Orlando was doing so well in school.

It was not a good week for me. As the days passed, I began to feel worse, and Leonel took me to the doctor. As it turned out, my mother was right. I was pregnant. Even though I had taken on the role of being a mother to Orlando, I was excited to carry a child in my own womb. I was excited about the experience. I would have been happy either way. I just wanted my baby to be healthy. I wanted to bring my child into a warm and open environment, one that I wasn't privileged to experience. That was now my sole purpose in life.

Leonel and I were so happy to share this blessing, but I was afraid to tell Orlando. Orlando was thriving in school, and I did not want to interrupt his progress. He was very sensitive, a product of his environment. After his parents divorced and with a rough start to *our* relationship, it was only normal for his emotions to take over at times. I did not want to hurt Orlando's feelings by telling him that in nine months he would no longer be the only person to receive our love and attention. I did not want him to think for a second that I would stop loving him, and that was what held me from saying anything to him. He would always have a place in my heart, as much as the unborn child I had not yet met.

We shared the same heart, and that was more than anything I could have wanted.

My husband and I decided that we would not tell Orlando about the baby for a couple of months, and we would surprise him with a dog. We bought a beautiful Cocker Spaniel. When Orlando opened the box, his eyes sparkled. Within no time, Orlando began calling him Blondy, and the two became attached.

Having a dog taught Orlando responsibility. He learned the value of taking care of something that could not care for itself. Leonel insisted that the dog sleep in his own bed, so we followed his request. The first night Blondy cried, yet after twenty minutes he began to quiet down. Leonel woke up at 6:30 the next morning to check on the dog.

When he returned to our room he said, "Sweetie, you were so right."

"What could I possibly be right about?" I responded.

"You want to know why the dog was nice and quiet last night?" he asked. While I did know the answer, I refrained from saying anything. "In the middle of the night, Orlando took it upon himself to take Blondy into his bed and cuddle with him so that he wouldn't be scared."

We finally told Orlando the news and he was so delighted. He would even save his toys for the baby. Throughout my pregnancy, Leonel was kind, considerate, and patient. I was not sure what to expect from being pregnant, but luckily, I had the most amazing experience because of the unconditional love and support my husband provided. I threw up every morning for nine months. I was under the impression that those symptoms would only last for the first trimester but I was wrong. I was frequently hungry and wanted to eat everything in sight. Unfortunately, as soon as I opened my mouth, I would throw up. All smells made me feel nauseous.

From the first moment we heard our baby's heartbeat during the sonogram, we knew we would be the happiest parents alive. Pregnancy is an exciting time and a big change. It was the most marvelous thing that happened to me even though it was a tough pregnancy. I could only think how something so small made me feel so strong. When I felt a kick for the first time, I knew the true meaning of life. The baby's small heart was my strength, my treasure. I didn't want to rush time, I promised myself I would enjoy every moment of this baby's life. Like any mother, I knew my time was limited and I would prepare myself to let him go when it was time. I was determined to give only the best of myself. My desire was that the baby would have values, empathy, compassion and strength, and intelligence to make its own decisions. At that moment I would have loved to find a book to teach me how to be the best mother in the world. But I never had access to something like that. All I knew was that I was determined to give it my all and more.

My delivery was anything but ideal. The last two months I suffered from preeclampsia, which was caused by an increase in blood pressure, making the delivery process very difficult. At the time, the doctors explained our options to Leonel and me. In situations like this with a high-risk birth, parents are usually asked to choose between lives, meaning if things were to present themselves as potentially fatal, who should the doctors prioritize in saving? They could not hear the baby's heart beat. Leonel suggested the doctors save me, but naturally, I told the physicians to save my child. My blood pressure was extremely high, but I refused to accept any medication until my child was born. Under no circumstance would I do anything to jeopardize my child's health. The doctors feared I would experience thrombosis if I did not accept any of the standard medications to treat this condition, but I knew that medication could harm my baby. My pressure was so high, and I had been in labor for so long, that I just wanted to know that my baby was okay. We were running out of time and the doctor was trying to save my life. Because I was convinced that my baby was alive, the doctor agreed to do an emergency cesarean. The only thing I remember was hearing a slight baby cough. The noise slowly faded out. I had passed out from the medication that was given to me after the delivery.

Our son was born early one morning in March, 1988. My mother and husband were at my bedside, anxiously waiting for me to wake up. When I finally did, I was in so much pain that I could not move at all.

"Where is my baby?" were the first words that came out of my mouth.

"Don't worry, he's fine." Leonel whispered in my ear, "I'm glad you're okay. For a few minutes there, I thought we lost you." As calm and caring as Leonel was, I couldn't care less what he had to say. All I wanted to know was where my son was and if he was alive and well. For all I knew, something terrible could have happened to my son, and they were not telling me so that I could heal.

"Leonel, where is my baby?" I asked again more intensely. The nurse touched my arm and smiled.

"Your baby is wonderful, Mrs. Ortiz. You have to heal so you can take care of him.

I need you to take care of yourself so you can go home." I started to cry. My face grew hot, and redness spread across my cheeks.

"Please, I just want to hold my baby." Seeing my son was the only thing that mattered to me at that moment. I felt like I was going to go crazy if they did not show my son to me. The nurse left the room, and moments later, she returned and handed me my son. When he was finally in my arms, I truly understood what happiness felt like. My beautiful baby boy. I soon looked up at my mother and had a new understanding of our bond.

"He is the most beautiful child in the world," I said as I looked at my mother.

She laughed and said, "Yes, of course. The best and most beautiful child in the world belongs to you."

I could not help but think how much pain my mother must have been in when they took Luis away from her. He was so sick, and there was nothing she could have done to make him better. All I wanted to do was go home. To make matters worse, the mother in the bed next to me had just lost her baby. There I was, enjoying the happiest moment in my life, and this poor woman next to me was miserable and overcome with sadness. When she went to deliver her baby, the doctors noticed how the umbilical cord was wrapped around her child's neck, and the baby did not make it. I can't imagine; I don't ever want to imagine.

She kept asking to hold my baby, and I was so conflicted. All I wanted to do was protect my child. I was scared she was going to have a mental breakdown and try to steal my child when I was sleeping. At this point, I had not slept for three days. Considering my labor was difficult, the doctor advised me to stay in the hospital for one week, given that my emergency C-section led to more stitches than the standard amount. I begged and begged the doctor, and he finally agreed to sign the paperwork as long as we were able to provide the means for a nurse to come and care for me for at least two weeks.

Chapter Twenty-Four

I could never forget that day at the hospital even if I wanted to. Orlando and his dog Blondy were waiting for us outside. The moment Orlando held his brother in his arms, I knew they would have a strong bond.

The nurse was with me for 2 weeks just like the doctor suggested, For some reason, my wounds were not healing at the pace they should have. My doctors had to change my antibiotics multiple times. I was so overwhelmed because I could not take care of my baby. Without my mother or my best friend Olga, I would not have made it. My mother and Olga not only took care of my baby, but me as well.

Olga and I had a very special friendship. My mother was not fond of her. If you have to hide your friendship, then maybe this is not a friendship. She came from a wealthy family that was well-recognized in the community. I laugh at how they got along so well now.

Taking care of my baby was one of the most beautiful joys in my life, but at the same time was one of the hardest things I have ever had to do. I always doubted whether I was doing a good enough job.

The one thing I had in my favor was that Leonel had more experience than me. He always had patience and was so helpful, especially when the baby cried. No matter what I did, sometimes Javier just kept crying. Leonel always knew what to do and how to handle the situation calmly.

When my baby was eight months old, we baptized him in the Catholic Church and named him Javier E Ortiz. Leonel came home excited with a beautifully-wrapped box. To my surprise, when I opened the box, I found four plane tickets to come to NYC. I could not believe my eyes. The next morning, we got up very early and went to apply for our visas. In our favor, it was granted immediately because my husband's economic status was very good. They gave us a visa. When my husband had our visas in hand he called his sister, who lived in New York.

That afternoon when I went to visit my mother and share the news with her, she was ecstatic for me. She also mentioned to me that my sister had stopped by and was thinking about coming back home. My heart sped up a couple of beats. I was so excited to hear that. If Sandra were home, my mother would not be alone, and I would feel much more comfortable leaving for America.

At dinner, I noticed Leonel looked worried.

"Is something wrong?" I asked.

"You know me too well," he said. "I am trying to get in contact with my ex-wife so I can take Orlando out of the country, but she hasn't gotten back to me yet. I've left messages with my daughter. Tomorrow I am going to drop off the papers for her to sign; otherwise, Orlando cannot come with us." I wasn't happy to hear this. The following week, we got all of Orlando's paperwork so he could leave.

Before we knew it, the day arrived. We packed our car full of luggage for the two weeks we would be gone. Prior to our travels, Leonel mentioned that he wanted to stop by his father's house to say goodbye, so we did. He got out of the car and went upstairs while I stayed in the car with the boys. When Leonel came back downstairs, I told him that I had to use the bathroom. I went upstairs while Leonel stayed in the car. While I was inside, I heard two gunshots. One of the bullets had broken the metal gate of my father-in-law's house. At the time, the well-organized cartel of drug traffickers played an important role in the economy. The cartel controlled 80% of the world's cocaine trade. The whole country knew that Bogota, Colombia, was not safe for anyone. I ran down the stairs in pure panic. My heart was beating out of my chest. My mind was moving faster than my feet, and I tripped on the last step. My knees hit the concrete and started to bleed. I pulled myself up off the ground and moved to open the garage door where I had gone in. My stomach dropped as the garage door opened, and I immediately thought the worst. I saw my husband walking toward me, holding the baby covered in blood. Orlando was struggling to get up off the street. I could not understand what was happening. The only thing I knew was my baby was covered in blood. I did not know if Javier was dead or alive. My body started to grow weak, and everything around me went dark. All I could think was, "*I am going to pass out, I am going to pass out.*" I forced myself to sit on the curb until I regained full consciousness. By this time, everyone started coming out of their houses. I was so confused. My arms were limp. I could not hold my baby, as all my strength had left my body. A few minutes later, we all made our way into my father-law's house through the garage door.

After going back into the house, his family tried to accommodate us as best as possible. They brought us hot water and towels with which to clean ourselves. At this moment, I still had no idea what happened. Crime in Colombia was so prevalent that we had no idea what the reason was for this attack. It could have been a kidnapping, a carjacking, or maybe both. My husband broke the silence, stating what had happened in the moment. After I got out of the car, two men approached the car. One of them went to the driver's side and the other man went around the passenger door which was unlocked. The man pointed his gun at Leonel's head and told him to follow his orders, or he would be shot. My husband's reaction was instant. He turned around and grabbed the baby from the backseat. The man was angry he hit him with the gun right in the forehead. At the moment Leonel started to bleed and dripped onto the baby. The man unlocked the door so his accomplice could get in. When the guys opened the door. Leonel pushed the door and got out of the car, trying to run away with Javier in his arms. The men started driving the car and that is when Orlando chased after them. At that moment, the attacker was caught off guard and began firing his gun in a different direction, completely missing Leonel and hitting the metal gate. We assumed that the kidnappers wanted to take Leonel. Fortunately, Leonel kept our passports and his money in his jacket pocket, and the two men had no idea. If that part was true, they were unsuccessful.

The attackers hit Leonel in the middle of the forehead and that's why he was bleeding so much. It fell on the baby and this was the image that stuck in my mind. I only imagined the worst. Still, it could have been a lot worse, and we were grateful to have all made it out alive. We were all confused and unbelievably shaken up. Even so, they did succeed in instilling persistent fear in our lives.

We soon made our way to the emergency room to get checked out, and physically, everything was okay, but emotionally, the experience was traumatic. The only person who needed medical care was Leonel. He required seven stitches in his forehead.

The next thing to do was get the authorities involved. While we were filling out the police report, the cops asked standard questions such as, "Do you have any enemies who knew you were planning on leaving the country?" Leonel stated that he had no enemies, and the only people who knew we were leaving the country were our families and his ex-wife. The police assumed that because my husband was economically stable, we were perfect targets for an attack.

I do not hold any grudges against my country. Colombia is one of the most beautiful countries in the world, with stunning scenery and landscapes. Colombia is also home to many, many hardworking individuals who have fallen subject to the misinformed and corrupt government. As in all countries, there are good and bad people. Change is necessary, but it takes a good person who is willing to lead the challenge to support the greater good of the population.

Somehow my husband decided that we were not going to give up our trip. Leonel sat me down and was adamant about going to New York. We packed our clothes once again and booked our flight exactly as we had planned before.

When we arrived in New York, I finally met Leonel's sister for the first time. She welcomed us with open arms but had so many questions about what had happened. We spent a couple of days with her and her family.

One night during dinner, Leonel received a call from his brother in Colombia. The police had called to inform him that the car had been located. We had no idea that this was just the beginning of the nightmare to come. Leonel decided we should cut our trip short, return home, and discover any information we could.

When we returned home, his brother picked us up from the airport. He explained that someone in the neighborhood had stolen Orlando's dog. We were devastated. We had already gone through so much, and I wasn't sure how much more we could take. This already traumatic situation just kept getting worse. We did everything in our power to help find Blondy. From this experience, we all had frequent nightmares and felt unsafe. We tried to comfort one another as best as we could to make the healing process a little bit easier, but it wasn't possible. We were all coping and living this life in a different way. Never once did our family imagine that we would go through something like this.

The moment the police found our car, it was hoped that the situation would solve itself, but this was only the beginning.

The following Monday, the first thing Leonel did was go to the police station to pick up the car. The police informed Leonel that four people had been found inside. My husband made it clear that only two people attacked him. The policeman understood what Leonel was saying but explained that these individuals belonged to a group called Nortenos, who made a living by kidnapping people and demanding ransom money. In this situation, Leonel was the target, and I would have been the one they would have blackmailed into giving them the money so they could return my husband. The police also asked my husband to participate in a police lineup. This would help identify one of the individuals who tried to kidnap him. At that point, Leonel and I were extremely nervous. We mentioned to the police officers how we feared for our lives, but the police officer assured us that we would be looking through a one-way mirror, and the perpetrators would not be able to see us. Sure enough, one of the men was recognizable.

Leonel identified the man, and almost instantly, everything in our life changed.

The next day Leonel started receiving phone calls through his office, cell phone, and home line. We were constantly being threatened. The purpose was to scare us, so much so that we would drop the charges. The message was clear. If we did not drop the charges, we would pay for it. By this point, these people knew everything about us. How? We had no clue. We forgot that our stolen car had been packed with our luggage containing all of our personal information, but although they had access to all of our belongings, it still made no sense how they figured out where my husband worked or where Orlando went to school. To us, it seemed like someone from the police department tipped the criminals off and gave them intimate details of our life. It was frequently common during those times for the police to give over personal information to the gangs. We were under a lot of pressure. My husband was under so much stress. It had been three weeks thus far, and we were living in complete and utter hell. My husband was terrified that these criminals were going to kidnap Orlando. He decided it was in Orlando's best interest to leave the country immediately, so he bought him a ticket and flew him back to New York. Leonel called his sister and asked if she would take care of Orlando for a while until things got better.

Orlando was not happy with this and did not take the news well. We were all heartbroken. I could not stand the thought of Orlando being away from us. For once in my life, I had a stable family, and slowly, things started falling apart. Sending Orlando to New York did not resolve the problems, but at least it gave my husband peace of mind that Orlando would be safe. We didn't sleep well. We couldn't move around our town freely. There was always fear in our hearts that we were going to be followed. We could not help but think about what was going to happen next. All we knew was that we had to act fast before something worse happened. We were dealing with a group of experienced and seasoned criminals who would harm anyone and show absolutely no mercy.

Everything had fallen apart in front of our eyes.

A short time later, we met with the judge who was in charge of our case and we conveyed all of our concerns and fears. To our surprise, the judge said, "Mr. Ortiz, you know how justice in Colombia works. There is no way to help. I have a family, too. I wish you all the best." At this point, I completely broke down in tears in front of Leonel.

My husband explained we had to move fast if we wanted to survive.

Chapter Twenty-Five

For once in my life, I felt like I had everything, and I was paralyzed at the thought of having to move and sacrifice the life I grew to love. No one should have to leave their home because of fear for their safety. The anger in my body pumped through my blood; the uncertainty nearly stopped my heart. What was I supposed to do with my mom? These decisions my husband and I were forced to make did not just affect us, it had a spiral effect on others as well. It was then that we had to assess the situation and decide what would happen to us and how this could impact our family's future. My husband was convinced that only we could handle this matter because of the injustice that grew sporadically in Colombia. Leonel decided that the only way for us to survive was to leave the country.

"I think the best decision for us is to move to America." Leonel paused, "I know you're scared, but this will all pass...I promise. We will come back in two years." I could not help but roll my eyes.

"Why can't we just move to another city?" I questioned, unable to hide my frustration.

"Another city is impossible. These people will find us if we stay here. The safest place for us to go to is America." I did not want to hear what he had to say. It made no sense. Neither of us spoke English or understood the culture associated with American living. We did not have jobs over there. How would we make a living?

"First, we will stay with my sister," Leonel said. "We also have savings. We will see how far that will take us." He had everything worked out in his mind.

I asked, "How long will it take to make this official?"

"It could take somewhere from two to three months."

I walked out of the room, and Leonel called after me, "In the meantime, why don't you take a course?"

"What?"

He was soft-spoken. "Like how to do nails or something, you know, something you can do in America."

I felt so overwhelmed. I made my way out of our apartment to take a walk outside to clear my head. I wondered if I was supporting Leonel enough. As a wife, I wanted to support my husband but not at the expense of losing myself. If I lost myself through the process, how would I be able to support my husband? I then took the initiative to enroll in a cosmetology class. Although moving to America was not completely my decision, I was still going to maintain the independence I always had. I am a worker, and I was not going to let this move take away my sense of self. The cosmetology course was a six month-long class but it was not practical for me, given that I had at maximum, three months left in Colombia. Therefore, I took the initiative to attend classes every morning and every night to get my certification in half the time.

I did not want to stress Leonel out too much by asking him too many questions about our move. I started packing and putting all of our belongings away because Leonel promised we would be back in Colombia in a year or two. We decided that we were going to store all of our belongings in Leonel's father's garage, with the intention of subletting our apartment to make a passive income. To make matters easier, we sold off all of our furniture. Upon purchasing our tickets to America, I had to inform my mother of my impending travel.

My heart broke when I informed my mother that we would be leaving. I promised her it would not be for too long. She had no intention of persuading me to stay; she believed that I had to stay at my husband's side. Tears began to stream down my face. It was not fair that I had to escape my own life as if I were a criminal guilty of committing a crime. It felt as if all of the hard work I put into getting myself where I was now was for nothing. Words could never describe how horrible it was having to say goodbye to the people I loved the most.

I held Javier tightly to my chest. I was so grateful that he had no idea what his father and I were going through. At that moment I walked through the airport in El Dorado without looking back. When we arrived at John F. Kennedy International Airport in New York, my sister-in-law picked us up. From across the room, I saw Orlando waiting for us. He was so excited to see us. He ran into my arms so fast that he nearly knocked me off my feet. We had missed one another so much. After all of our struggles, it was so nice to be together again. When we finally got to her house, my son Orlando was very excited to show us a surprise he had for us. Orlando had gotten a part-time job delivering newspapers, and with his earnings, he decided to buy three gifts. The first was a snowsuit for Javier so he could play with him in the snow. The second was a pajama set and snow boots for his father, and the third was a hairdryer and a curling iron for me because he knew I graduated from cosmetology school (without knowing those tools would be useful in the future). Orlando had also given me two little monkeys hugging each other. Somehow, this horrible situation was a blessing in disguise, transforming Orlando into the most generous, tender-hearted person I had ever known. All we had to do was be strong, but because we had one another, it seemed a little bit easier. With no idea of what each day would bring, I was grateful for the present as my family and I were finally joined together under one roof.

We arrived in New York in November, right before the start of the Christmas season. The winter of 1990 was our first holiday spent in America. The streets were decorated beautifully. I remember sticking my head out of the window, and the snow fell like tears on my face. I missed my home and family, and I didn't know when I was going to see my madre.

To ring in the New Year, we all sat down to have a big dinner. After dinner we went to the living room and they turned on the TV to watch a "ball drop." Suddenly, after the ball dropped, everyone wished each other a happy new year and abruptly went to bed. I was in disbelief at the lack of enthusiasm and excitement when it came to celebrating the new year. I was not familiar with their custom. In Colombia, we would celebrate New Year with a glass of wine, aguardiente, or whiskey. This was just the start of the festivities. People would dance in the street at four o'clock in the morning until a hangover sensation began to kick in. Colombian's cure for a hangover always consisted of tamales and a soup called caldo de costilla, which was commonly greasy and hot. The party would continue through January 1st.

When I walked into the small room where we were living, my son Orlando was waiting for us with orange soda and four plastic cups. We cheered with our orange soda and promised that next year would be better for us.

It did not take too long for me to break down in tears. I missed my people so much. I missed my routine and the life I had. Even though we had one another, I felt very alone and depressed. I didn't know how to hide it. That night, I went to bed with tears in my eyes as I held the picture of my mother that I always kept with me. Anytime I needed her, I would hold the picture close to my heart to give me the strength I needed to keep moving forward. After the New Year, we still were unaware of how we would seek employment opportunities in this new country. My sister-in-law was persistent in making us aware that if we didn't take the initiative to learn the English language, everything would be ten times more difficult. I was growing crazier as each day went by knowing that I was still the family provider back home in Colombia. I had to send my mother money to help out with her expenses, but with no income, how could I do so? Two weeks had passed in the blink of an eye, and I still had not found work. Each day I would look but had found nothing. According to my husband, only a few days had passed, but I felt like I was stuck in quicksand. My patience was slowly beginning to disintegrate. My husband and I were hard-working people; we wanted to work. We were willing to do anything, but we just needed direction on where to start.

I could not help but worry about my children. Their minds were like sponges, and I wanted to ensure that growing up was as easy as possible for them. I wanted to raise them with strong morals so they would grow up to be right-minded men. I wanted to make things happen for my family. I wanted everyone to succeed. I knew that for us to leave our country after how hard we worked, it had to have been for a real reason. "Good things were to come," I would repeat to myself. This was not the first time I would have stones on the road; this would only be another battle.

All I wanted was to find a job. Speaking English would have made life so much easier, but at this time, I didn't know enough. Believe it or not, in the two weeks that I had been job hunting, I had already learned a couple words in English. I was watching cartoons and began making sense of putting words together. The language barrier was not going to hinder me from getting a job. In the meantime, my sister-in-law offered me a job to work with her. She cleaned houses for a living. I was happy. Finally, I had a reason to get out of the house. For someone who was always working, it gave me sanity knowing I had something to do. Since I did not know how to use the chemicals she cleaned with, I would frequently come home with burns on my hands, but that was nothing I could not handle.

I made it a point to call my mother one morning, and spoke with Sandra and assured them that everything was ok. I promised my mother as soon as I got better economically, I would send money home for my sister and her. Each day that I had the chance to speak to my mother, she would always make it a point to question when I would be returning. With no clue as to the answer to her question, I would frequently deflect and change the subject of the conversation.

Over dinner one night, my brother-in-law mentioned something about a Spanish community. I questioned what that was. My brother-in-law explained that this community would find work for native Spanish speakers and immigrants.

"And you're just telling me this?" I questioned in disbelief. "I need the address right now. I am going tomorrow." My brother-in-law was a very sweet man.

"I did not mention it to you because I did not think you could do those jobs." I could not believe the words that escaped his lips.

"And what kind of job is that?" I questioned strongly.

"They just send groups of people to clean banks and supermarkets. They pay very little money, too. I think they abuse those without legal status." I didn't care about the workload or the wages I would make. All I heard was that there was a Spanish community. All I knew was that I needed money. I needed a job, and if these people were going to give me one, I would take it no matter what. Through the Spanish community, I found a job cleaning a building at night, seven days a week. Finally, I was able to send money back to Colombia to help my mother. Upon moving to America, the economic situation for my family members had become very difficult. Everyone was simply just trying to survive. Yet still, my biggest concern was my mother and her health. Her high blood pressure was killing her little by little. She had to take her medications at specific times, and sometimes she would forget. It was important for someone to remind her and look after her. My mother also suffered from terrible migraines. Sometimes she grew so ill from them that she would not be able to get up from bed for days. I could not find peace in not knowing what was going on with her. I needed to hear her voice to alleviate some of the stress. Each morning I would work with my sister-in-law in the morning cleaning houses, and I would clean the buildings at night. Even so, sometimes, I would go back to the Spanish community to see if they heard of any other jobs.

I liked going to the Spanish community. For instance, one day, a gentleman was talking about immigration. I did not know anything about this topic. I decided to sit in and listen to what he had to say. I gathered as much information as possible and took it home to my husband. Leonel agreed that all of this was useful information considering he liked to do everything legally.

In order to apply for a driver's license you had to acquire points. We did not have library cards, so we requested them and became one step closer to getting our licenses. We soon realized that having a car in this country was not a luxury, it was a necessity. As soon as I had the application, I put all my papers together, and we applied for our driver's licenses.

I was constantly asking questions. So much so that I think people began to grow a little annoyed with me. Asking questions was the only way to find answers, and luckily for me, I was never shy. I tried to call my mother before I went to work, but most of the time, I only heard bad news. Sometimes I did not want to call my mother because I could not handle getting anymore bad news. Within no time, calling her began to depress me. Subconsciously I began to blame myself for leaving her. One morning she let me know that Luis was giving her trouble—drinking a lot and not coming home. She would wait up all night for him, and he would just not return. This worried me so much, as I was in fear, knowing this could make her sick. She didn't need this burden and pain; she had been through so much already. Luis was very angry with me. He did not understand why I left. He and I were so attached that it was no shock that he did not take the news well when we let him know we were moving.

We were still living with my sister-in-law. Her home was a single-family house located in Central Islip. My sister-in-law's family lived very comfortably in the home, but with the addition of my family, it felt like we were all on top of one another. My family of four lived in one room in their house, and matters began to feel awkward.

Although my in-laws had been so gracious and generous to us, I could not help but feel like we were overstaying our welcome. I knew we needed to leave, but finding a place to live was even more difficult than finding a job. I appreciated everything that my sister-in-law did for us. She taught me how to clean with those vicious chemicals and let my family live in her home. Through all of this, the most difficult thing I had to do was leave Javier with a stranger. She was called a "babysitter." She was a lovely woman who came highly recommended, but my baby was so little. I tried to be as strong as I could, but sometimes I could not. I broke down as I walked from the babysitter's home to work. I was only one person and could only handle so much. This was not what I planned for my son when I first discovered I was pregnant. As life continued to teach me more and more lessons throughout the years, this was by far the most difficult one. All I wanted was for my mother to be here with me. She was the only person in the world with whom I would leave my son with absolutely no fear at all.

Chapter Twenty-Six

Moving to America was a very difficult adjustment for my husband. He went from being a well-respected businessman to not having anything. He lived a lavish life back home, and here he was forced to learn how to cut grass. There was no secret—my husband was unhappy. Yet throughout the entire process, he acted as if he was indifferent to all of this. I was changing Javier's diaper when Leonel came into the room and looked at me with empty and defeated eyes.

"We're not on a vacation, are we?" I asked.

He shook his head and spoke softly, "No, but don't worry. Everything is going to be okay. We're only going to stay here for a year, and then we'll go back home...to our bed... and stay for good." He reached into his pocket and pulled out his wallet. His eyes lit up as he opened it, and out came a driver's license. Leonel was so proud. He walked to a table beside us and opened the drawer where we kept our emergency cash. "I am going to use some of the money we brought from Colombia to hopefully find a car." I nodded and wished him luck.

America is often referred to as the land of the free, a country where dreams come true, and a country of endless opportunities.

Yet with all its simplicity, there still tends to be lots of complexity. The key to the "American Dream" is knowing people or surrounding yourself with people in order to establish wealth, regardless of whether you are born in the States or are an immigrant. We knew living in America was not a lottery ticket with a free ride to success, but it was the only opportunity we had to survive. The only thing we could do was share this unity; family was crucial. We needed one another to survive. At times, we were challenged with this task, but this was the only way we would succeed in living the "American Dream" we were destined to conquer. In a new country filled with great opportunities, we were left to question, "Where do we begin?"

When Leonel told me he had found a second-hand car for us to use, I was elated. I knew he was planning something big with this car; he would not spend our small amount of savings on just anything. The only thing I could make sense of was that it had to do with sales. That night at dinner he shared with me the idea that he had.

"What do you think about me packing the car with Spanish products and driving to different stores and trying to get them to sell these products to customers."

Without hesitation, I said, "Okay, so when are you going to start?"

"I noticed there are a lot of Latin places around here, so I was thinking I would start with them."

I nodded. "I think that's a good idea. What are you planning on selling?"

"With the money we have left from the car, I was thinking about selling coffee, flour, cookies, candies and bread." The next day Leonel bought all the items he had thought of and promised he would not come home without selling every item he had gotten. Sure enough, he was very successful and sold everything he had planned on. Eventually, this led to Leonel meeting a man who owned a bakery in Queens who asked him to sell his products in Spanish communities. Leonel was pleased that he found a legitimate business partner, and within no time, his business was starting to become a success. I knew people were going to fall in love with Leonel and his little idea of selling Spanish products in Spanish communities.

My brother-in-law introduced us to the kindest and most thoughtful Puerto Rican family I have ever met. He knew we needed our own place. It was not easy living under their roof. He found out that they were renting out one of the apartments in their home. The apartment was located on the second floor and was deemed a legal and habitable place to live. My brother-in-law thought it was a great idea for us to move there, which it was, but the only problem was that we had spent all of our money on Leonel's start-up business. To our surprise, in America, the rental agreements are as follows: tenants are required to pay a two-month security deposit with the additional first month's rent—we had nowhere near enough. Sometimes playing hard to get was not always the right approach when it came to making a deal. I believed that by being honest, it wouldn't hurt when negotiating. I told the owners, "I love this apartment, but in all honesty, we do not have the money to provide you with some sort of security deposit." The family appreciated our honesty and let us move in, contingent on the fact that rent would be paid by the end of every month. Every ounce of my body was grateful for that moment and appreciative of the chance this family gave me and my family. They treated us as their own from the initial moment we met them.

As much as we wanted to return to Colombia, we were informed that the hostile environment we had left was still the same. If anything, the conditions had only worsened. The only thought on my mind was my mother safe. While the conditions in America were safer, the concern of financial stability was one we couldn't escape. There's a saying that those who go from having something to having nothing face greater challenges than those who had nothing but became something. While I was the product of having nothing and gaining something throughout my life, my family was not. My family was used to the lavish lifestyle we were living in Colombia. Every time Leonel and I touched on the subject of going back to Colombia, he became defensive. If we went back to Colombia now, we would never be able to come back to America, but if we stayed here longer, I would lose precious time that I could be spending with my mother. To start acquiring papers to stay here, we would need an immigration lawyer, but we did not even have the money to think about getting one.

My husband and I were working seven days a week, and with what little free time we had, we would try to spend it with our boys. Orlando, now a teenager, continued to go to school and was working part-time. Time was passing by so quickly that we were already celebrating Christmas and New Year's Eve again. When we had saved up enough money to meet with an immigration lawyer, someone who came highly recommended by Leonel's associate, we drove to his office in Manhattan. We were bombarded with so many questions: where do you work, how much do you make, if you have bosses are they willing to sign documentation stating that you are working for them? In order to start a case, they needed a lot of information.

The lawyer said, "In order for us to start this process, the fee will be eight thousand dollars, and this only covers my expenses as your attorney." He emphasized that we would have to pay him upfront before anything could happen. I was in disbelief.

He continued, "What I need from you is your tax records for the time you worked, and your boss must come to my office to sign the petition." When my husband gave this lawyer the eight thousand dollars, I felt sick to my stomach. I wanted to throw up; this was our entire savings. The lawyer explained after payment was received and all paperwork was completed, Immigration would send a confirmation letter that they received our petition.

Three months had passed, and there was no sign of any forms or documentation. I checked the mail every day, sometimes two and three times a day, knowing that the mail person only came once a day. I decided to take matters into my own hands and call the lawyer myself. A woman answered and explained that she was unaware of why we had not received a letter and would find out where the discrepancy was. She explained that something like this had never happened in the past. A month later, we still hadn't received anything. I called the lawyer's office once again, but this time no one picked up. At this point, I started to get worried. I suggested that my husband and I drive to the city and speak to the lawyer in person. When we did, the office was closed, and the lawyer was nowhere to be found.

Unfortunately, while one would view this scenario as uncommon, it actually happened quite often. Scammers would promise unsuspecting individuals like my family citizenship, and after taking as much money from them as they could, they would fall off the grid. We were upset to find out we were just another victim to them, but what concerned us more was that these individuals had our passports. Without them, we could not start this process over again. All I wanted to do was talk to my mother about this, but I couldn't, it would cause her more stress than was necessary. All that was left for us to do was to start saving again.

A month later, I checked the mail and found a yellow envelope containing all of our passports inside. God must have heard every one of my prayers.

I must say, life had gotten a little bit sweeter when we moved into our own place. Having a kitchen was so much better than ordering takeout every day. Even though the apartment was small, I was so happy to have a place to call our own. After all the hardships we had gone through, being able to come home and be alone with my family was all I needed. In the corner of the living room, I had a small rolling chair with a vanity mirror. Little did I know that this was the sign that I, too, was going to start a business.

The following Sunday, I wrote my name and phone number on little pieces of paper and handed them out to every woman I saw at church. The day that the passports had come back, I took it as a sign that I needed to do something bigger than I had ever done before. We saved our money for rent and food and caring for our children, but that was not enough for me. I wanted to live just as well as everyone else, and I wanted to bring my mother to America. I now had a home and a place of worship with women whose stories and feelings resonated with mine. I wanted to empower them and make them feel as good as they possibly could, and that was what I did. The only problem was I needed to find the financial means to do so.

My husband worked so hard. He woke up every day at 3:00 a.m. so that he could get to the supermarkets before they opened to the public, but he was doing well. He was thinking about purchasing a bigger car. This made me happy because I thought maybe I could have a smaller car instead of taking the bus and train every day. That morning I spoke to my mother, and she sounded distraught. Sandra had just started seeing Moises again. I tried to comfort my mother as best as I could. It made no sense to me why my sister would do this again. On top of that Luis was also misbehaving. I was feeling helpless. I could not do anything from miles away. I was feeling guilty for leaving them.

And still had no idea when I was going back.

Chapter Twenty-Seven

After a long day of work, Leonel came home excited to talk about his day. Through the conversation, he explained how he met a woman at one of the bodegas where he was selling his products. She was the cashier. In addition to checking out people at the bodega, she was selling Mary Kay beauty products. She asked my husband if he would be interested in selling the products, but he explained that it would not make sense for his brand as he was exclusively selling food. After thinking for a couple of moments, he asked if it was possible to bring me in, as he thought I would be interested in continuing down the path of being a saleswoman along with branding out into a new area of sales, beauty.

The woman agreed and gave my husband a card for me to call. Of course, I did not think twice, as I was excited to have an opportunity to work and get back into sales. The next day I contacted the cashier with no hesitation, and by the end of that week, I was selling Mary Kay products. Sales gave me this power that stemmed from the adrenaline that would kick in when I spoke to new people, especially when it came to finalizing a purchase. It was contagious, and all I wanted was to be on an adrenaline rush. I felt like I was improving consumers' lives with the products that I had at my disposal, and it gave me satisfaction in knowing how quintessential I was. The colleague with whom I was working was around my age. She was a nice Dominican woman who also ended up in the States trying to live out her American dream. It felt so easy and gratifying to work alongside her because we resonated with each other on so many issues and personal life decisions. Working in a foreign land and unfamiliar with the language, we were both just trying to do the best that we could. Eva and I had a great connection, and because of this, she exposed me to Dominican culture. I did the same with my roots in Colombia. She introduced me to her family, and I instantly felt like I belonged. At first, I was under the impression through what I had seen and heard when around her family that they were angry and constantly arguing with one another. This was a result of the way they spoke to one another, which was in a loud and vibrant manner. In reality, I soon began to grasp that among Dominicans, it was common to speak very loudly and quickly. Dominicans were very passionate when it came to talking about what they do. Not only did they welcome me into their home but they also welcomed my family. We fit right in; it felt like we knew them forever.

Out of everyone I met in that family, Eva's mother happened to be the most amazing human being I had ever encountered who was *not* my mother. Everyone called her Mama Rosa. She had the largest smile and welcomed everyone into her home. She graciously fed us and made sure everyone was taken care of. It's sad how life works. Although she was a truly genuine person who should have been given the world, God had other plans for her. Cancer decided that her time on Earth must come to an early end. She will always have a place in my heart, and I hope that one day I can be to others what she was to me and everyone in her life.

I worked for Mary Kay after 5:00 p.m. and on the weekends. I went door to door trying to sell beauty products as I did back in Colombia when I was selling encyclopedias. Here in America, I was selling skin care products to women who did not have the time to go to the store and find products specific to the level of care their skin needed in particular.

At the same time, my husband also found a second job at a supermarket. He was on the cleaning crew and would clean the freezers at the end of every night. It was not much, but it gave us the extra money we needed to survive. Obtaining citizenship was still a main priority of ours, so finding another lawyer to help us through this process was imperative. The cost of seeking legal aid was significant compared to the small amount of money my husband and I were making. People are so quick to judge when individuals are living in America, but most of the time, they are unaware of the circumstances people are dealing with. More often than not, people are traveling to America to escape their dire reality. The last thing I wanted to do was leave Colombia, but I did not want to subject my children to danger. I had to constantly remind myself that I wasn't alone. There were, and still are, so many people in my situation. Luckily, I could say I had it better than others. Applying for citizenship is anything but easy. That is not to say that all people are genuine and that no one tries to take advantage of governments, but it is important to note that so many people are only trying to do what is best for themselves and their families.

My husband was friends with a man who was dating a woman who worked in a beauty salon as a nail technician. He mentioned to Leonel that the salon was looking for a coat room attendant, and of course, my husband thought it was a good opportunity for me. I agreed, as I usually never turned down work. My husband thought that there would be a possibility for me to do hair eventually if I stayed at the salon long enough and was able to be taken on as an apprentice. Although this seemed like a great stepping stone for me, there was a clear challenge. I had no way to get there. I did not want to lose this opportunity, so I had to figure out a solution to the problem.

The next day my husband drove me to the salon, where I had an interview with the owner. The man spoke Italian and a little bit of Spanish. All I understood from the conversation was that I got the job and that I would be paid only in tips rather than receiving a normal salary. This concept made no sense to me. My boss explained that for every coat dropped off, a client would drop at least a dollar into the tip jar, and I could easily go home with seventy dollars in cash. Back home in Colombia, only homeless people did this. Only beggars would ask for money. I was not a beggar. I worked honestly for all the money I had ever made.

The coat check seemed only to make sense as a winter job, considering that come the spring and summer months, the weather would be too warm for jackets or sweaters. I knew I wanted to stay at the salon, so it took weeks for me to convince the boss to let me stay with them. The hair salon was huge; there were over forty employees. Every hairdresser had an assistant, and everyone spoke English. The only people who did not speak English were myself and the man who cleaned the salon. Each day I made it a point to express to my boss why I deserved to be put on staff. I was willing to make coffee, shampoo the clients, and greet everyone as they entered the salon. I wanted to do my best to look like everyone else; I desperately wanted to fit in and assimilate into American culture. I tried my best to learn at least five English words a day. It was important for me to be able to communicate with everyone because I wanted to set myself apart from the rest.

Every morning I woke up at dawn and brought Javier to the babysitter. After that, I would take the train to Hicksville, Long Island, and then would take a forty-minute bus ride to Great Neck. The day started at nine in the morning, no matter what, and I needed to be punctual to make a good impression. The days were extremely long; I was exhausted. I stood for hours and hours on end at work and was so grateful that Leonel would pick me up every day at 5:00 p.m. I missed my children so much. There is no greater joy than being a mother, and I wished I could be with them as much as humanly possible, but it was not feasible. I had their future to think of.

I was humiliated by my little tip jar but knew I was in this for the long run. After work, my friend and I would go out and sell our Mary Kay products. We would schedule our appointments a day in advance. The business was doing well, and we were selling products at a steady rate. Most nights, I would come home to find Leonel making a quick dinner for himself and the kids. I spent weeknights and weekends plugging in so many hours to make money and maintain the household that I realized I had barely spent any time with my children or husband. Leonel had no problem being with the kids, but it made me feel so guilty that I could not be with the boys as much as I wanted.

At this point, I began cutting people's hair in my home. With my little vanity, I created my own mini salon. There was just too much on my plate, and it started to become overwhelming. It was not at all because I was money hungry, but I was desperate to provide for my family. It's just in my nature to be a provider, which stems from my childhood being raised by a single, independent mother.

The little vanity was set up in my kitchen. The conditions were not ideal, but I made it work. My goal was to obtain legal documentation and bring my mother to America. I did not want to lose any opportunity to work because bringing her to the States was my main goal. I needed to have my papers in order. Not to mention it was sickening to walk around every day without legal documentation.

My boss called me into his office one day and asked if I had my license in cosmetology. My stomach jumped. I explained that I did, and he asked me to bring it the following day. That night I went home and looked through all of my paperwork and found the license. I was grateful that Leonel suggested I take some classes here and there and get a license in as many areas of work as possible. That way, if the time came and I needed to find work, I would be able to do so. The next day I went to work with my cosmetology license, and my boss scoffed in my face when he saw my paperwork. My license was issued in Colombia, which was not valid in New York.

After he finished laughing, he spoke. "I can wipe my ass with this piece of paper. This is America. This won't do." He dropped my license on the floor. I picked up my paperwork and made my way to the bathroom with tears in my eyes. The manager noticed I was distressed and asked me if something was wrong. In the minimal English I had learned, I tried my best to explain the situation to her. She asked me to follow her, and so I did. It was then that she went on to skim through the Yellow Pages to find me a number.

"Call this number in Albany. They'll help you get your license. Don't worry, they'll have a Spanish-speaking representative to assist you." I had always believed in angels, and this woman was an angel to me. She guided me to the right path without even knowing who I was. I called the number and spoke to someone in Spanish. They were extremely helpful. I needed to get this license as soon as possible for the sake of keeping my job. When I sent all my paperwork to Albany, I realized that I never obtained the required amount of hours needed to get my license. In the meantime, I was cleaning the salon and bringing lunch to all the hairdressers. Albany was lenient when it came to working in the salon. They credited those hours toward the required hours, but I still had a ways to go. I did whatever anyone needed in the salon. Once I met the required hours, I was able to sit and take the New York licensing exam. I also needed my boss to write a letter verifying my employment at his salon, which he graciously did. On top of all the things I was doing, I made it a requirement to study every night. There were nights that I would multi-task and study while sitting next to Javier's crib. The guilt was haunting me, knowing that I was not spending enough time with him. Everything that I did was for him and Orlando. Although I missed most of Orlando's childhood because I was not with his father yet, I felt less guilty because that was not of my own doing. I did not want my boys to grow up in the same environment my siblings and I were raised in. The only thing I wanted to do was give my kids access to the best education so that they would never have to endure the same situation that I was in. So, I completed the necessary hours and took— and passed—the exam on the first try. I was persistent and worked extremely hard for my goals. I knew if I did not take the opportunities that were presented to me, there might not be an option for a second chance.

Each day I'd take the bus and would constantly be repeating English words to myself over and over again. Javier was going to start school sooner than later, and I knew I was going to have to help him with his homework. I wanted to be there for him in every way that I possibly could.

Chapter Twenty-Eight

I was very excited when my husband told me he had purchased a used truck. His business started to grow rapidly. My husband is one of the most professional men I have ever met in my life. I have so much respect for him, and I always will. Leonel's work ethic was amazing. He was persistent and would never give up, no matter how difficult the situation might have been. Without speaking a word of English, he began his own company in a foreign land. This is how "Lejoos Food" came to be and still is in business.

This implied that I would get our first car and essentially no longer be using mass transit to get to work. I was relieved by this news. Now with the car at my disposal, I didn't need to stress, and during the cold winter months I didn't have to stand in the freezing cold or be subjected to any delays. I will never forget the first time behind the wheel when I was on Interstate 495, I was driving next to 18-wheel vehicles that could potentially crash into me and this made me nervous. When I got to work my legs were still shaking. I just had to get used to driving. And just like that my car became my best friend.

I was finally able to get my Cosmetology license, I felt like I won the lottery.

Immediately I took it to my boss. The first thing I said was, "Don't wipe your ass with this one!"

He laughed a lot, and looked at me and said tomorrow you will start in the shampoo area. Remember if you give the client a good neck massage they will be generous with you. Getting my license allowed me to work as a shampoo assistant and continue to learn as well. I always knew shadowing quietly was the best way to learn. And that's what I did.

On Sundays and Mondays, I cleaned houses, offices, and buildings near my home and worked at the salon Tuesdays through Saturdays. At night I would cut hair for the Spanish community. Just like me, they had the same work schedule. They didn't have the luxury to go to a salon that day. I chose not to charge a lot because I knew how hard it was to make a living.

There were not enough hours in the day to accomplish all of the tasks I needed to do. I wished that the days were longer or that the week had an extra day. My mother and siblings were on my mind all the time, and the only way I could let them know I was thinking of them was to provide for them and make sure that my siblings were taking care of my mother. It took us a long time to save enough money to hire an immigration lawyer. Money was tight, which made saving difficult when having expenses for a household of four.

Javier was finally in school, and after my long day at work, I would assist him with his homework. In reality, Javier was the one teaching me English. He was brilliant, and I knew within no time he was going to do big things. That's why I had to make sure he was always on track with his studies.

I was working in the shampoo area for almost a year. My trick was always to include a nice head, neck, and shoulder massage. This tactic was used so frequently in the salon that I ended up getting the title of Golden Hands because I was good at my job.

Clients were relieved of all the stress they had in their bodies after I massaged them. Although I was doing a good job, my boss was not particularly happy. Clients were requesting me left and right and were waiting to be shampooed at my station. This was holding up the other hairdressers and limiting the number of clients that could be taken during the day. Being that my boss was a very smart businessman, he decided that if clients were going to request me, he was going to designate my time to perform an oil treatment that would cost the clients an extra fifty dollars. Not only did the clients have to spend additional money, but they also had to arrive twenty minutes before the appointment time for my services. The oil treatments became very popular, even more than my boss could have ever imagined. Since I was doing so well at the salon and my oil treatments were incredibly successful, all seemed to be going well for the salon.

I on the other hand felt I wasn't growing. That's when I decided to take skin care classes at Christine Valmy. This course was only for a year and classes would be at night.

It was time for me to expand my horizons and grow.

* * *

One of the church members from our parish recommended a lawyer. Leonel and I decided to make an appointment, but we arranged to do it through my job. My boss was happy to work with me and decided to assist me in petitioning for citizenship if I committed to working for him for ten years. I thought that this agreement was fair, and so we proceeded forward. I was excited to be moving in the right direction. It was then that we were finally able to move to Glen Cove, Long Island. This move cut my commute immensely and allowed me more time at home.

I was grateful to have a full-time job, but leaving my son for so many hours was killing me. At times, I was jealous of my babysitter, which stemmed from being afraid that, over time, Javier would love her more than me. I knew what my place in Orlando's world was. Being that I came into his life when he was a little older and how we were able to work through our differences only instilled in my heart that blood meant nothing and family is the people who choose to be in your life.

Each day, Javier needed me more and more. Those early years are so important, and I needed him to know he was a priority. Moving to Glen Cove was a blessing for all of us.

As soon as we moved, we fell in love with our new home right away. We were close to the water, with a church and Catholic school nearby. I had my heart set on Javier attending this school. At the time, Orlando was enrolled in a public school and was not pleased whatsoever. It was such a bad experience for him that he expressed no interest in allowing Javier to follow the same path. Orlando was such a good older brother. He was always thinking about what was in Javier's best interest. Orlando even offered to work part-time to help send Javier to the Catholic school. You can teach your children to be good people, but ultimately, it is up to them to decide if that is the person they want to be. Generosity cannot be taught; it is innate and a characteristic that Orlando possessed so beautifully. He always aspired to do and be better for his brother, and I wanted to give them both the world.

Balancing school, work, motherhood, and being a wife became overwhelming. I desperately wanted my mother to live with me, we mutually needed each other. I dreamed a lot. I wanted my own business. There is a saying, "Dreaming doesn't cost a dime, I did a lot so I wouldn't forget anything is possible." But what I could do is continue my education. I continued taking classes at Christine Valmy for skin care in Manhattan. I would take the 5:30 evening train from Great Neck to Penn Station with only ten minutes to run from the train station to class. No matter how fast I ran, I was always a little late to class. My teacher understood why I was late and never questioned me. My tardiness wasn't intentional.

Getting home was easier, but it was still exhausting. The class was four hours long.

It started at 6:00 p.m. and ended at 10:00 p.m. The train leaving Penn Station was at 10:20 p.m. and I would usually arrive home after 11 pm. The process to obtain a skincare license would take a year. I had to be patient and remind myself this is just the start. My goals were clear and I still had a long way to go.

Chapter Twenty-Nine

Each day my morning began at 5:00 a.m. and did not end until well after 11:00 p.m. I admit there were many days I wanted to drop out. I felt like I was the worst mother on the planet. I left my child for hours and hours on end to work and get my license. On occasion I would cry, which made me feel better. People on the train would see me cry and never question me. Upon returning home every night, I would find Javier already sleeping. I was afraid he was going to forget me. I was always in a rush. I could never play with my son. I constantly had to remind myself that this was temporary. I wished and wished for this year to fly by.

Culturally, Hispanic men are considered 'macho men.' Hispanic men are typically breadwinners, while the women stay home to cook, clean, raise the children, and be homemakers. Leonel never once treated me as a housewife; he knew I liked to dream big and always supported me in anything I wanted to do.

Leonel would leave the house at 4:00 a.m. and would return at 3:00 p.m. This gave him time to pick up Javier from school, go home, make dinner, wait for Orlando to come home and have a meal with him. He would take care of them when I wasn't around.

There are not enough words to express my gratitude for all the support that he gave me.

He knew that everything I did was to benefit our family.

At last, the immigration papers were submitted. The waiting period was taking forever. I felt so much pressure. It was like the weight of the world was on my back. I possessed so many identities and almost forgot who I, Esperanza, was. My mother's health began to deteriorate again. I was constantly in a state of worry and guilt, knowing I was not by her side to help. The only hope I had was to see her.

Before I knew it, I was graduating from the Christine Valmy School. The date was May 2, 1994. Both my husband and children had come to support me at the graduation. With flowers, hugs and kisses, they let me know how proud I had made them. All of a sudden, every minute on the train became worth it. I had to miss so many moments in my children's lives in order to graduate and work at the same time, making this moment even sweeter. I would continue to learn and accomplish my goals for a better future for my children.

Every Sunday, we would go to church and have breakfast at The Pancake House. We would then usually go to the park so the boys could play and finish the day off with a nice family dinner. I always looked forward to spending time with my family after a long work week.

Glen Cove was just one town over from Sea Cliff, so I made it a point to begin running every morning. I would run to the beach in Sea Cliff and then make my way back to our home. I loved starting my day off with the sun on my skin and the fresh air in my lungs. One day on my daily run, I noticed a beautiful home with a lovely garden that had flowers outlining the house. I could not believe that I had passed this house so many times but never realized how perfect the home was to me. Right in front of me stood a woman who was tending the flowers she had planted, and I decided to introduce myself. I complimented her on the garden.

Her eyes were big and kind. We began talking and surprisingly she was also a hairdresser like me. While I was just starting my career as a beautician, she shared with me that she was just about to retire. I expressed my admiration for her home, and she graciously invited me inside. The house had the odor of cigarette smoke and I could hardly breathe. Despite the pungent smell, it was the most beautiful home I had ever seen. Three bedrooms on the upper floor, a bathroom, living room, kitchen, and garage. I smiled and asked if she would consider selling her home. She informed me that at the moment the property was not for sale. However, she agreed to call me first if she ever decided on moving. I wrote my name and number down on a crumpled piece of paper and ran back home.

I was so happy to meet someone new. When I got home, I told Leonel all about it.

"What would happen if this woman called tomorrow and said she wanted to sell the house?" He had a devious smile on his face, and I laughed.

"I don't know," I said and placed my hands on my hips.

"Huh?" he asked as he laughed. "With what money are we going to buy that house?"

"I don't know!" I said once again.

Leonel grew serious. "I don't want to ruin your day because you sound so enthusiastic, but the lawyer called today asking for more money." I nodded, and just like that, my dream home disappeared.

Our immigration process was moving incredibly slowly. Patience was not a virtue of mine. The lawyer informed us that this was going to take some time, but I did not expect it to move as slowly as it did. On the bright side, we already had our EIN number and permission to work legally. Unfortunately, at this time, we were unable to leave the country because if we did, we would not be able to come back. This meant that seeing my mother was not in the near future. Until our residence was approved we could not leave.

* * *

In the blink of an eye, a year had passed, and I received a call from an unknown number. To my surprise, it was the woman I had met on my run just one year earlier, and she kept her promise. She was selling her house and intending to move to Florida, and I was the first person she called. She asked if I wanted to come over with my husband to see the house. I was nervous but happy. I was excited to show Leonel what I had fantasized about. I could not believe this was happening. As soon as Leonel got home, I told him what had happened. He was silent for a while and seemed disinterested.

"What do you want me to say?" he asked with frustration in his voice.

"I want you to come and see the house with me." My answer was simple. I was not asking for much.

"Is this what you want?" Leonel questioned.

I did not answer. Instead, I grabbed his hand to turn him around and pushed him through the door.

Of course, as soon as we arrived, Leonel fell in love with the house. He looked into my eyes, and I knew exactly what he was thinking. Neither of us knew where we were going to get the money from, but I knew Leonel was going to do anything humanly possible to buy this house. We quickly applied for a mortgage. As first time buyers you only had to put down a 5% down payment. Waiting for the bank's approval was the most difficult part. The first bank denied the loan, but giving up was not an option. After bank shopping, we were finally approved and able to buy the home.

My children were elated as they would finally be able to live in a real house and have their own room. We split the garage in half. One part salon and the other part was storage for Leonel's business. Orlando was elated. He was working a part-time job at McDonald's, and with his own money, he began to buy stuff for his bedroom. We were applying for a credit card and furnishing our new house. We bought everything from IKEA, given that their prices were within budget. Although the items were reasonably priced, we never expected the furniture to be so difficult to assemble. The instructions were difficult to read, and there were entirely too many pieces. The process was tedious but well worth the difficulties. My boys finally had a consistent home to grow up in.

* * *

One morning after living in the house for a couple of months, I heard Orlando scream. I rushed upstairs to see what was going on, and Orlando was in tears. Javier decided he was going to cut Orlando's hair while he was sleeping. He said he wanted to cut hair just like me. Orlando was such a good brother and always defended Javier. When I was disciplining and yelling at Javier, Orlando begged me not to be upset with him. Little did Orlando know that I was not going to be able to salvage any of his hair and that I was going to have to shave him bald.

Chapter Thirty

Now that I had my esthetician license it gave me the opportunity to join the skincare industry. I began doing facials. My boss was pleased that product sales had begun increasing significantly. I would make recommendations after every facial, and clients would leave with products to help their skin. I was now in charge of the skincare department, anything that was related to the face and body.

My days in the salon were intense, working from nine to five. It would take me thirty minutes to get home. When I would get home, Leonel would make dinner, and I would sit and do homework with Javier. I would read him a book and put him to sleep. Then I would head into the garage where a client was waiting for me, and then the next. I would work until eleven p.m. My son, Orlando, generally came home late from his part time job. We would spend some time together trying to be quiet since his dad had to be up early in the morning.

I understand now that everything has a price in life . Being away from your family is a big sacrifice, but with a move to the USA and living here for a couple of years, finally you get used to the culture and begin to set roots down. This was my reality and luck was on my side. It wasn't right to complain about anything. I should just be grateful for what life has given to me.

* * *

I made a promise that I would take my children to Disney World on a vacation. I began saving all the tips that my clients generously gave me . The funny part was our first cruise led us to a new family tradition. We agreed this was only possible if the children kept their grades up or else there would be no trip. I wanted them to treasure studying with enthusiasm and commitment. It was an idea that gave me great results.

We believed in education and wanted to provide them with every possible opportunity. We placed much emphasis on their studies, so they can have the tools to succeed in life.

Around this time, I found out that my brother Julio had applied for his tourist visa, and he wanted to come and visit us. I was thrilled. Finally, after eleven years, I was able to see someone from my family. We decided we were going to meet him in Florida for a mini vacation and then bring him back to New York to show him our home. We knew we were not going to be able to devote all of our time to him, so it made more sense to give him the best of both worlds. We worked incredibly long days, and we did not want Julio to feel like he was unwelcome. Our family would benefit from having some time away, as well.

The week we spent in Florida was amazing. As much as I wanted Julio to enjoy his time with us, I think it might have deluded his perception of what our life in America was actually like. He was going to stay with us in New York for an additional two weeks, and I knew by the end of his trip, his expectations were going to be let down significantly.

To a foreign person, living in America was the dream, but little did they know there was a price to pay. We lived in a comfortable home, had two cars, and had children who attended good schools. What could we possibly complain about? Julio noticed how we never spent time at home. And when I was home I continued to work late hours in the garage. He found this astonishing.

One day he said, "Your sofa is beautiful." I said, "Thank you." He looked into my eyes and said, "When was the last time you sat on it?"

I took a breath and stood quietly. After a long pause I said probably last Christmas. He was not pleased with my answer.

The routine of the life that I was used to was the only way to succeed. This was the life I chose, and I was going to make the best out of it to provide for myself and those around me. It was sad when it was time for Julio to leave. Our eyes filled with tears as we said goodbye, and we longed for the next time we would see each other. When Julio arrived back in Colombia, he expressed the difficulties of living in America, but no one believed him.

Chapter Thirty-One

In January 1994, I received my Green Card. I was beyond grateful. The lawyer explained that if I continued to contribute to society, pay my taxes, and have no trouble with the law, I would be well on my way to becoming a permanent resident and in the future I could apply for American citizenship.

I asked the lawyer, "And then, will I be able to petition for my mother to come from Colombia?"

"Yes," the man nodded. "In the meantime, if you would like your mother to come and visit, she can come on a tourist visa."

"We've tried." For whatever reason, my mother was frequently denied a tourist visa. It felt like it was going to be impossible to get her here.

I made it a point not to let my family back home in Colombia know how difficult the process of becoming a citizen was. There was a major misconception that those in America walked on pavements made of gold with money hanging from trees and flowing down onto the streets. Unfortunately, no one knows the process and difficulty it is just to get a status in America. Only those who have been through this can understand.

After having my status legally, I prepared for my trip home. I was excited to return and reunite with my family. Thirteen years had passed since I left. I went shopping that day especially for the children. Unfortunately, it was not possible for the whole family to go. So I only bought a flight for myself.

When I arrived in Colombia, nothing was the same. There were buildings that I had never seen before, and the town looked unrecognizable. Seeing my family for the first time after all those years was remarkable. I was extremely happy to see them and we shared tears, hugs, kisses and smiles. My mother told me I was too skinny, and I told her the same. I held her for as long as I could before we left the airport.

When I arrived at my mother's home, I was in utter disbelief to find her living in such harsh conditions. This was not at all the situation I had left her in when I first went to America. My family tried to explain to me that the economy in Colombia was significantly worse than when I left, but it did not make any sense. My mother was living with my younger brother Luis, sharing one bedroom. There were two twin beds and a coffee table in the middle separating their areas. Months ago, my mother mentioned wanting to buy a television, so naturally, I sent her the money. When I asked where the television was, she told me she never purchased it and used the money to buy food instead. I was devastated, as well as in disbelief. I could not understand where all the money I sent had gone. I was angry, and that was the last thing I wanted to do—talk about money.

Although Luis was living with my mother, he was not taking care of her as well as I hoped he would. My mother was concerned that Luis was drinking a lot, and sometimes he would disappear for days. She explained that when Luis was not home, she was in a constant state of worry. I did not want my mother to have this stress. It was not good for her health. We sat and cried with one another for hours.

The next day I woke up early to find an apartment for my mother to live in.

Fortunately, I found exactly what I was looking for. I paid six months' rent in advance; that way, my mother had nothing to worry about for some time, and I furnished the apartment with the money I had left. At least this money was being used properly. Before going home, I took my mother to the doctor. She had anemia and her high blood pressure was not being controlled — she had not been taking her medication. I bought her vitamins and all of the medications she would need to stay healthy for the next couple of weeks. Before returning to America, I spoke to Luis about his drinking habit. Luis promised to do better. I reunited with all my brothers and sister and asked for their cooperation in taking care of my mother and not cause her stress.

I wanted to spend time with my family. I wanted to spend quality time with my nieces and nephews, but it was impossible. Time flew by and I had to return to New York. This time I felt a bit better. I was leaving my mother in better conditions. Time was quickly coming to an end and I was returning home soon. I was getting extremely sad that I was leaving her again. But this was reality, this was life.

I promised my mother as soon as I got my citizenship, I was going to sponsor her so she could live with me. She smiled with tears in her eyes and said she would be fine right where she was. "Hijia, don't worry about me anymore. I am fine where I am now."

I had an idea, I suggested my sister move in with my mother and brother. Sandra agreed to move back in, and I was happier with this arrangement. That way it would be easier for me to help them.

When I arrived back in New York, there was only one thought on my mind. I wanted to buy my mother a house. I did not care how big it was, I just wanted to buy something that was hers so that she would never have to worry. My family was elated to see me when I arrived home. I missed the smell of my house and the faces of my clients., even though I was gone for only ten days.

I began working on Sundays again, and by the following year, I had the down payment for my mother's house. In reality it was worth it, this brought peace of mind to me. Thank God my mother and Sandra never left each other's side until her dying day. Three years had passed since I went to Colombia. I had been taking a history class in the library preparing for my citizenship. Classes were intenses but I learned a lot about this country.

While I was preparing for the class I received a call from Colombia. The news was not good. Luis was still having difficulties managing his drinking and was hopping from bed to bed with different women. He was a brilliant mechanic and could have done such positive things with his life, but due to his addiction, it made managing multiple areas of life difficult.

I did not mind working extra hours to make sure all of my mother's expenses were covered. I wanted my nieces and nephews to be cared for, as I did not want them to have to grow up knowing what being hungry felt like. I knew Sandra would care for my mother as I would, but I was afraid that she was going to leave again. Sandra had gone through a lot over the last couple of years, but the only thing that mattered to me was that she and my nieces were cared for.

After seeing how my family back home in Colombia continued to struggle, I developed a deep appreciation for the life I have been building here in America. I have had opportunities to accomplish anything and everything I have ever wanted. If I had stayed in Colombia, I would have had to make double, if not triple, the amount of sacrifices I have had to make here. My dreams would not have been made possible in Colombia. Staying honest and persistent has given me the life I have today, and I will forever be humbled.

Before I knew it, three years had passed since my trip back to Colombia, and I was taking a history class at the library. To become an American citizen, I had to take the citizenship test that was composed of historical American facts. The test was extensive, and most natural-born citizens would not be able to answer the questions. Having a Green Card was not enough for me. I needed to be an American citizen so that I could sponsor my mother and bring her here legally.

While I was applying for the citizenship exam, I received a phone call from my family in Colombia. They explained that my mother had an aneurysm and had to have surgery. Just as I expected, my mother was against having surgery and refused to speak with the doctors. I was extremely worried about her. The doctors explained if she did not have this surgery, her life would be in grave danger. After a while, my mother finally gave in and agreed to have the surgery. Unfortunately, while under anesthesia, she suffered a stroke and became partially paralyzed. She lost all feeling on the left side of her body, and the doctors did everything they could to save her. I was overwhelmed with guilt, as my family was going through so much, and I was so far away.

I was devastated that I could not be at my mother's side. I felt as though I was doing nothing because I was not physically there with her. All I could do was send money, medicine, and the things she needed to be healthy. Even though Julio saw how we struggled in New York, my family in Colombia still believed I had more money than anyone. If I went back to Colombia to take care of my mother, I would feel obligated to spend money that I did not have. Staying here at least gave me the option to send what was financially available.

The last time I went to Colombia, I noticed that my family was spending the money I had sent them in ways I had not intended. I purposely sent money to buy my mother a television, but when I arrived, they did not have one. All I could do now was hope that the money I was sending for medicine was used for that exact purpose.

The days grew long and challenging. I felt like I was going to lose my mother. Each day I called her in the morning and the evening. At this point, the doctors were in communication with my family. They were happy with my mother's progress but believed she would be unable to walk again. After two long weeks, my mother was finally sent home, and through physical therapy, the doctors were hoping my mother would recover.

Sandra was taking care of her as best as she could. The only reason I was not in emotional turmoil was because I knew my mother was not alone. After a couple of months, we noticed the physical therapy was not working in the way the doctors had hoped. Buying a wheelchair was our next step in my mother's recovery process. Knowing that she would never walk again was a harsh reality for all of us. One never truly values their body until something is wrong with it. We are only temporarily moving bodies, and within seconds, those moving bodies can stop working.

Chapter Thirty-Two

Even though my mother was going through one of the most difficult chapters in her life, there was still some good happening.

One day after work, I noticed there was a letter from immigration. My mother had been approved for her Green Card in 1997. This was supposed to be a happy day, as we had been waiting for so long, but I did not know how to feel. I was conflicted because of how sick my mother had become. Of course, I wanted her to be with me, but I was not sure if traveling would be safe or if I would be able to care for her in the way that she needed. I was rarely home as is, and taking care of her would only mean an increase in the stress I was already going through.

I sent the paperwork to Julio, including the date and time for my mother's interview to receive her Green Card. I was nervous my mother was not going to feel up to going to the interview, so I let him know it was okay if she had a change of heart. To my surprise, my mother wanted to speak to me on the phone. She was excited and willing to go to the interview. I was thrilled that her spirits were up. Tears began to fill my eyes, and I heard the crack in her voice. She promised she would come to visit after all these years.

The process of applying for a visa was incredibly difficult, but I did not want my mother to feel obligated to be here with me. For so long, I was only thinking of myself because I missed my mother so much. Having almost lost her put so much in perspective for me. I just wanted her to be healthy and happy wherever she was, even if it was difficult for me.

"Are you sure you want to move to America?" I asked hesitantly, scared of her answer.

"I have waited many years for this day. Of course I want to move to America. I want to finally meet Mickey Mouse."

I was surprised by her sympathetic humor. My mother was experiencing physical and emotional pain, especially when she found out she will never be her old self again. I was so surprised at how optimistic she was. As soon as my mother received her Green Card, I sent her a ticket. When she was ready, she could come at any time.

I started preparing her room. I wanted the room to be beautiful when my mother arrived so I painted it and bought a new bed frame and mattress. I decorated the room with an area rug and candles. I wanted my mother to have everything. Sandra called me in a panic, reminding me that she needed care 24/7. She was not the same person as before. She was concerned I was not going to be able to take care of my mother. She was constantly reminding me that she was in a wheelchair and was no longer the same as she once was. I grew worried. I tried my very hardest not to let Sandra hear my sadness as well as my apprehension. There was nothing I wouldn't do; my mother was nearly here, and I promised to take care of her. I appreciated the phone call because she helped me realize I was not ready at all to care for my mother.

This was supposed to be a happy day, but instead, it was one of the most painful experiences of my life. As I approached JFK I saw my mother in the distance, but she did not see me. My sister was right; that person was not my mother. I began to shake, and my stomach felt hollow. My fingertips were frozen, and my palms were sweaty. I went to the bathroom for a minute.

"Why my mother? She did not deserve this!" I whispered to God. I could not believe she found enough strength to make the trip. I cleaned myself up with cold water and paper towels and made my way back to where she and the flight attendant were. I knelt in front of my mother and put my arms out to hug her. We cried and cried for entirely too long. When we arrived home, my mother looked exhausted. I suggested that she lie down, and she agreed. While she was napping, I made some chicken soup, and I was excited to finally share a meal with my mother.

Unfortunately, my mother was unable to get through the night without a problem. In the middle of the night I had to call an ambulance. My mother was having trouble breathing. I did not know what else to do. After being in the emergency room for what felt like hours, the doctor finally told us that my mother needed a pacemaker in order to survive. The surgery was scheduled for the following day. They had to put a temporary tube in her throat. I wanted to believe that this was all a bad dream, but I had to stay strong to make sure my mother was getting the care that she needed.

I was scared that this procedure was going to cause more harm than good. My mother's stroke occurred while she was having a procedure done for her aneurysm, and I did not want to be the reason she fell ill once again. The doctors assured me that she would live very comfortably with the pacemaker. I agreed, as they knew what was best for her, but I was still concerned that I was doing something wrong. I would spend the night at the hospital with my mother and go to work as soon as I woke up. Constantly running around with little food in my system, I inevitably lost ten pounds.

I was exhausted, but that was not a problem. I was used to being tired. My problem was that I knew my mother was unhappy. My mother was very angry with me. In some ways, it felt as if she was blaming me for what had happened to her. She did not want to be in the hospital anymore, and due to the language barrier, she had no idea what was happening to her. My mother had gone through so much in the last year, and to make matters worse, she was losing her cognitive abilities. I tried my best to explain to her what was happening, but I had no idea if she understood what I was saying. All I knew was that she spent her days crying. Every time the team of physicians would go to see my mother, she would scream at the top of her lungs that she wanted to go back home. Without knowing it, my mother broke my heart. She did not want to be with me; all she wanted to do was to be back in Colombia and live her life as she was. I promised her that as soon as she was feeling better, she could go back home. There was not a day that went by that she did not ask about my brothers. She missed Luis most of all.

It was hard for me to grasp that my mother preferred to live in Colombia. For once in her life, it was about her, and she was not happy. I know her health was a significant factor in making her unhappy, but it felt like much more than that. Although it broke my heart, I loved my mother too much to see her unhappy. If sending her back to Colombia is what she wanted, then that is what I was going to do. All I needed was clearance from the doctors.

When my mother was discharged from the hospital, I sat her down and let her know that I wanted to take her to Florida before she went back to Colombia. At this point, I did not know when I was going to be able to see my mother again, so I wanted to make every minute count. She agreed, and two weeks later, she felt better and stronger. We went to the doctor to see if she was cleared to fly, and all was well. I took a week off from work and packed up my boys and my mother for the trip.

To my surprise, as soon as we got to the amusement park, my mother wanted to go on the *ET* ride. I did not know if that was the best idea, and I conveyed my concern. I was worried that it would be too much on her body. She was not amused with anything I said.

"If I am going to die, then let me die happily," she said.

I said to myself, "She knows what she's doing." My mother and I got on the ride together, and I could not wait for it to be over. When it finally finished, my head was spinning and I wanted to throw up. My mother was excited and wanted to go again. I didn't know whether to laugh or cry. I knew she enjoyed every second of this trip and I was so happy to witness this.

A week later we were back home in New York. As promised, I put her back on a flight to Colombia. Although it broke my heart, this is what she wanted, and I wanted her to be happy. Colombia was her home, and I had to understand that.

I worked hard to pay off all of her hospital expenses in New York. It was all worth it, in the end, to know that my mother was able to breathe and sleep better. She was still in a wheelchair, but her quality of life was significantly better thanks to the pacemaker. Each call ended with a promise to call her the next day. I always asked if my mother needed anything. She would say to take care of my siblings and she'd be okay. I continued to send money, until one day, she asked me for a bird. Out of all the things she could have asked for, she decided a bird was what she wanted. Her request was a bit specific; she wanted one that was yellow and red. I called Julio to advise him of my mother's strange request.

"Where exactly would you like for me to get this bird?" he asked, laughing.

"I don't know, but I expect the bird to be at my mother's house tomorrow." I do not know what Julio had to do, but somehow, the bird was there the next day. I would do just about anything to put a smile on my mother's face. Not too long after getting the bird, my mother told me she saw the cutest dog on a television show, so naturally, I sent the picture to Julio, and he found the dog for her the very next day. Two weeks later, my mother told me she no longer wanted the dog in the house because it was making a mess, so I told Julio the dog had to go.

"What would you like for me to do with the dog now?" Julio asked.

"I don't know, figure it out. Take it to your house or give it to Edgar." We laughed. Now and then, my brothers got a little upset with me for spoiling our mother, but they were just as bad because they always ended up helping me get her whatever she wanted.

My mother went to the doctor a few weeks later, and they told her that drinking goat milk would be good for her. Finding goat milk was very difficult, so I did what anyone else would do and bought her a goat. When I told my brothers, they thought I was crazy, but they went along with it. One goat turned into another and then another. My mother had goats for a very long time, and she had milk to drink every morning. I always made sure to provide my mother with anything she wanted.

One of my biggest regrets was not seeing my mother more when she was well. I traveled back to Colombia a few times, but only because my mother was incredibly sick and needed my help. Although I made sure to provide my mother with everything that she needed, I know she would have preferred seeing me. It was a difficult decision, but I knew the money I could send was more useful as it would provide her with better care.

My mother was never able to walk again. Every time I saw her, she looked more frail. The strength in her body was gone. She was unable to feed herself, and she had bed sores all over her legs. The doctors tried to heal them with cream, but nothing worked. They suggested surgery that would improve her condition, but it was very expensive, and insurance did not cover it. I could not bear the thought of my mother suffering anymore.

My siblings would describe my mother's screams of pain. It broke everyone's heart. My mother was hardly eating anymore and was exclusively on a liquid diet. All she could keep down was Ensure drinks. I felt hopeless, and I was going to do whatever it took to make sure she did not suffer.

On one unsuspecting day, I received a call from my family. They told me my mother was in intensive care. I explained the situation to my boss, and he completely understood. I was on the next flight to Colombia to see her. Every fiber in my body was praying that I made it to her in time. I had no idea if these were going to be my mother's last days on Earth. Upon my arrival in Colombia, I went straight to the hospital to see my mother. The doctor explained she was dealing with ulcers all over her body. The pain was intolerable, and she needed surgery to aid in the healing process. The doctor wanted to remove skin from her buttocks and transplant it onto her legs, but they were not sure if my mother's body was going to reject the graft. I paid for the surgery and gave my consent in the hopes my mother would no longer have pain. I stayed in the hospital with my mother for a week. She was healing nicely and was discharged. I was pleased that my mother was finally doing better but disappointed that I had to go home so soon. I had to get back to work to pay for whatever additional treatments she would need. I could not afford not to work anymore. I had credit card debt and bills to maintain.

To make matters worse, I felt as though I could not tell my family about how I was feeling. I just wanted my mother to be okay and for my family to understand that she meant everything to me. I left her in the care of my sister and returned home.

Chapter Thirty-Three

When I returned home from Colombia, I went to work the very next day. I put on my pretend smile and tried to make my clients feel as special as possible. They came here to relax, not to hear someone complain. My personal life was just that, personal, and I had to keep it away from work. Sometimes I felt like a therapist without the title. When people were in my chair, they would vent the entire time, and I would just listen. Everyone has baggage, and everyone has something going on in their life that is causing trouble. I realized then that I was not alone, and no matter how much money people have, the challenges of life will never go away.

Being stronger than those stones on my road was the only way to move forward. I knew that I worked a lot, but I had no other choice. Somehow I needed to have a type of work-balanced life. But I didn't. Every time I called my sister I heard the same thing—she wasn't getting better. The wounds on her legs were getting worse. Even though I wanted to give her the world, her quality of life wasn't the best. Her health was deteriorating everyday. As much as I loved my mother, I was confused about why God had not taken her already. God is almighty and takes care of His people. If God was so good, how is it that so many people suffered? It made me question God. Why did she suffer so much? It was inhuman. I was so resentful and angry.

At home, it was like nothing had changed as long as we followed the rules. My husband never asked any questions about anything. to the point that his silence was cruel. He was a passive man that never complained about anything. Being quiet and nonconfrontational was in his nature, which he did without knowing his silence hurt me.

This I more than accepted, but never agreed with.

I called my sister that afternoon. It was not good news. The surgery was not a success, and my mother's body rejected the skin graft. The doctors wanted to amputate her leg, but I knew in my heart my mother would not want that. After declining the amputation, the doctors stated that there was nothing else that could be medically done to heal my mother. We decided that natural medicine would be the next best thing simply to make her comfortable and to specifically stop the pain.

My mother used natural treatments for about six months. The holistic route made her comfortable but didn't improve her sores. She could hardly move, and she barely ate. Liquid supplements like Ensure were the only nutrition she received. Her physical mobility was nearly nonexistent; she had to be carried to and from the bathroom. Having not seen my mother in six months, the phone calls meant the world to me. Each day we spoke, I noticed she was getting weaker and weaker. I knew she did not want to hang up the phone as she had more things to say, but her body would tell a different narrative.

Watching someone's body betray them is horrible. Sandra constantly had to turn my mother around. It was difficult for Sandra to constantly lift my mother, and she did it with such grace.

"Madre, do you want me to come back?" I asked, feeling guilty that I was not with her.

"No, hija. Your place now is with your family. They need you." She paused as she needed a break in between sentences. "Your sister is taking good care of me."

My heart broke piece by piece. So much time had passed. I had not noticed that this was around the time my family and I would usually take our family vacation. As much as I loved my boys, I was more concerned with my mother's health. Sandra agreed that I should go on the trip. Two weeks had passed, and I heard nothing from Colombia. No news was good news, but I still did not feel I was making the right decision. I began packing my bags for our yearly cruise, but something told me I was making the wrong decision.

Two days before the trip, Sandra called to tell me something was wrong. My mother was coughing and not doing well. Instantly, I knew my reservations served me right, and I was ready to book a flight to Colombia. Sandra disagreed. She explained that my mother had been to the hospital many times and had always returned home. This was nothing out of the ordinary. I could not help but think that just because it was ordinary did not mean something along those lines would not change. I did not feel right.

Something kept telling me things were not how they usually were.

"Madre, do you want me to come?" I questioned once again, hoping she would say yes to give me a real reason to see her without looking dramatic.

"No, hija, you look forward to this trip every year. Everything is fine; I will be fine.

Go on," she said.

Again, my heart shattered into little pieces.

"Madre, bless me, please." Before my mother and I would terminate our calls, I would ask her to bless me. Having my mother's blessing and approving thoughts meant everything to me.

"Dios te bendiga. Hoy, mañana y siempre. Porque tu eres lo mejor que le paso a mi vida." (God bless you today, tomorrow, and always because you are the best thing that happened to me.) We hung up simultaneously, and within an instant, tears were streaming down my face. Something just did not feel right. A short time later, I called Sandra, and she let me know they decided to admit my mother to the hospital.

"Okay, I am going to get on a plane right now and come to you." My face was red, and my heart was beating very hard; I could feel it in my temples.

"Why? For what?" Sandra questioned, and I was in disbelief. "This is not the first time that Madre is in the hospital. It's just a cold. She will be fine, and when she gets better, they will send her home."

"Are you sure?" I questioned her, not knowing what decision I should make.

"Yes, they are going to keep her overnight because she's been coughing a lot, but other than that, she's perfectly fine, believe me."

I nodded as if she could see me. "I'm going to call you tomorrow before we take off for Florida. If things get worse, Leonel will go on the cruise with the kids, and I will come to you immediately." I wanted Sandra to know that no matter what, I was only a plane ride away.

After days of feeling nauseous about the outcome of my mother's condition, when I spoke to Sandra the following day, she had great news. My mother was doing much better. She had even requested chicken soup for lunch. Even though Sandra let me know my mother was improving, I still had a feeling in the pit of my stomach that something was wrong. After years of worrying about my mother, I guess it was impossible to turn off my nerves.

The next day, Sandra told me our mother was eating soup and doing well. At this point, I became more nervous as my family and I were boarding the cruise ship in the upcoming hours. I let Sandra know that my cell phone would not have a signal since we would be in the middle of the ocean, but if needed, they could call the cruise ship. I should have been elated to go to Mexico on a beautiful cruise with my family, but I was not relaxed; I could not stop overthinking. In front of my family, I tried to pretend like nothing was wrong, but I was convinced that something horrible was going to happen. I had an impending sense of doom, and it was not going anywhere, no matter how hard I tried to stop it. My soul felt drained, and I could barely focus on my family. Poolside, I opened a book to try to distract myself from reality, but it didn't work—nothing worked. The kids were so happy and it seemed everyone was having a good time.

That night when I returned to the cabin after dinner, I noticed a red blinking light on the phone. Someone had left a message. I assumed it was from the boys trying to call the room. I pressed the button, eager to hear what they had to say. In a meek tone, I heard the subtle voice of my coworker.

It was April 21, 2003....."Hola, Esperanza. We tried to call you, but we have not been able to get in touch with you. I am so sorry that I have to leave this message, but your mother just passed away." Within an instant, I felt like the world around me was moving so fast but with no formal direction. All I heard was silence. Leonel was in the bathroom, and the boys were not around. Without thinking, I ran to the elevator, looking for an exit. It did not matter that I was on a ship in the middle of nowhere. I just knew I needed to go. I needed to go to Colombia. Running out onto the deck, I could not help but notice my eyes were growing heavy. My heart began to beat slower and slower and slower...*boom, boom, boom.* Everything went black.

I finally woke up in the ship's medical office with Leonel by my side.

"What happened?," I asked

He answered with anguish. "You ran out of the room onto the deck and passed out into this guy's arms," Leonel said. He pointed to the man who brought me here.

The man said, "I thought you were gonna jump out of the ship. You gave me a scare!" After thanking him and apologizing, I closed my eyes and tried to remember what happened. But the truth is I didn't know what was going on. A few minutes passed when suddenly I remembered it all.

All of those reservations began to resurface about coming on this trip. My mother was not with us anymore. I started to cry uncontrollably. Later they told me I was walking towards the water and the man held onto me because I was ready to jump. To this day I can't remember what happened.

I was angry and disappointed in myself for not listening to my gut. Now I was in the middle of the ocean, and I needed to find a way to get to Colombia. As difficult as it was to admit, I felt as though my mother did not want me to be around, not only at her death but at her funeral, as well. I did everything I could for my mother and wanted to be there for her in every possible way, but it seemed as though she had different plans.

Instantly, Leonel and I spoke to the captain about how I could get off the ship. He expressed his deepest condolences for me and my loss. He said I had to wait one more day for us to be close enough to Cuba so I could take a flight to Miami. From Miami, I would fly to Bogota. I prepared to go. I had to say goodbye to my mother for the last time or I could never forgive myself.

Chapter Thirty-Four

When I finally got in touch with my family, I asked them to hold my mother's body for one more day. I could not stand the thought of not being able to see her one more time. That night was immensely difficult. When I was a child, I remember sitting in the grass watching the planes fly by, longing for the day when I would be able to travel and not have to worry about where my next meal was coming from. I felt small, but I had the drive and passion in my heart to make a life for myself. Yet, there I was all those years later, brokenhearted and waiting to take a plane to lay my mother to rest.

The next morning, my body felt stiff when I woke up. I had hardly slept; I was living in a haze. As I turned over, I looked at Leonel sleeping so peacefully. In my moment of grief, I was glad that he was there for me to turn to. I needed all the strength that I could find to get me through this time. When Leonel opened his eyes, he turned toward me and spoke words that shattered my being in more ways than I could ever have imagined.

"Make love to me," he breathed. I blinked my eyes in the hopes that maybe I was not seeing or hearing clearly.

"What?" I questioned, thinking I must have heard him wrong. There was no way that my kind-hearted, gentle soul of a husband would have asked me to make love on one of the hardest days of my life.

"What's the problem?" he questioned. My stomach twisted, and I grew queasy.

"You're leaving, so why can't we do it?" I was in disbelief. At that moment, the image of my perfect loving husband was gone. The man before me was no longer someone who supported me but one who wanted from me at a time when I needed to be held tight.

Without saying a word, I got out of bed, took a pen and paper, and left the room. I don't know why I did that, as I had no plan to write anything.

In moments alone, my mind was constantly at work. My mother always asked about my happiness, to which I never responded. That question never crossed my mind until I stood back and reflected on the answer. I was so accustomed to living on autopilot that truly feeling my emotions was unrealistic. If I let myself feel all of the emotions associated with the human experience, I would have never been able to accomplish anything. My two boys brought me so much joy, and I loved being a mother. My sons were the light of my life and fulfilled me in a way that only a mother could understand.

Are you happy? At that moment, the only feeling that surrounded the question was emptiness. My mother took most of my strength with her when she died, and Leonel took whatever was left when he asked me for my body this morning. I had never experienced grief like this in all forty years of my life. My body physically ached. I was hollow. There was no energy left in me; I felt like I was paralyzed. As the pen touched the paper, I created a little poem for my mother.

Wherever you are

I stand here thinking about you

I witness all your sufferings

No matter my pain

I accept your departure

Because I know you are in a better place

I will try to be the best version of you

I sit here and think how will I continue my life without you.

A hole was left in my heart

Help me not miss you

So I don't feel dead inside

When I finally gathered myself together and wiped my tears. I went back downstairs to explain to my children what was going to happen. Orlando promised me he was going to take care of Javier. I left my family on the ship and made my way to the Cuban airport in preparation for another flight.

From Cuba, I flew to Miami, and from Miami, I flew to Colombia. I could not sleep at all. My mind was fluttering with thoughts and memories. Minutes before we landed I went into a deep sleep. While I was sleeping, it felt like someone was kissing my forehead, and when I woke up, I had arrived. Was it my mother? At that moment, it felt as though my pain disappeared. Somehow, all of my energy was restored. I allowed myself to believe that this was my mother's way of saying goodbye to me. Whatever it was, it gave me the strength I needed to get through the next few days.

As I left the airport, I remembered how my mother never wanted to be involved in drama, especially at a funeral. She hated when people were hysterical at funerals as she believed that meant they felt guilty about something. She made it a point to let us know that she wanted her funeral to be a celebration. She wanted her children to be strong and proud of the life she lived. I promised my mother when she was alive that when it was her time to go, I would honor her request.

Somehow, I mustered enough strength to smile at her funeral. I did as my mother wished, and I did not cry. I smiled and took pictures. Sandra was disgusted with me. She could not believe how I was not grieving as everyone else was. She let me know this was a funeral not a birthday party. What I didn't know was that my siblings had prepared themselves for my arrival. They believed that I would be inconsolable when I saw my madre's casket. They were waiting for me to be uncontrollable. But to their surprise, I did not react like that. For that reason I apologized to my siblings for the way I acted. I was only honoring my madre's wish.

I know that Sandra got the short end of the stick. I found out later when my siblings picked me up at the airport, she had to confront my father alone. Surprisingly he took a chance and showed up to my madre's funeral. He wanted to see her just for a few minutes. But my sister asked him to leave and respect our sorrow. There was no reason for him to be there. He had made her suffer enough all these years. His forgiveness was not welcomed. It was in his best interest that he leave immediately before I arrived.

Although it was hard, I knew my mother was finally at peace. She suffered so much and for so long that I was glad she was no longer in pain. I knew she was in a better place, and there was no reason to be upset. This was a celebration of a beautiful woman's life, who suffered for far too long and was now at rest.

From the corner of my eye, I could see my Uncle Abraham with his head down, holding a napkin soaked with tears. I knew he was heartbroken. He and my mother had a lovely relationship; they loved each other so much. I hugged him and told him that my mother would not have wanted him to be upset and thanked him for being such a good brother to her. As difficult as it was, my family seemed to be holding together very well.

The funeral was beautiful, and so many people came to pay their respects to my mother.

My mother was blessed by watching them grow up, but I did not have the same pleasure.

I could only sit and watch them. I hardly knew them.

My family told me that it rained every day that week except on the day of the funeral. I did not believe them. That day was so beautiful I could not believe the days prior were stormy.

When we finally got back to my mother's house, I walked into her bedroom alone.

On my mother's wheelchair, there was a bottle of peach soda. That must have been the last thing she drank before she died. On the seat of the wheelchair, there was a blanket that smelled like her. I held it to my chest and could no longer hold it together. I sobbed uncontrollably for hours. I cried myself to sleep that night, and my family gave me the space I needed with her belongings. We were all in pain, but every single one of us was worried about Luis the most. He was drinking everyday and showed up drunk at my madre's funeral. He was crying inconsolably. Luis was the baby and was very attached to my mother. We did not want him to do anything he might regret during this time of grief. Sandra told us when my mother was in the hospital Luis said he would take his own life. We were also scared that he might try to hurt himself so all eyes were on him.

Unfortunately, I couldn't stay for very long as I had to return to New York. All of my siblings came to drop me off at the airport. We said our goodbyes with sadness and tears but without me promising anything. I took off, not looking back.

Chapter Thirty-Five

Even though my father is alive, somewhere in this world, the truth is I'm not interested to know, given that I had no relationship with him. Losing my mother made life unbearable. Every fiber of my being had shattered into a million pieces, but those around me had no idea. I had no real expectation of how my family would help me cope when I returned. I put every effort into acting normal in my daily life. My emotions were uncontrollable because I was mourning all by myself.

Javier didn't have time to get to know my mother. Given the stress we endured when leaving Colombia, he only managed to spend time with her when she came to America for that short trip. My son thought he would have a sweet grandma like the ones he saw on TV. but it was far from the truth. At that time, my mother was already wheelchair bound and recovering from surgery. There was not enough time for them to create a bond like the one I imagined. I remember one funny night. My mother was in her room resting. Javier started screaming and ran back to me as if he had just seen a ghost. He had entered my mother's room to find her dentures soaking in a cup. He was in disbelief, to say the least.

"Oh, my god! Teeth! There are teeth swimming in a cup!," he screamed as he barged into the bathroom. I could not contain my laughter. "I am never going to drink juice in this house ever again!" Javier was under the impression that my mother was going to put her teeth in all of our cups, which made me laugh hysterically. His paranoia was so bad as a result of the denture incident that he forced me to purchase plastic cups for him because he refused to drink out of any other household cup. Javier was sweet and funny, but my mother did not care for his humor and found it disrespectful. She always said that everyone spoiled him.

On another occasion my mother called Javier into her room to assist her in finding her glasses. In the process of looking around, he suggested examining under the pillow. She had no luck looking for her glasses, and when she looked in the mirror, she realized her glasses were on the top of her head. He found it funny as he knew that they were already on her head. Orlando did not find it funny either and reprimanded Javier. He did not allow him to bother his grandmother.

My mother loved Orlando. Orlando worked at McDonald's, and when he would come home, he would sit with my mother and listen to her stories. She always appreciated her time with him. They would make each other laugh. I would hear them laughing from the garage where I was doing the clients at night. It always made me smile, knowing my mother got along so well with Orlando.

I did not expect my children to grieve in any way, as mourning was not a reality to them, given they did not have a long-lasting relationship with my mother. I know it was hard for them to understand what I was going through, and how deep my pain was.

However, I yearned for my husband's support at this time.

My husband had lost his mother a few months before meeting me. I did not have the opportunity to meet her. His parents were never really a topic of conversation between us, as it always seemed to be a sore subject. I was always respectful around this topic, but for me he knew how much I loved and cared for my mother. For this reason I found it strange I didn't get his emotional support. In some way he believed that if we ignored the loss of my mother, the feelings would disappear with time. Ignoring those feelings only served as a catalyst for a much bigger problem.

I suffered in silence until I couldn't mentally and physically take it anymore. I felt a lingering pain in my chest that couldn't be cured with anything. I couldn't focus at work and struggled to keep a smile on my face. Everybody at work began to notice it. My boss wasn't happy about it. It was so evident that I was called into the office a few times. This was a first for me. I was never called to the office for my conduct in fifteen years. My boss asked me to concentrate a bit more and change my attitude. He suggested that I take some time off. I understood completely how people felt around me. It was something very hard for me to manage. Nothing seemed to go right. My husband was angry with me too. Nothing at home was functioning as it was supposed to. This situation only made me feel guilty, irresponsible for the instability around me. As much as I tried to play my part, I felt more empty.

On many occasions and without anyone knowing, I called Colombia the way I used to, pretending for a second that my mother was going to pick up the phone, and I could hear her voice again. I really thought I was going crazy. I began losing my appetite and lacked sufficient sleep, which was probably why I couldn't function at home or work. It came to a point where I didn't want to get out of bed and made excuses for not going to work. I only wanted to sleep and not see anyone.

It was then that my boss called me for the third time to his office. He was bothered and very direct with me. He said, "We cannot work like this. You have missed work many times. I think the best thing for us is that you train someone else. In fact, she is waiting for you downstairs." At the moment his words didn't mean anything to me. I felt like a zombie. I just listened to him and followed his orders and trained the new cosmetologist.

Two weeks later when I finished training that girl, my boss wanted to talk to me again. I could not forget that day. He didn't even care that my child was with me. He called me into his office and sarcastically told me to take two weeks off. I felt horrible at that moment because my son was present and witnessed all of this. I didn't say a word, I went to my station and cleared it completely in front of all the staff. I took my belongings, put them in my car and left with Javier, not looking back.

For three weeks, I only got out of bed to use the bathroom and send Javier off to school. Orlando was the oldest and he was very responsible. I didn't shower for ten days. The only desire I had was to sleep all the time. I was trying to handle the house the best I could so my kids didn't notice anything. I was so well-coordinated that I would set the alarm to wake myself up before Javier arrived home. When the kids asked, "Why is mommy going to bed so early?" my husband would respond, "Your mother doesn't feel well." That is when my husband spoke with me and suggested I see a doctor. It was obvious that something was wrong with me. The next morning I made an appointment with our primary doctor.

It didn't take long for him to notice I was in a deep depression and that I should see a specialist. I was hesitant about doing so. How was I supposed to talk to someone who had no clue who I was? I convinced myself that I didn't need anyone to talk to and that I would take matters into my own hands.

The following morning, I woke up and decided that today I would be present in my life and make the effort to carry out all the tasks I had forgotten about. I took a shower, cleaned the house and put fresh flowers on the table. I am a horrible cook, but I attempted to make lunch for everyone. Since it was such a nice day, I decided to walk to the beach, something I used to enjoy doing every morning. On my way back, I struggled to make it home. I felt a cold rush into my body. I was feeling a bit dizzy and had a hard time breathing. It felt like I was going to faint. I got scared and I sat for a time on the grass curb and began taking deep breaths. I didn't know if I would be able to make it home. I felt as if a truck had run me over, and I didn't have the strength in my body to lift myself back up. It took everything in me to get back home. When I got home I ran to the bathroom and threw up. I fell to the floor and into a sleeping state. When I woke up all I wanted to do was sleep and never wake up.

That same day my husband came into the room and spoke quietly and said, "I don't know how you're going to handle this. You need to seek help like the doctor told you. If you won't do this for yourself, do it for your children."

The next day, I called the doctor that my doctor had recommended. I didn't know what I was getting myself into. I was asked multiple questions, which I answered to the best of my ability. When I finally hung up, I had the biggest headache and felt like I was about to throw up. Was I sure I could do this? The office scheduled an appointment to see the psychiatrist for the following week. While I wasn't thrilled about going, it became necessary, given how horrible my situation was. It was now something that I could no longer control, and I needed professional help.

The day finally came. I took a shower and dressed myself. I drove and didn't know how I got there . All I know is that I was sitting in front of a stranger asking me a million questions. At that moment I could only think about what I went through in my life. This was only temporary. Everything will get back to normal. Meanwhile, she was trying to have a conversation with me. The only thought in my mind was how I let myself go.

Coming to this place was a waste of time. The strength of my mother is second to none.

I couldn't wait to get out of there, but it was evident that something was wrong with me.

She seemed concerned, given that I had black and blue marks under my eyes, and asked, "Mrs. Ortiz, are you sleeping at all?"

"To be honest, I am not. Would you mind passing me some water? My throat is very dry all the time."

"Not a problem. Please wait for me here."A couple of minutes later, she came back into the room with a woman by the name of Doctor Felipe, or as I called her, "my guardian angel." She asked my name. We talked for about an hour. Later, I was diagnosed with a chemical imbalance. This imbalance can be treated with medication. That is exactly what she told me. This was all new for me. I never heard of this. I returned home with a prescription for 20 milligrams of Prozac, which I was to take once a day and go for therapy twice a week. I admit I was very ignorant about this topic. However, I became doubtful and decided that I was not going to take the medication.

When my husband arrived home I discussed with him what Dr Felipe said. I told him I needed to attend the twice-a-week appointments and take the prescribed medicine.

My husband was very happy for me and he went to pick up the prescription.

I was apprehensive about taking medication. I hid it in my nightstand. I did continue my therapy. After a couple of weeks of sessions, I did not see any improvement. It was the opposite. I forgot everything, I didn't want to get up. I had no intention of going back.

Both doctors thought that I should have progressed further. This was because they were under the impression that I was taking the medication. While I knew that what I was doing was not right, I couldn't come to terms with putting myself on medication. I felt that it opened the door to side effects and complications, and I could not help but worry that it would alter my personality.

It was then that my husband confronted me. I was not prepared to have a conversion with him. He insisted. He wanted to talk to me. You could see the frustration he had. He realized I was not taking the medication when he decided to check to see if I needed a refill. The next time I was in bed, Leonel came and sat right next to me. I knew what this meant, and I wasn't ready to have another conversation.

"I want to talk to you." he paused. "You're supposed to be the role model here, and I don't know if you understand that the state you're in is affecting all of us."

I kept my eyes closed because I couldn't bear the embarrassment and humiliation I felt. My family was not at fault for my mother not being in this world. I didn't have the right to interrupt the peace in my family. That made me feel horrible and responsible for what was happening.

When I opened my eyes I remembered the look he had. He was very bothered by me. In his hands he held my medication. "How can you get better if you're not taking your medicine? You know Javier is very young and still sensitive to everything." I did not speak one word. "If the doctors are advising you to take the medication, then you should do as they say." He let out a defeated breath. "I can't do this anymore." And just like that, he left the room without another word.

Before I knew it, I was sobbing uncontrollably. I didn't even know what I was crying about. My body began to tremble. I was ready for bed.

Within an hour, my willpower had run out. Somehow, I pulled myself out of bed, took a shower, made a cup of coffee, and took my medication for the first time. At this point, I was still skeptical about taking the medication, but I knew I needed to make a change. After one month, I began seeing colors I had not noticed in so long, and my focus returned. I was able to sleep, and finally, the burden of holding all the pressure in my chest had left. I felt like I was reborn again.

Chapter Thirty-Six

I remember that weekend. I decided we were going to have a barbecue. My husband was so happy. He didn't even recognize me. Not only did I host people the following day, but I decided to attend church. My spirits were so high that I even went to the movies with Javier to see "Marley & Me." Everything was turning back to the way it seemed before. I felt everything return to normal. But deep inside I was terrified to think this was only temporary because of the medications. Nevertheless, I did not want to return to that stage of my life again.

Due to the events at that time, I lost my job. Sixteen years of loyalty, working six to seven days a week all for nothing. The person I trained took over my position and my presence wasn't needed. That is when I remembered what my boss had told me," No one is indispensable and everybody is replaceable!" Life continues. I will rise again no matter the stones in the road.

I had to devise some kind of a plan. The bills still kept on coming. I started to see my clients at home once again. Little by little they started coming back. The clients were happy to see me reopen. That gave me the opportunity again to offer my facial services at home, hoping there would be great results.

***

At home it was prohibited to argue or say any curse words. If my husband or myself were not on the same page, it was to be discussed in private, and when the children were not present. This is the reason the children never saw any arguing, physical abuse or disrespect between us. If I ever escalated my voice, he would simply walk out of the room or leave me talking by myself. He always said that for an argument to be had, there must be two people. He would leave the house and when he returned I knew I couldn't bring up the topic. Everything would have to go back to normal.

I admit this was frustrating for me. But I agreed with his rationale for many years, because this would benefit our children. It was then that I discovered in therapy that everything I did at home was not normal and it was far from healthy for the kids. There is nothing wrong with confrontation. Arguing does not always imply the absence of love but shows that two must fight to make things work.

Keeping emotions and feelings bottled up is not good for anyone. Pretending and maintaining a perfect family harmony is not possible. When children have to face life on their own that confuses them. When I would share the talks I had with my therapist with my husband, he did not share the same belief.

I remembered he said, "I hope these sessions really help you because what you are saying does not make any sense. Can't you see for yourself the results.? Our children are excellent and it's only thanks to the stability we have given them. That is why it is important that you don't get confused."

In each of my sessions I would recover another part of me. I could express myself without fear. I could do whatever I wanted without needing approval. I didn't want to ask permission anymore, or follow the rules, being scared of confrontation. I didn't know I had so many repressed feelings inside of me. I felt like another child at home.

And I wanted to be a companion or wife, not a daughter.

I loved the feeling of the air on my face and the smell of the surrounding ocean. Running is where I felt free to be me. If I was angry, sad, or excited, I ran. I was lucky that in this way I could reset my mind. When I arrived home, it would be a different lifestyle. I knew my husband wasn't willing to make changes at home. He still believed that it was my responsibility to keep stability at home and this was not negotiable for him.

By September 2003, working from home was going so well. I was excited to be able to see the boys when they came home from school. I decided to set up a facial room in the room we decorated for my mother when we hoped she would stay with us. It was difficult to be in it, but I was in the process of trying to learn how to handle my emotions. The room was beautiful and only needed minor changes to make it a skincare room. The space was super clean and smelled amazing. I decided to set up candles to mimic the look of a little five star spa. Surprisingly all my old clients from my previous job found me and made appointments. They showed their full support. I would continue to work early morning until late at night. I would run every morning and on Mondays to therapy with Dr. Felipe. On Sundays we had to go to church and later have brunch at a diner. And just like that a year had passed.

In one session, my therapist said, "So, Mrs. Ortiz, how has it been with the transition of working full-time from home?"

I responded, "I am very pleased to say it is going well, I never got the opportunity to see my children come home from school. But I think I am working more than usual."

It was evident from her facial reaction that she wanted me to talk more about this topic. My therapist was curious about the emotional support system I had at home, and I was not sure how to respond.

"I hardly see my husband and it's impossible to sustain a conversation with him. He leaves for work very early in the morning and I am always busy with my clients."

"How does your husband feel about all of this?" she asked.

"To be honest, I am not sure how he feels. I believe he is happy with the progress I am making.By the time morning rolls around, my husband is gone before I wake up."

"If your husband was in front of you right now, what would you like to tell him?"

Instantaneously, I began laughing, not because I found the question funny but rather because I felt uncomfortable and nervous with the topic. The laughing began to die down as tears began to drip down my face, and a knot developed in my throat. She hit the nail right on the head. This was my spot of weakness and a topic that was painful for me to grasp. This was such a sore subject that I wished this topic of conversation never came up. This is like a piano with a broken key that is camouflaged by the keyboard, but it is never used to play a melody.

"Mrs. Ortiz, if your husband was in front of you right now, what would you like to tell him?" She said it again.

Before she could finish re-asking the same question, I began speaking. "I always feel like the third child of the house. Why is it so hard for you to see me as your wife ?" I said with relief. "That's what I would say."

After my mother's passing, of course, I needed to lean on my husband. I was devastated and fell into a depression I didn't even know existed. I don't want to blame anyone. But I would have loved his emotional support.

"Does your husband know how you feel?," she asked.

"No No." I said. I replied without hesitation.

"Would you like to work on your relationship with him?" she asked.

"Yes of course. I would love to communicate better."

"Why don't you bring your husband to the next appointment?" she suggested.

I thought this would be a great opportunity for us to work on our marriage. I was willing to do anything to keep us together. Even though I knew we had become distant, we had a whole life together. Twenty five years weren't easy to throw into the garbage. We were two human beings with values. We had two beautiful children. Personally, I didn't believe divorce was the solution. Only to think of that made me nauseous.

After therapy I drove home and I could not stop crying. The tears just came and would not stop. She touched a topic that I tried to avoid. What I do know was it made me feel good to cry. I felt peace within me.

Chapter Thirty-Seven

When I finally got home, I could see from the car that Orlando was putting up the Christmas lights. Although it was only Thanksgiving, he liked to be prepared ahead of time. He knew how much his dad loved seeing the house decorated. When I finally entered the house, I saw my husband in the kitchen holding up the turkey. He asked me to season it like I always did. My husband went right upstairs after he put the bird down. I had not spoken one word. Never was I asked how therapy was or how my day was. Not once did he ask if I was okay. He never checked in on me to see how I was doing. Maybe I should have told him without him asking. But I didn't have the time to tell him. I, more than anyone, knew his routine. He would go upstairs and I would not see him for the rest of the night.

Thanksgiving, the traditional American holiday, always managed to lift my spirits. Living in America for so many years, the holiday and its traditions grew on me, and it became a customary holiday in my household. My home always managed to smell heavenly, and pumpkin pie was a must given that it was my favorite holiday dish. For Americans, Thanksgiving signifies welcoming all family members under one roof to share a festive meal to give back and show what they are truly thankful for. I enjoy the fact that Thanksgiving never revolved around presents and gift-giving but rather brought everyone together for a day to eat and laugh. This holiday was truly an opportunity for me to spend more time with my children, decorating the house and making the classic, traditional Thanksgiving day meal.

Javier was no longer a little boy. He was turning into a man and had everything going for him. Javier was a senior in high school on his way to college. While I was so excited about what opportunities would come his way, a piece of my heart couldn't bear watching him grow up before my eyes. He was driven and focused on doing well in school while also partaking in extracurricular activities, such as soccer, where he and his team played well. Javier opened so many opportunities for himself, and throughout it all, he managed to succeed. I know on many occasions I pushed him too hard but I knew he had it in him.

We made it my purpose for the next year to schedule meetings with college counselors, take campus tours, and gather all the documentation for the college application process. It was now, more than ever, that my son needed me the most, which meant I had to stop thinking about me and that is exactly what I did.

After the holidays we applied to different universities. Thank goodness my son had more knowledge than me of the application process. We always worked as a team. The most important thing was to let him know he was not alone. I wanted to give him the opportunity that I didn't have. I would do anything to make it happen.

When Javier told us he would like to go away to college, my husband was not thrilled. The two of them shared an indescribable bond. When it came to letting Javier go away to school, my husband and I were in disagreement. I trusted Javier and knew that he was capable of moving out, while my husband was fearful of his son leaving. It was time to trust him and let him experience life on his own and make mistakes like all college students do. I strongly believed that by not letting him go we were cutting his wings and leaving him with no opportunity to learn how to fly. I admit I was not the one to change his mind. Javier convinced his dad and he acquiesced.

On the other hand, Orlando was on his way to becoming a pilot and graduating from pilot school. One day, Orlando decided to take us up on a small plane, towards Manhattan. It was gratifying to see him accomplish such a milestone in his life, and I was so proud to call him my pilot. We had sacrificed a lot, but it seemed as though it was all worth it. Orlando always loved life and lived it fully. He never gave up on love. And if given love he gave it his all. Orlando and Javier grew up together and there was no jealousy between them. The love and respect they have for each other is admirable. They are my pride and joy. When we got the news that Javier was accepted to the university, with love and laughter, we celebrated with him. It was a stressful month. I tried to remember everything he needed. When we finally had to drop him off at college, I wanted to die but I made sure he did not see my tears.

It was only when I got home that I noticed Doctor Felipe had left me a message.

She was worried I had missed many sessions. My mind was so distracted by Javier's move that I lost track of canceling my appointments. I owed her an apology and that same day I made an appointment.

The last conversation had ended with her suggesting that my husband join the following meeting. To no surprise, I knew this question she would not have forgotten.

The first thing she told me when I entered her office after a month was, "So, Mrs. Ortiz, I thought your husband was coming."

To which I responded, "No, maybe next time."

"Why not, Mrs. Ortiz?" she asked. I offered no response.

"So, how are you feeling?"

"To be honest, I'm feeling numb. I concentrate on what needs priority attention, I solve it and continue on. That's what I have always done." I laughed and told her why I had missed my therapy sessions.

She only listened. That day she said, "Mrs. Ortiz, you must try and work on what we talk about. Remember to think of yourself. Now that your children are no longer with you, take some time for yourself. Do something you haven't been able to do," she insisted.

Everything started to register in my head and I thought it was a good idea. I had hoped I didn't have to rely on medication forever. But in reality it helped me so much, but I believed I was ready to stop.

"Mrs. Ortiz, please do me a favor and promise me that the next time you will bring your husband to the session. I would also like you to be consistent when it comes to attending therapy."

When I got home, for the first time, I told my husband it was important for us to talk. Just by his facial reaction, I knew this wasn't going to be easy. He gave me a look like I was going crazy again.

"In a passive voice he asked, "Are you taking your medication?"

I felt offended but I gathered my patience and said again, "I don't understand what one thing has to do with the other. All I would like to know is if we could go out to dinner and talk."

"I have work tomorrow, and I have to get up early. Is this extremely important, or can this conversation wait?"

As always, I put my emotions and feelings aside. "It's not important, but I would like us to talk." I then left so he could get some sleep.

To my surprise, when Saturday afternoon rolled around, my

husband asked me if I would like to go out for dinner. Nervously, I responded that I would love to.

Immediately upon being seated he looked into my eyes and said, "What happened? Talk to me. I'm listening."

The truth is I didn't know where to begin. So I said, "I would like to ask you a favor and ask you a question."

With him I knew I had to get to the point like it was a business transaction. I gathered the courage to say, "I would like you to do me a favor and go to a therapy session with me. The doctor thinks it would help me with my recuperation. And the question is, do you think there is a problem with our marriage?" There was a long pause.

"Now that the children are not home maybe we can try to communicate more, don't you think?" I asked. He looked at me seriously.

"There is nothing wrong with our marriage. I think this is all in your head. Instead of blaming this on our relationship, why don't you take this time to figure out what is wrong with you? I did everything to support you. I allowed you space when you needed it. And I took care of the household when you couldn't manage it. I managed to do everything a husband should do. I am an active father who shares a presence in our children's lives. I have been faithful to you. I don't smoke; I don't go out with friends and don't come home drunk. I am faithful and loyal to my family. The only person I see here in the wrong is you. What happened to my wife? What have you been doing in therapy for a year? I feel like I am living with a stranger. You don't want to even sleep with me anymore, let alone look at me. So why do I bother having a wife? Why don't you let me know what you want."

It was very hurtful to listen to him speak with such resentment. My intention wasn't to get my husband's anger up but rather to express my feelings, which didn't go well.

But it served me well to know he was bothered. For me this was a win. He never expressed anything.

"I appreciate your sincerity," I said. "I am happy you are talking and letting me know how you feel. Can you please answer my question? Is something wrong with our marriage?"

"No, there's nothing wrong with our marriage. There's something wrong with your head. You are not making this any better. The happiness in our family is in your hands." He quickly asked for the bill. Within no time, we paid and left the restaurant. Silence enveloped our drive home, each of us lost in thought. He went to his room as usual. The following morning, he woke up as if nothing had happened the night before.

I lost all hope of communicating with him. Keeping busy at work was the only way to disconnect myself from my reality at home.

I made it a priority to attend my therapy sessions. Hoping to stop the medication, it was hard to believe that I might have to take them for life. I hardly left my home. I worked long hours and without knowing it I returned to my old habits. The people around me always saw a smile on my face. I was the only one who knew my reality. The only space I felt free to express myself in was in therapy. It was a difficult part of my life. My children were not at home, I felt alone more than ever. Especially when I finished my long shifts. What I felt internally could not compare to the facade I created for myself. I would walk around, masking how imperfect my life was when, in reality, I felt dead inside. I was not allowed to complain because to the world, my life *was* perfect: I married a great guy, raised a beautiful family, and had a roof over my head. What else could I ask for? But the only thing I wanted was to reconnect with my best friend, who desired a relationship between two adults, who fought for a strong family. And now more than ever we have the opportunity to take care of one another. I didn't have a magic wand to make all our problems disappear. But I wanted with all my heart to save our marriage. We lived under the same roof but I felt more alone than ever. My only distraction was my long hours of work.

When I finished for the day, I would sit in the kitchen by myself and watch la novela, which consisted of Spanish soap operas, to ease my mind. As usual, my husband would already be in bed sleeping. All I could think about during those evenings alone was the last conversation I had with him and how he blamed everything on me. This was how the days passed. Each day we grew further apart. It was clear he didn't like this new version of me.

Chapter Thirty-Eight

One day, I opened up the mail to find an invitation for us to attend the wedding of the daughter of one of my clients. I immediately closed it up and hid it before he could see it. The last time I was invited to a wedding, he did not have any desire to attend. We were constantly invited to barbecues, sweet sixteens, baptisms, and engagement parties, but he always used work and attending church as an excuse to miss the events. This time, I really wanted to go since he was a really special person to me, so I decided to ask him.

That weekend when he arrived home from church, I approached him and said, "Before you give me an answer, I want you to hear me out. Why is it that every time someone invites us to do anything, you don't want to go?"

"Just because I don't want to go doesn't mean you can't. You are always welcome to enjoy any invitation that is sent to us. I just prefer staying home."

"But you're my husband. Aren't we supposed to attend these events together? Why do I always have to go by myself?"

"Remember the last time we attended an event like this together? You weren't happy at the fact that I wanted to leave after dinner."

"Of course I was not happy with that," I said. "When someone invites you to their party, you cannot just come to eat and then leave right away. You have to take some time to talk to others who are in attendance and try to have a conversation before leaving."

"The last time we were invited to a barbecue, we arrived 30 minutes late, and within an hour of being there, you wanted to leave. Your reason was that you wanted to go home and watch television. You thought there was nothing wrong with that. While I did understand where you are coming from, I want you to see my perspective, to see how this looks."

My husband was tired of hearing what I had to say and brushed me off by repeating that I am free to go wherever I like. I went back to the kitchen and started cleaning. I was in no mood to talk. He followed me.

"Why are you crying?" he asked.

"I am frustrated and not sure what I am supposed to do. You don't want anything from me. What is happening to us? The only thing we do is work, sleep, and eat. Is this the life you want for us?" I said.

"Everyone does the same thing," he said. "We go away on vacation every year while so many families cannot afford to. I don't know what you are complaining about." After a silence I told him, "One of my clients invited us to a wedding, and I would like us to go."

"All of this for a wedding Okay, so we'll go," he said. He always managed to keep his composure, even when he was angry.

* * *

Orlando was living in Newark, and Javier was in college. They were the ones that kept the joy at home. Now the home was more than empty. I could feel the loneliness in each corner of the house. I was on Javier's bed smelling the scent of his room. I missed him so much. But I was the one who pushed him to leave. We would be separated for four years. The reality was he had to learn to live without us and experience life on his own. I was sure he would be an outstanding, educated man because I gave him the best of me. I didn't want to get emotional but I couldn't stop crying. I decided to go walking on the beach. It was very satisfying. Upon my arrival back home, I went upstairs and heard Leonel laughing. It was amazing how he could disconnect from life and make it seem like nothing was wrong. Maybe he was right, I was the real problem. Somehow I managed to find a way to convince my husband to come to therapy with me.

The following Monday after therapy, one of my clients was waiting for me in her car which frequently happened. What I didn't know was this was becoming a nuisance to my neighbor. I didn't think the neighborhood was being affected. But my neighbor thought my business was inappropriate. So she decided to call City Hall and issue a complaint. I didn't know what was about to happen until one day I received a summons to appear in court. I admit I was shocked. I was far from committing a crime. For the first time in my life I appeared in court in this country.

I remember the judge asked me, "What business do you run?"

I told the truth. I worked for a salon for sixteen years and lost my job a year ago. I had to help my family with the bills so I started cutting hair in my garage. And I do facials in the guest room.

The judge smiled and asked, "Do you have a license?"

"Yes, sir. I have four; Cosmetology, skin care, laser tech, and teacher."

The judge asked, "Do you pay taxes?"

"Yes and I have them here with me. When he had my taxes in his hands, he said, "I'm happy that you have everything in order. The only problem we have Mrs Ortiz, is that you live in a non-commercial zone. I am sorry to say you can not continue your business from home. Today I will not fine you. But if you continue to work from home you will have a big problem."

I thanked him and went home.

I was worried and I had to find a solution quickly. Things happen for a reason. Maybe it was time to open my own business. I thought I would go into town and look for a space. When I told my husband, he said, "if there is someone who is ready to start again it is you." In reality his words soothed me. Like a professional he admires me a lot. Less than a month later, Tom Suozzi was cutting the ribbon to my new business, *Hope Aesthetics*. One of my dreams was becoming a reality without even planning it. From experience, I know at the beginning it's hard work and sacrifice. We worked seven days a week, something not new to me. Only now I had an obligation and rent had to be paid the first of the month. I had to pay rent, pay utilities and much more now. It was a hard year. This was the place where I spent the majority of my time. Professionally, I was doing well. My clients supported and followed me to the new location. I started having new followers. I thank God and this country for giving me this opportunity to follow my dreams.

I would like to take this time to thank all of MY clients for their love, patience, loyalty, generosity and for believing in me as a Professional. Thank you and blessing to all of you. And also a special thank you to my neighbor! If you never made that call perhaps I wouldn't have had the courage to start my business, and follow my dream.

Going to therapy was a priority for me. Especially now that the doctor was lowering my dosage. It was only a matter of time when I would be off the meds.

One day we decided to pay a visit to Javier at college. It was a two-hour drive, and given that we were alone, I thought this was the perfect time to talk. When we got in the car, Leonel turned on the radio to listen to music. As he began driving, I began expressing how I felt. Leonel interrupted, "I cannot hear you because the radio is on."

I knew that meant he was in no mood to talk, so I pretended to sleep for the duration of the car ride. There was not one word said between the two of us. As soon as we saw Javier, it was as if Leonel's attitude flipped, acting like a completely different person from the man I was just driving with. We were both so happy to see Javier. We decided to get lunch together and catch up with Javier to see how he was doing.

As a parent, all you want in life is to see your kids content with who they are. I was ecstatic to know that he was so happy in college. He couldn't stop thanking us for everything we did for him. Within our conversation, he expressed his interest in taking up the college opportunity of studying abroad in Spain for a semester. The only requirement was upholding a good academic standing. While we were a bit hesitant about letting him go that far, we promised him that we would think about it and let him know. On the way back home it was the same. I closed my eyes and I felt like I was being punished. Once we got home, we went our separate ways.

I went to therapy as usual. The first question the doctor asked was how I was doing without the assistance of the medication.

"I am doing really well. I am looking forward to not having to use it again." I shared with her my visit to see Javier and expressed how I would love for my husband to attend one of the therapy sessions with me but I didn't know how to bring it up again. She was extremely happy to hear me say it. You can tell him this would help you in your progress.

This was a great idea. When I arrived home and approached his room, it seemed I was a stranger. I told him, "I would like to tell you that I have been off the medication for over three months. I would like you to accompany me to my next session."

He agreed. I couldn't believe it. It was the longest week ever. I was anxious and just hoping the day would come soon.

We were sitting in front of my therapist in complete silence. It froze the room. Dr. Felipe broke the ice.

"So, would anyone like to begin?" she asked. "Mr Ortiz, do you have anything you want to express to your wife?"

Immediately he responded, "No, I don't have anything to say."

"Mrs. Ortiz, do you have anything you want to tell your husband? Feel free to start wherever you would like."

"Honestly, I am not sure where to begin." Looking right into my husband's eyes, I was eager to get my thoughts out. "The reason why we are here is because there is a lack of communication between us. We have constructed a life together, forming beautiful children. But I don't know how important our marriage is to you now."

"Our marriage?" he said sarcastically. "I didn't know our marriage was a topic in your therapy. I was under the impression that we are here to solve *your* conflicts."

Leonel was very angry. It was the first time I realized how much animosity he had towards me. He continued talking.

"In this marriage the changes were made by you! The only thing I have done is respect your decisions, the ones that you don't want to face now. To be honest, doctor , I don't know why I'm here."

After a long silence, the doctor asked, "Mr. Ortiz, would you like to do couples therapy? I think it would be good for you both. Again, I am not specialized in couples therapy, but I can recommend a few therapists who are."

He answered, "Truth is doctor, I appreciate your time but I don't think it's necessary." The tension was so intense. He abruptly got up and shook her hand, like he was closing a business deal.

Looking at me, Dr Felipe said, "Mrs Ortiz, I will see you next week."

On our way home I asked again if he would like to go to couples therapy. "If that works for you, then be my guest, but I will not be going. Did you bring me here to embarrass me? Why couldn't we share this conversation in our own home?"

For the first time in my life, and with no fear and losing hope, I mustered up the words to tell him that if he didn't try going to therapy then maybe it's best we divorce.

My husband looked me in the eyes and said, "Whatever you want, and until you want. I have been preparing myself for this moment for a long time. I always knew this was going to happen."

I couldn't believe what he was saying. This whole time he was preparing himself for this moment and all I was doing was trying to save our marriage.

I was raised without a father in my life and I wouldn't ever want my children to grow up like I did. Divorce was never a thought. At that moment he gave me no way out.

When I got out of the car he said, "Wait! Think carefully about what you are about to do and how much this will affect our children. I would appreciate it if you would wait until after Javier finishes law school. He's doing well, and I don't want to ruin it for him."

I went to my room speechless. I lost the biggest battle ever. I never expected him to say those words, let alone think it in his head. Like any marriage disagreement, one would assume that before making any irrational decision such as getting a divorce, both parties would try to reconnect with one another. He was clearly not looking to fight for our marriage.

I went to his room and I said, "I will agree to your request." I told him I would not want to hurt my children. I wanted this divorce to be peaceful. I wasn't looking to argue with him. I wanted to end things on good terms and part ways whenever he believed it was best for our children.

Chapter Thirty-Nine

Hope Aesthetics was going well. I couldn't complain. It was the only thing that disconnected me from everything. I learned to listen. It's amazing how it feels to listen to other humans. Each person has a story to tell and I was here to listen to them. That's where I got my title "Hair Therapist."

Everything seemed to be going well, but from one day to the next I started having changes in my body. It was hard to fall asleep. I felt dizzy, with a lot of pain in my neck. I thought I was working too many hours. What worried me the most was my chest pains. I felt a pain that made it hard to breathe. I couldn't concentrate. I had brain fog. I was looking for things that were already in my hands. My clients started to notice my exhaustion. I wanted to avoid their questions. I would wear makeup to cover my circles. I was worried. I thought I had a disease. At my next appointment with the therapist I told her my concerns. Immediately the doctor told me to start taking the medication again.

Bursting into tears I asked, "What is happening? Isn't my progress going well?" The doctor understood how I felt, and reminded me what a chemical imbalance is.

"Mrs. Ortiz," she said, "Our progress is not over. Your symptoms today are not the same. I will start you on a low dosage to avoid you getting worse."

The way she explained it, I understood, and that's when I started my meds once again. She also suggested I take some time off and maybe think about visiting my family in Colombia. Three years had passed and I missed them so much. Back home in Colombia, my family had no idea what I was going through concerning my marriage. I never wanted anyone to worry or be concerned about me. Somehow, I was always the protector and never wanted it any other way. Marriage was a sore subject for me, as I always believed it was better to keep any problems we had between my husband and me to myself.

This time, my intention to get my life back in order wasn't for anyone else. Rather, I was doing it for myself. I even started going to the gym again. It was a great way to meet new people.

One of my clients offered me an opportunity to train in her scuba school. I always wanted to get certified, yet I never had time to do so. I decided to challenge myself and get my certification. She told me that if I was certified, I could attend the annual trip, which consisted of scuba-certified divers traveling to various countries. It was a great opportunity for me to travel. I decided to save all my tips to pay for the upcoming scuba trip.

I flew to Bonaire, an island prominently known for scuba diving. The trip lasted a week and allowed me to network and meet new people with similar interests. Being by myself was incredible, and I was so excited to travel and see more of the world. Growing up adjacent to a river, I loved the water because it gave me a sense of freedom. This was an experience I will never forget. When I arrived home, my husband didn't even bother to ask how it was. I was convinced if I wanted a change in my life, it was up to me.

Otherwise everything would remain the same.

Going back to work was the best therapy for me. My clients were like my second family, and in a weird way I missed them. After the loss of my mother, which was difficult for all, each of my siblings lived with her absence in a different way. We tried to stay united as we promised her, even though we were far apart.

I spoke frequently with Sandra. She would keep me informed as to what was happening with the rest of my family. I remember that afternoon we talked and I was surprised to hear the news that we had unclaimed property where we grew up. My sister was so excited. I heard every single word she said. It confused me as to why she was so happy to receive this news. It saddened me a bit. I was not interested due to the horrible memories of what my family and I endured. The first thing that went through my mind were all the hard times. Why now, when we are all adults?! We suddenly get property that is available for us. That place was not valuable to me. My mother was no longer with us. I didn't want anything that reminded me of the past and that is what I expressed to my sister. I told her I didn't want anything to do with that land. When I told my brother Julio he was not thrilled, probably because he shared the same feelings about the property as I did, and didn't want to have any involvement either. However, my sister was adamant about it and wouldn't stop insisting. I asked her to listen and understand where I'm coming from.

She listened and surprisingly she said, "Now you are going to listen to me! Do you understand that that land can be ours now!? You are only right about one part. You don't want to return! But have you asked yourself if Edgar, Joaquin, Luis, Julio or myself want the same thing you want? We do want to return."

Sandra tried to convince me by saying that our mother would have loved for us to return to the place where we grew up. You only remember the ugly part: Soata is a beautiful place, the climate is incredible. I listened but I still didn't understand why they would want to go back! Deep in my heart, I knew they were just waiting for my approval. I didn't have the right to make decisions for them. Afterwards, I apologized and told her to do whatever she thinks is right. In the end, they started the paperwork to claim the property. In reality, it was easy to get it under their name. I couldn't help but think why the property was so important to my siblings, especially to my brother Edgar. He was willing to sell his house and everything he had to invest in constructing his new home on the land. When the property went to our name the deed surprisingly already had a name "Balneario La Esperanza." *Sometimes in life you cannot explain how ironic things can turn out to be.*

My siblings back in Colombia had big plans for themselves, opening up a new body shop, building a restaurant with a pool, and my sister wanted to make a cabana where she could spend the weekends. I kept my thoughts to myself but respected their ideas.

Immediately, they started demolishing our old childhood home that brought me such horrible memories. In no time, my brothers were sending me pictures of breaking down walls like they were trying to bury the bad memories and start a new story in Balneario La Esperanza. For many months, Edgar and Luis kept working hard. They wanted to turn this place into a paradise. They decided to plant trees, fruit, and flowers giving it a fresh look. They invited me to Colombia to see the property and insisted that I come back. After much thought I accepted and with all my strength I decided to go.

When I arrived at El Dorado Airport a million feelings went through my body. My siblings waited for me with hugs and tears. Almost immediately we traveled to Balneario La Esperanza. My hands were cold and sweaty. Thoughts and memories flooded my head.

When we finally arrived, I was amazed to see how quickly it was built. Nothing looked the same. In front of my eyes was beauty. In the midst of construction, trees were ready to bloom. In reality they made a paradise. I didn't know if I should laugh or cry. I always admired and respected my brother Edgar. But, what he was doing with this property was truly admirable. My brother Edgar approached me and asked what I would like to do next.

Without hesitation I said with a smile, "I know what I want to do. Tomorrow I'd like to host a huge barbecue and invite the entire neighborhood. Please make sure there is a sufficient amount of food. I want everyone to eat and drink as much as they want."

My brother laughed and said If you want that to happen you need to kill a cow. He knew quickly I was serious.

"If that's what you want, that is what we shall do."

The next day food would be made. The elders and children of the neighborhood stopped by for a meal. Everyone could not stop thanking us for our generosity. He made me a promise that he would never say no to anyone who needed a meal. Wherever my madre was, she was so proud of us.

The trip to Colombia made me feel good, especially seeing my siblings with good spirits. They were so driven with their projects. I was so happy for them.

When I got back home, I went back to my routine. I continued going to therapy and went to the gym twice a week. I was saving my future tips for my next scuba trip.

Scuba diving is a passion of mine. I didn't have time to think of anything negative. Everything that was happening in my life was going well. My children were doing well and that was important to me. In Colombia my siblings continued their projects, going on with the construction.

A few months had passed since my trip to Colombia. I remember the day my brother Luis called me. We talked quite a bit. Luis was thrilled and looking forward to opening up an auto body repair shop. He was so excited about all the plans he had with Edgar, and shared how beautiful the house was becoming. I had never seen him this enthusiastic or driven before. He was preparing to travel to Bogota. He hadn't seen his children and missed them very much. Before hanging up, I told Luis how I truly loved him and was excited to see what he and Edgar would do next. As soon as they would finish the restaurant I would be the first one there.

Luis arrived in Bogota later that night and stayed with my sister. It was 2013.

In the morning, he had breakfast with Sandra and decided to play soccer with his friends afterwards. Even as a child, Luis loved playing soccer. He was dating a woman at the time who was living in Bogota, and decided to stay with her that evening. The following morning, Sandra received a call from the woman. She sounded desperate for help as Luis wasn't feeling well. Within no time, Sandra arrived there and found Luis lying on the couch. Sandra could see something was wrong, as his appearance didn't look right.

Luis was rushed to the hospital. It was extremely crowded and unable to accommodate with immediate assistance. Luis was on the cusp of dying, and no one was taking the initiative to save him. Sandra decided to call our cousin, Manuel, who had two daughters that were registered nurses in the hospital.

I was worried but happy knowing I had family there to help my brother. Manuel's daughters were extremely accommodating and tried to help to the best of their abilities. They managed to transfer my brother by ambulance to Clinic Santa Clara. After a couple of hours, the doctors entered to explain what was wrong with Luis. He had an aneurysm in his brain, and their goal was to try and drain the blood because he had an additional one there that had to be taken care of. The swelling was excessive, and we all knew he was not in good condition. Sandra called Edgar to explain the situation. The following day, Edgar drove to Bogota. Everyone was concerned. Luis was the baby of the family. No one ever thought Luis would be walking around with an aneurysm in his brain. It felt as though it was just a bad dream.

When I received the news from Sandra, she advised me to remain calm and she would keep me posted on Luis's condition. Every day, Julio and I would sit by the phone waiting to receive good news. As the days went by, the news didn't sound promising. There was a slim chance of Luis surviving, but only if he had surgery, as the swelling in his brain was not subsiding. He was very alert and able to hear and see what was happening around him, but it was painful to see this, given that there wasn't much we could do to help him.

I was not in good shape with the news of my brother. I was trying to overcome my own battles and elevate myself again, and then this happened. When was I going to catch a break?

Ever since Luis was a child he struggled with his health. He was hospitalized at two years old, fighting for his life. Now again, he was in the hospital, struggling to survive. It was hard to comprehend this situation. In our last conversation, he sounded so happy and full of life, making plans for his future. A few months earlier, he began working with Edgar on the property, rebuilding the house we grew up in.

Edgar took the news of Luis very hard. My family was falling apart, and so was I. My nightmares began again, and I kept dreaming the same thing—someone was knocking on my door, and when I opened it, no one was there.

The following morning, my brother Julio knocked on my front door. He never came into my home, and when I saw him through the window, my heart began beating very fast. At a loss for words, he just hugged me and cried. I knew my little brother had passed away, and I couldn't even say goodbye.

It was nearly impossible to find a flight to Colombia, as the following day was New Year's Eve. Regardless, I knew I needed to be there to support my family. In my heart, I knew that Luis wouldn't want my last memory of him to be in the hospital. It was a dark and gloomy day as it rained all afternoon. I could barely breathe, and my heart only began to ache more. We could not speak without falling apart. It was as if we were a puzzle missing its last piece. I decided to sit in the chair and look out of the window.

"Maybe if I was there, I could have saved him," was all I kept hearing in my head.

Ever since I moved to America, I dreamed of spending Christmas and New Year's with my family in Colombia. The holiday season is considered the happiest time of the year when people have parties, play music, watch fireworks, and scream "Happy New Year!" in the streets, excited for what the coming year would bring.

They say in a city packed with countless people, you pass through life, existing invisibly among the hustle and bustle of that city. One gets lost in the crowd, and no one notices your tears, sadness, and pain. That was how I felt when I lost Luis.

Each one of my siblings had their own way of coping with grief. While I tried to be the glue that held the family together during this rough patch, I realized it was difficult given that I had been in the United States for so many years. I always thought that with courage, one could have the strength to go on, but I was in no shape to do so. I needed time to process this pain, and my situation at home made it even more challenging.

It was New Year's Day and with my family we were in a funeral home. Many people came to pay their respects for our loss, many being unfamiliar faces to me. Each one had a story to tell of how Luis touched their life in so many ways. A gentleman who had caught my attention told us he met him not very long ago. He started to say that his family had gone away for the weekend. In the midst of driving, his car broke down. They had been on the road for more than two hours trying to get help. But, no one would help. He called the tow company and they said they could be there the next day. The gentleman was anguished when suddenly Luis appeared on his motorcycle and offered his help. After taking a look at the vehicle he said the starter was damaged and that he would go to the capital and purchase the part. The gentleman thanked him but didn't believe Luis would go and come back. Surprisingly after two hours Luis did come back, with the needed part and refreshments for the family. After my brother fixed the car he gave him his business card and said next time you probably have to stop by.

None of these stories surprised me. This was the type of person my brother was; humble, caring, empathetic . He always had a smile on his face with little room for sadness. Luis lived fully to the day like there was no tomorrow. I personally think his style of life was a happy one.

If I was once the glue that kept this family together, I could no longer be that. I was finding it very hard to process this on my own.

Suddenly I felt someone squeeze my hand. When I raised my head it was Orlando. He was next to me, somehow he seemed to be there when I most needed him and his love at that moment supported me. The only thing that was consoling me was that my mother and Luis were now together and no one could separate them. I felt like there was nothing more to give. We were raised with the mentality that we would always stick together even if things were rough because together, the possibilities were limitless.

Now though, I was the one who found it hard to stay happy. We were unconsolable and tired of mourning our losses. But, why my baby brother? Losing my brother was not easy. Each of the siblings mourned differently. It was hard to process the death of my brother, and it's still hard to believe it. Time will heal all wounds.

After the funeral we went back home. I spent the rest of New Year's locked in a room wiping my tears. A couple of days after that, I packed my bags and returned home to New York. Saying goodbye to my family was never easy, especially in times like this when we needed each other the most. As I sat on the plane, I contemplated where home really was for me.

Edgar and Sandra continued on with the construction. I can't imagine how they had the strength to continue. I decided I needed some space from everyone, yet I felt guilty because I felt responsible for my family.

At home the same routine continued. I don't remember the first time I did something for myself without analyzing how my actions would impact everyone around me. Time was running against me and the years would be passing me by. I didn't do anything to change and try to be happy.

My children were professional grown men. I am a proud mother. I have two beautiful, successful, grown-up sons. Orlando is a pilot, and Javier is a lawyer. I have no doubt they will continue to achieve great things. How many more excuses was I going to have before thinking of myself?

Chapter Forty

I was at the beach lying on the sand. I was thinking about the last conversation I had with Sandra. She said we buried my mother and then my brother.

"More than a year has passed and you haven't come to visit us. It seems like we buried you too. I don't know what I have to do for you to come back to Colombia." I went home and thought about it. I confronted my fears and traveled again to Colombia. I didn't have any more excuses. After Luis's death it was very upsetting to go back to town. But the first thing we did was go to La Esperanza. Construction was done and my siblings wished I would come and see it.

When we finally arrived I burst into tears, not because of sadness but pride, because in a short amount of time the construction was done. My brother Edgar with his own hands made his dream come true. The restaurant was open for business to the public. Many families would come by on the weekends for the delicious cuisine and to enjoy the pool. My sister Sandra started to build her cabana and was excited. She proposed that we finish the cabana so we can enjoy it in the future. In reality we thought about our children. If they one day wanted a place to get away to, La Esperanza would be a place to look forward to.

On my trip to Colombia I had the chance to have dinner with a wise friend who I admire as a professional and as a human being, Dr. Ricardo Gonzalez. He sat me down for dinner and enlightened me with his words, giving me answers to so many questions.

He asked me first, "Do you know what a debt is?"

I answered, "Yes! Debts owed or favors that were done, I personally believe debts should be paid." I shared with him all the debts I had paid and I remembered many of the times my mother had to hide from places where we used to live, because she didn't have the money to pay the rent. But I never forgot those debts. When I had the opportunity to go back, I paid them for the times when my mother couldn't. Some would remember and others just took the money and said, "Thanks." It was important for me to do so.

After he heard me out, he looked at me and said, "And have you paid your own debt?" His words were full of wisdom.

Unfortunately, I didn't understand that I owed myself something.

He said, "Every time we take our own life and decide to place it in the hands of others, we become indebted to ourselves. Sooner or later, we have no choice but to pay ourselves back."

I was speechless because his words of wisdom truly resonated with me. I felt like I was in debt to myself, and it was time for me to take care of my soul and heal from each pain that I had endured. His words meant so much to me. For many years I was indebted to myself and I didn't even know it. We said goodbye with the promise of meeting again soon.

On my return to New York, I was content leaving my family. They seemed to continue with life. Now more than ever I had to think about myself. I had to wake up and now it seemed like it was a new day to approach to its fullest, because I didn't know if this was the last. I never had any fear to start over but this time it was different.

There are no good or bad people. Each person is a world and from each world you learn, big or small. When all is said and done, the most important thing is to respect the experiences of other people, especially the ones we love. While one might not understand why people do certain things, it is good to accept and come to your own understanding without passing judgment.

Just like that, a week later we came to an agreement to start the divorce process. I remember the lawyer asked if I knew my rights. I said I did. He asked, "Why are you not demanding anything?" and continued by saying, "You have businesses, cars, accounts, assets from the marriage. It should all be divided down the middle. With the house someone can buy the other one out or you are welcome to put it on the market. Any questions?"

We stood in silence.

The lawyer broke the silence by saying, "Since both parties are in agreement please sign."

After we left the office, I told the father of my children, "You can stay in the house as long as you want . We can put it up for sale when you think it's right. I will never demand anything from you. On the other hand, I would like to thank you for everything you did for me. I will leave when I find a place to live. I would like it to be me who tells the children."

He agreed.

There the four of us sat in a restaurant. My sadness hurt my soul. It was one of the most difficult things I had to do in my life.

I gathered my strength and said, "I am leaving the home."

I will always remember Orlando's touching words: "Mom, even if you divorce my father, I will always be your son. I just want the two of you to be happy. You both deserve it."

On the other hand, Javier said nothing. The silence was killing me and causing more heartache, knowing that because of my actions, he was in pain. If I didn't do this now I would never do this. I knew this would cause a lot of distress to those I loved the most. It took courage to take this step, but I couldn't live like this any longer. If I stayed in the home, no one would be able to move on. I wanted things to change, it was time to take matters into my own hands.

That weekend I took my clothing and my children's photo album and left my house without looking back. I moved into a small studio close to where I worked. For once in my life, I did not feel alone. I felt invincible, willing, and able to handle any problem that came my way. I finally knew my worth and what I deserved in this world. Even though it wasn't going to happen overnight, I was determined to make myself happy no matter how long it took. But if I could see the new light I can start again.

Legally my marriage was over. But on top of everything I always knew we could count on one another regardless of the circumstances. We always had a true friendship. We ended our marriage on good terms and with the understanding of always having a good environment for our children.

It was hard for me to see how Javier was taking this news. I always wanted to avoid this embarrassment and sadness. I didn't want to hurt the person I loved the most. I waited until he was grown thinking it would be easier. But even in that I was wrong. It does not matter how old your children are, a divorce will always be tragic and painful to them.

He didn't want to come to the house anymore, preferring to see us in his town.

He'd rather we go see him in his apartment. The times when I would see Javier, I felt a distance between us. I had to be stronger than ever and not feel so guilty. I knew I had to give him his space to get through this. In the process, I constantly reassured him how much I loved him, and no matter what, my love for him was always unconditional. Even if this takes a lifetime, I will be here with my arms wide open.

My ex-husband and I always had a great friendship so the process for us was easier. Even when we would all get together they found it curious how well we got along and they thought we were faking it again. But in reality it wasn't like that. I will always help him if he needs my help.

I remember when we had a cup of coffee the last time. He gave me a book. To my surprise the book was called, "I Love You, But am Happy Without You." Curiously, it was the most romantic he had been in a while.

I was a strong believer in the quote, "You can only pick from the ground what you harvest." My ex husband and I planted the seeds in our children, and today we see the result; two beautiful, strong men ready to achieve anything in life. We gave them a great childhood, a good education, a happy life where they never had to want for anything, and a support system where both parents constantly showed affection. We were proud of the children we raised. I know I wasn't the perfect mom but I gave as best I could. I would like to take this time to say, "I'm sorry if I hurt you in any way."

Diving allowed me to travel the world to places like Fiji, the Maldives, Dubai, Bonaire, Florida, the Mexican Riviera, the Caribbean, San Andres, Cartagena, Canada, and Costa Rica. I was so excited about traveling to Fiji. On one of the trips, I shared a room with a nice lady who worked in real estate. Through our conversations, I mentioned that I was a hairdresser and had my own place, but I was tired of paying so much rent. She said she would be happy to help me find a new space. Before we parted ways, I decided to take her up on her offer.

The first week back to work was challenging as my customers counted on me to make them look beautiful. It started to feel like I was developing a family with my clientele. When one has a true passion for their profession, they tend to have a higher success rate, and I was very passionate about my work. It felt gratifying to make a difference in people's lives by changing their aesthetics or listening to them speak about their lives for just five minutes.

* * *

It had been one year since my brother Luis had passed. In speaking to Sandra, I could still hear sadness over the phone. She was the closest to Luis and in reality they had many great memories of him. Every time I had a chance to see my children, I would share with them, even if it was only for a few hours. Each one of them had their own responsibilities but we tried to stay united.

A few weeks later, the realtor contacted me and said she would like to show me a place. I felt nervous because I wasn't prepared, I remember opportunities only come once. I took the news in a positive way. I was very excited about it, given that my lease was about to expire. I didn't have any type of money to make such a big purchase. I dared to dream and that afternoon I went to see the property. Before my eyes stood a small house that was falling apart. She started to say that the property needed a lot of work. That didn't scare me because it was in an incredible location. I closed my eyes and manifested my business there.

The next day, I began the paperwork process. It was not going to be easy, but I knew I would rise above the challenge. The banks were extremely strict. Given that my income was low, the loan would not be approved. Luckily, I had Javier's support.

When he found out about this project, he grew concerned and nervous for me. He wanted to make sure I could afford it and tried to support me in any way possible. The only way for my plan to work was if Javier would buy the property with me. He earned a higher income than me. Once the bank approved us, the only thing I needed to worry about was the initial down payment. "What savings do you have?" they asked.

Laughing and crying, I answered "Nothing. Nada!" The small savings I had, I shared with my loved ones. Because I was never attached to anything, I had to think quickly now that we had the approval.

That is when I called my trusted friend Jeff Trugman. I met him when I was 23 years old. At that time I did not speak English. Jeff visited me in my first employment position. He gave a talk to the staff at that time. That is when I learned the words SEI, IRA, SEI Roth, SEI TOD. I did not understand anything. When he finished I asked him if he spoke Spanish. He answered, "No."

I didn't imagine that the next day he would come back with a Spanish interpreter. He sat down and explained all I wanted to know. Since that day, I have started saving for my retirement. When I called Jeff, I discussed my project. Not only was he happy, but he gave his unconditional support. He told me I can count on the money and I wouldn't be fined because I was using it to buy property.

The following week I had the initial down payment that was required. I called him later and invited him to the Grand Opening. I promised him that I would return every cent to the account, I was only borrowing it, and that's exactly what I did. Thanks to my son and his support I could purchase the property. Without his support it would have been impossible. Later, after receiving the key, the hardest part was remodeling the space.

Throughout the process, I endured challenges from the city of Roslyn, which was strict on the properties in the area, given that they were deemed historical landmarks. They were not agreeable to making any big changes and insisted on following codes.

Their intentions were to keep the charm intact while doing cosmetic, minute renovations.

I wanted to keep the township happy, and that's what I did. The most stressful part was paying rent on my current space and carrying the mortgage. Many times I thought I wasn't going to make it. It was a struggle and stressful. I constantly reminded myself that I was a fighter and that it was up to me to keep going.

One year later, I sat in my car admiring the new home from across the street. It was finally complete and looked so beautiful. It seemed like a dream, and I couldn't believe this was my reality. I began crying hysterically, yet they were tears of joy. I was happy to know all my hard work was paying off. On February 16, 2018 friends and family supported my success at my Grand Opening.

Two years later, everything was going better than expected until we got an unfriendly visitor in our homes. I was a victim too and it almost took my life. Without asking permission it took our liberty leaving sadness and death, destroying lives, causing unemployment and destroying families and marriages. It caused terror and pain across the whole world .....COVID 19.

Once again I had to get strength and start again. I was a survivor from this disease and I wasn't going to take life for granted.

Hope Aesthetics opened its doors again one year later with unconditional love from my clients and Jeannette, the person who has been by my side for over thirty years.

Jeannette who knows my sadness, my failures, my achievements, and my true happiness. Jeannette has been there unconditionally. She came into my life without me asking, like a gift from God. When I met her she was just a child but we stayed connected through our mutual involvement in a charity. Our bond grew stronger each day. With a twist of fate, she came to live with us and was raised with my children. She has been the daughter I couldn't have. Together we opened the doors to Hope Aesthetics once again, with the same dedication and persistence to serve the public. We are in this together.

At a young age I fought to survive in the middle of a storm with little opportunity. My madre had always taught me to love life like a gift. You can only depend on yourself to change things, as many times as you have to. Confront your obstacles without fear. I will always be ready to fight any battle, because I am the daughter of a fighter, my madre.

Today I can clearly see the road I've walked on. It's not important how many times I fell or how many stones I discovered on the road. The only important thing was to rise again and face the world. Each time I have the chance to be happy I will do it. Because I only have one life to love and I am the only one responsible for making it happen.

I only have one thing left to say. If I can do it, you can do it! Dare yourself. Your life is your story and you can turn it into a bestseller. With love to anyone who has the chance to read my story, I remind you to remember that not one leaf on a tree moves without the Creator's permission.

Epilogue

What motivated me to write this story?

My goals were always clear. I didn't know what destiny had in store for me.

However, I always knew what I didn't want in my life. My father's abandonment led me to face my fears and the sudden changes in my life. All this was with my only support, my mother. That has inspired me to fight every day of my life. Likewise, and without proposing it, another of my motivations was to have a better quality of life not only for me but for my family and loved ones.

Now I recognize the cruel and heartless abandonment of my father, his refusal of the opportunity to see me grow up, his being the one who was never interested in protecting me, advising me or giving me any love. Thanks to his vile and cowardly memory, I was forced to get ahead. Today I know that I will never need him. His abandonment made me strong. He taught me to take care of myself and protect what's mine.

I also know that I carried a heavy load on my back, which sometimes led me to think that I could not live with it: thanks to time, it became less intense and much more bearable. Sometimes I wonder if I would travel this path full of so many stones again and my answer is always the same: Yes, I would do it again, because just remembering my mother's sweet look inspires me to start again, as many times as necessary.

What was my connection to God?

Someone asked me what my relationship with God was. I didn't know how to answer but when I was alone I asked myself that same question. For me, God is my first love. I have known him since I was a little girl. Thanks to the teachings of my mother, I had a very strong relationship with him. He knows everything about me. He's my confidant, my best friend. On many occasions I've fought with him. I was asking him for answers I couldn't understand. It felt unfair in the moments when I needed him the most. He wasn't listening to me. Many times I asked why my mother suffered so much in her lifetime. Why did she have to be bound to a wheelchair in her last days with wounds on her body that never healed? Why did my younger brother pass away at such a young age?

Why so much poverty and suffering? Never will I understand why. But I'll keep believing in Him, because my life would be sad and empty without his presence. I'm the one who seeks him because it's the only way I feel alive. My mother always taught me that I had to go to Church, willing to talk to God. But time taught me differently. God is my creator, My Father, and now I know regardless of anything he's always with me. I'll always be connected to Him and communicate with Him even when I don't agree with His decisions, because I don't know how I can live without His strength which keeps me going and living each and every day as if it were my last.

Thank You

Montana A, Desiree Y, Tracy and Barry Stopler, Jeannette F, Ellen N, Maria Esperanza Avendano, Kathy Perez-Creative Director.

About the Author

Maria Esperanza Pinzon grew up in Soata, Colombia. She became a young entrepreneur to feed her siblings and herself, meeting her partner, starting a family. Getting death threats, Maria had to leave her country and begin a new journey to live in the USA, not understanding the culture or language. Maria found a career in beauty and fashion, starting with her education to be an esthetician. A beautician by profession, Maria is the founder of Hope Aesthetics. Working for over 30 years, Maria has truly brought smiles to her clients' faces by expressing her passion for beauty. Maria is a true example of an immigrant achieving the American dream. She is newly remarried and lives with her husband and their two dogs in Long Island, New York. She has a lovely relationship with her sons, and excitedly awaits the birth of her first grandchild.

Edgar, Joaquin, Julio, Ma Esperanza, Sandra and Luis

Edgar, Joaquin, Julio, Ma Esperanza, Sandra and Luis

www.ingramcontent.com/pod-product-compliance
Lightning Source LLC
Chambersburg PA
CBHW030545080526
44585CB00012B/267